"What is the work of works for man if not to establish in and by each one of us, an absolutely original centre in which the universe reflects itself in a unique and inimitable way? And those centres are our very selves and personalities."

Teilhard de Chardin

# The Mystery of Personal Identity

## Michael Mayer

International Standard Book Number 0-917086-54-6

Cover Design by Laurie Ortiz


Printed in the United States of America

Published by ACS Publications, Inc.
P.O. Box 16430
San Diego, CA 92116-0430

*This book is dedicated to
all fellow travelers:*

*"Keep Shining Like the Stars You Are"*

# Also By ACS Publications, Inc.

All About Astrology Series
The American Atlas: US Latitudes and Longitudes, Time Changes
    and Time Zones (Shanks)
The American Book of Charts (Rodden)
The American Book of Nutrition & Medical Astrology (Nauman)
The American Book of Tables
The American Ephemeris for the 20th Century [Midnight]
    1900 to 2000
The American Ephemeris for the 20th Century [Noon] 1900 to 2000
The American Ephemeris for the 21st Century 1900 to 2100
The American Heliocentric Ephemeris 1901-2000
The American Sidereal Ephemeris 1976-2000
The Asteroid Ephemeris: Dudu, Dembowska, Pittsburgh, & Frigga
    (Stark & Pottenger)
Astrological Insights into Personality (Lundsted)
Astrological Predictions: A Revolutionary New Technique (Whitney)
Astrology: Old Theme, New Thoughts (March & McEvers)
Basic Astrology: A Guide for Teachers & Students (Negus)
Basic Astrology: A Workbook for Students (Negus)
The Body Says Yes (Kapel)
The Cosmic Clocks (M. Gauquelin)
Cosmic Combinations: A Book of Astrological Exercises (Negus)
Expanding Astrology's Universe (Dobyns)
The Fortunes of Astrology: A New Complete Treatment of the
    Arabic Parts (Granite)
The Gauquelin Book of American Charts (F. and M. Gauquelin)
The Gold Mine in Your Files (King)
Healing With the Horoscope: A Guide to Counseling (Pottenger)
The Horary Reference Book (Ungar & Huber)
Horoscopes of the Western Hemisphere (Penfield)
Instant Astrology (Orser)
The International Atlas (Shanks)
Interpreting the Eclipses (Jansky)
The Lively Circle (Koval)
The Mystery of Personal Identity (Mayer)
The Only Way to. . . Learn Astrology, Vol. I
    Basic Principles (March & McEvers)
The Only Way to. . . Learn Astrology, Vol. II
    Math & Interpretation Techniques (March & McEvers)
The Only Way to. . . Learn Astrology, Vol. III
    Horoscope Analysis (March & McEvers)
Planetary Planting (Riotte)
Planting by the Moon 1983/84 Including Grower's Guide
    (Best & Kollerstrom)
The Psychic and the Detective (Druffel with Marcotte)
Psychology of the Planets (F. Gauquelin)
Secrets of the Palm (Hansen)
Small Ecstasies (Owens)
Stalking the Wild Orgasm (Kilham)
Tomorrow Knocks (Brunton)
12 Times 12 (McEvers)

# ACKNOWLEDGMENTS

It seems impossible to think of any given thing as one's own without remembering how it always springs forth from the wider whole of which one is a part.

In this light, deepest thanks are given to:

My Doctoral Committee:

**Sam Keen, Ph.D.** — committee chairman, whose penetrating insight led me to question my every assumption, whose warmth and sensitivity gave me room to develop my own way, and whose eloquence stimulated my imagination and served as an inspiration to my inner journey.

**John Beebe, M.D.** — whose aesthetic sense of language, therapeutic sensitivity, and intellectual rigor pushed me forth to define concepts clearly, to remove that from my writing (and my self) to which I was most unduly attached . . . to treat my work as I would my soul.

**Gordon Tappan, Ph.D.** — my first mentor at the Humanistic Psychology Institute, who led me to explore the shadow of astrology, and my own; who helped to initiate my going forth on my Vision Quest.

**William McCreary, Ph.D.** — whose support and nurturing spirit, unique communication style, and vision of wild horses breathed life into my work.

**Forrest Orr, Ph.D.** — for clinical advice and support.

Without these committee members' efforts and encouragement, my dissertation certainly would have been less potent and my self less rich.

**Sandy Rosenberg** — doctoral fellow, fellow traveler, friend — whose deep understanding of phenomenology and endless hours of intense discussion helped to fire the Sagittarian arrows that enabled my work to continually move to new horizons.

**Dane Rudhyar** — from whose works the intellectual seed of this dissertation grew. Your presence stood as the mark of a man having the courage to venture forth into forbidden territory. May my work build upon the land that you so richly developed.

**Jim Shere and Chalon Crawford** — astrologers who helped me to develop a symbolic understanding of this ancient language.

**Eugene Gendlin, Ph.D.** — who helped me to appreciate the importance of the body's felt sense when working with symbols.

**Sifu Fong Ha and Sifu Ken Cohen** — my Tai Chi teachers who introduced me to this ancient way, from which I learned the Tao of Counseling...one of the greatest gifts of my life.

My friends, **Cynthia Yaguda, Deborah Knighton, Debbie Gallo** — whose patience with my focus on my dissertation, and being there for me between the lines, gave me a base of love and support to write from. With special thanks to all those friends who helped to edit, constructively criticize, and form this work.

**My parents** — whose brilliant minds stimulated my intellect, whose warm hearts gave sustenance to my being.

**The Humanistic Psychology Institute** (now Saybrook Institute) — which provided fertile soil from which mutated plants can grow.

**Neil Michelsen** — special thanks to the publisher who provided the vehicle through which this work can reach a wider community of souls.

**Tasha Pera and Maritha Pottenger** — editors extraordinaire, who helped to turn an academic dissertation into a book for a larger audience...who helped to change a writing task into a labor of love.

**Deborah Knighton** — for her conscientious attention to detail in indexing, and her devotion to the spirit of this book.

# CONTENTS

# PREFACE

This work is about the quest into the mystery that underlies each of our personalities. In ancient times this pursuit was often associated with the search for one's "true name." If I were living in certain ancient cultures, a part of my initiation would consist of being given a new name through which I could come to terms with my life's meaning. (See Chapters One and Two for a more in-depth discussion of "naming" in ancient cultures. The Plains Indians' cosmology and their view of naming is discussed in Chapter Three.) In a sense this work is an expression of the search for my "name." Although it initially took form as a Ph.D. dissertation focused upon how the modern psychotherapeutic relationship could help aid a person in coming to terms with his or her identity, its roots went back much further into my early life . . . much further than I knew when I began writing as a Ph.D. student.

The first interest I remember having in this area was around my seventh birthday when I recall spending long hours watching people at the local ice cream parlor buying ice cream cones. I wondered what the way they bought their cones said about who they were as people. I remember creating metaphorical names for these people to express qualities carried over into their everyday lives. There were the lip smackers, the careful considerers (of the chocolate, vanilla, and strawberry varieties), the indulgers (You know, the three scoops with marshmallow topping kind.) and on and on.

Each of these individuals had a unique way of relating to the world. It became my interest over the years to study what it was that constituted the uniqueness of a person's personality. This unfathomable task took me through a wide variety of subject areas, including philosophy, anthropology, mythology, comparative religions, and metaphysics. Finally, psychology, specifically personality theory, became my area of concentration in graduate school.

At the Humanistic Psychology Institute (now called Saybrook Institute) as part of my research program, I decided to actually go out into the woods, as an ancient initiate might have, to see what would emerge. After clearing the red tape though school, I made a commitment to be in the woods for forty nights and deal with my fear of being there alone in the darkness.

# My Vision Quest

After about three weeks of sleeping in the woods, about three miles from the nearest mark of civilization — it came. I was asleep alone on top of a ridge with a water hole nearby, and was in a state of lucid dreaming where I was conscious of my surroundings, but was at the same time aware of being in a dream. I noticed that a group of seven deer were approaching me. I was particularly aware of the leader who had very large, golden, glowing antlers, and eyes so emblazoned that I was not sure if it was really a deer or a Shaman wearing a mask trying to trick me. I was afraid that he might eat my eye out of its socket, but I thought that if I pretended to be asleep perhaps he would just pass me by. My left eye was quivering, however, and I thought that surely this was going to give me away. The deer approached, and gently kissed my eye. A warm energized ecstasy filled me like nothing I had ever experienced before. A moment later, though, I was terrified as I realized that my eye was no longer in its socket. . .it was in the deer's mouth. In my panic, the first thought that came to mind was that of my parents saying, "I told you so. We always told you when you slept out in the back yard in New Jersey, 'Why do you have to do things like this? Why can't you just sleep inside like everyone else? If you had only listened to us you wouldn't have lost your eye.' " This thought of my parents "I told you so" was as bad as the image of crawling back to the nearest mark of civilization with only one eye.

Even amidst these horrifying fantasies I somehow realized that regardless of the consequences, all this had a place in my destiny. . . . I breathed, letting go to my fate. I noticed the deer in a new way. I realized that he was doing something with my eye that was not malevolent. He was rolling my eye around in his mouth, like some kind of ritual, as if washing it. He then placed my eye back in its socket. . .but it was not an eye, it was some kind of jewel — a green emerald. I was awestruck.

My next recollection was waking at dawn and feeling for my eye. To my surprise it was just an eye again. I then noticed a large number of fresh deer tracks around me. Had the deer actually been there? Was it a dream, a vision? For many days thereafter (and even to this day) I was filled with a sense of wonder.

When I returned to my Doctoral advisor and group after the forty day period someone suggested I read the book, *Seven Arrows* which is about the process of Vision Questing among the American Plains Indians. Here amongst the legends of the people of the land that I had lived on, I found a starting place on to my personal path. You will read in Chapter Three how these people's symbolic names gave them a sense of meaning and purpose in life. I, like an Indian brave might have many years ago, began to enter into the metaphor that lay hidden in my experience in the woods, searching for my "name."

I realized that I had long had a sense that each of us has a vision unique to our purpose in life. Like various ice cream eaters, each of us has our own way of taking life in, and choosing from its many flavors. Throughout life I had also noticed that people seemed to suffer from wounds due to their unique way of seeing life: from all the "too's" — you're "too sensitive, too expressive, too shy" etc. It seemed to me that many people had fears about their ways of being in the world. So much suffering in our culture seemed to be from people's lack of seeing how their different styles were a sacred gift. We had no cosmology to help people find their "names" in the Western World.

Perhaps, I thought, my path lay in becoming like the deer of my vision. What a quest it would be to kiss eyes like the deer had kissed mine — to help people find how their ways of seeing the world were like precious gems, to take others' eyes and wash them and to allow them to do the same for me, to help people find their ways and their names. If I could only do this gently, then I would be like a "Deer Kissing Eyes."

It was from this "name" that my doctoral work began. It culminated in a Doctoral dissertation exploring how ancient cosmologies could aid the modern psychotherapist in helping a client discover a path into his or her life's meaning and identity. This book is a rewriting of that original dissertation: "A Holistic Perspective on Meaning and Identity: Astrological Metaphor as a Language of Personality in Psychotherapy."[1]

---

1. Mayer, M. *A Holistic Perspective on Meaning and Identity: Astrological Metaphor as a Language of Personality in Psychotherapy*, Ann Arbor, Michigan: University Microfilms International, LD 00166, Vol. 3, Issue 1, March 1978.

# My Genetic Roots: The Baal Shem Tov?

Another step in my personal quest came after I returned home to New Jersey after finishing my Ph.D. dissertation. My eldest aunt Hannah on my father's side said that she had a secret to disclose that had never been told to me. My aunt said that we were direct descendents of the Baal Shem Tov, Israel Ben Eliezer, the founder of Hasidism in the early 1700s. His name, Baal Shem Tov, translates to Master of the Holy Name. Chills went up my spine.

Could it be that my lifelong interest in naming the essences of personality and my last five years of writing my Ph.D. thesis had roots in my genetic code, my blood? How was this transmitted? Another layer of the mystery of personal identity was unravelling.

# My Task as a Personality Theorist

With the interest I had in personality description, I noticed myself becoming increasingly disturbed, along with other personality theorists, that so much of the language in the psychological profession is oriented towards describing the sickness of the human personality. Within the terms themselves, such as obsessive-compulsive, hysterical, neurotic, there seemed to be no route toward healing as there was in certain of the ancient languages of personality I had studied. This became my quest: to find a language that was expansive enough to speak of personality in a way that included the sacred dimension.[2]

In this light it is not so strange that I chose astrology as a language that could speak about the astronomical number of differences in the personality qualities of various human beings. At first I had much resistance to the pseudo-scientific claims which correlate the patterns of celestial objects to human behavior. When I was younger and studying to be a lawyer, I enjoyed arguing vociferously against the claims of astrology with "believers." What a strange twist of fate that later in my life, while studying psychology, I found that certain aspects of astrology's holistic nature as a symbolic personality system appealed to me.

As the reader will see, I set about to change the pretense of

---

2. The use of the word "sacred" is not in the sense of traditional religion, but more in the sense brought forth by Mircea Eliade. (See *The Sacred and the Profane*, New York: Harcourt, Brace and World, 1959.) He speaks of the contrast between an alienated, profane world and a "sacred" one where there is a link between heaven and earth, an orientation to the wider cosmos around us through the power of symbols.

objectivity within most theories of astrology, to glean that which is useful in the language itself. With the reformulations that the reader will find in this work, I hope that the sacred dimension of this symbolic language will be more accessible to those interested in unraveling the mystery of their personal identities.

# INTRODUCTION

To develop a language for describing the unique essence of a human being is no easy task. The power of the Name is such that it is not easily changed. Just as most of us will never change our Names[1] (and resistances may come up when one even thinks such a thought) so is it with the psychological lexicon. It seems that psychology itself would need to take a Vision Quest, to enter into its own soul, in order to find a new Naming system.

To many thinkers in the field, it seems imperative that such a journey be taken soon. A new language is needed to do justice to the aesthetic qualities of the human being. E. Fuller Torrey[2], Special Assistant to the Director of International Activities of the National Institute of Mental Health, puts it this way, "The first thing that is needed is a suitable name for the people with problems of living. Names are important for they carry both implications and connotations." James Hillman in his far reaching works on depth psychology says,

> Therapy might profit were it to take a fresh interest in rhetoric...We need again what was common in the Renaissance — belief in the verbal imagination and the therapeutic incantational power of words...The contents of psychiatry and philosophy are of prime importance but the language they use to express those contents is soul-killing...Soul-making needs adequate ideational vessels.[3]

---

1. The majority of women in our culture do change their last names at least once, when they get married. As the women's movement has increased women's (and men's) consciousness of such issues, it seems an increasing number of women are hyphenating their old and new names. This suggests the view that the woman is adding her husband to her identity. The former, nonhyphenated practice suggests the woman is incorporated into the man's familial world. She gives up her family name and the ability to have that identity carried by her children.
2. Torrey, E. *The Death of Psychiatry*, New York: Penguin Books, 1974, p.164
3. Hillman, J. *Revisioning Psychology*, New York: Harper and Row, 1975, p.214.

Chapter One discusses how the mystery of personal identity has been connected throughout time to the quest for one's "true name." The language through which one describes one's identity colors the way that each of us sees our self. It becomes the lens through which we view our identity and the structure through which we experience our life's meaning. In this light, it seems most serious that the psychological tradition describes people within a medical model — which views the person in terms of illness.

Chapter Two begins with a general review and critique of personality theorists. We see how personality theorists have felt the need to move towards creating a holistic language of personality. Although there has been much criticism about psychological language by the public and within the psychological field, less emphasis has been placed upon introducing a viable alternative. Our major thrust is to focus on this quest.

In Chapter Three, certain premodern identity systems are examined to find an alternative to the medical model. The language of astrology is focused upon because it seems to be the most complex of premodern identity systems, and seems to provide a holistic means of describing the uniqueness of a human being.

Considering the use of such a system may be an exercise in putting old prejudices aside. Some readers might have similar reservations to those this author once had, feeling that the ancient, foreign territory of premodern personality systems has little to contribute to our sophisticated, modern homeland. Perhaps as my xenophobia was transformed, so will these readers be. Finding alternatives to the way our civilization views personality demands an openness to new territory.

The task of this work is to salvage that in astrology which could prove useful to the psychologists' interest in the areas of meaning and identity. This necessitates raising astrology from the quagmire of fixed beliefs about the objective relationship between cosmos and personality. Here, astrology is revised in line with the meaning reorganization point of view of phenomenological thinking[4] and the archetypal point of view introduced by James Hillman. Bringing these points of view to astrology creates a departure from both the causal stance of traditional astrology (which assumes the planets are making things happen on earth) and even the synchronistic orientation of humanistic astrologers such as Rudhyar. (Synchronistic theory assumes correspondences between planets and people, although it

---

4. Fingarette, H. *The Self in Transformation*, New York: Harper and Row, 1963.

is not seen as a cause and effect relationship. Nevertheless, the assumption of an interrelationship between cosmos and humans is made.) The term "astro-poetics" (in Chapter Six) is coined to align astrology with the phenomenological and archetypal viewpoints.

I do not preclude that a correspondence between cosmos and personality might exist, but merely create a means whereby the psycholinguistic center of the system (its function as a symbolic language) is the focus of attention.

In exploring the symbolic nature of the astrological system, the structure of symbols in general is examined. This discussion takes place in the course of attempting to make astrological language more communicable to the larger counseling community. We show how the essential core of the metaphorical language used by poets in the description of personality rests upon an isomorphic (iso = same; morphic = structure) perspective, i.e., that it derives from the perceived similarities in structure between qualities of one's everyday surroundings and one's way of being. The poet might proclaim, for example:

> Some say love, it is a river that drowns the tender reed.
> Some say love, it is a razor that leaves your soul to bleed.
> Some say love, it is a hunger, an endless, aching need.
> I say love, it is a flower and you its only seed. . . .[5]

Just as the isomorphic perspective yields a poetic language by using metaphors from nature, so does the astro-isomorphic perspective yield an astro-poetic language by using celestial metaphors to speak of personality. I argue that a possible alternative to the current medical terminology would be to combine the use of metaphors from both nature and the cosmos and call it "astro-poetics." This gives a range of terminology from which one can speak with varying degrees of complexity about qualities of human being.

The astro-poetic language is discussed (in Chapter Six) as providing a holistic perspective on psychotherapeutic systems. By using the astrological mandala to organize therapies, a higher order psychotherapeutic system is envisioned which includes all systems within its framework. This metasystem encircles the orientation of this work and shows its place on the metasystematic wheel (based

---

5. This poem, originally composed by Amanda McBroom, was sung by Bette Midler in the movie, *The Rose.*

on astrology). By so doing, astro-poetics is presented not only as a language but also as a way of thinking.

For the first time to my knowledge, astrology (astro-poetic language) is demonstrated in use as a symbolic language in the psychotherapeutic setting. Although there have been some demonstrations of the astrological chart as a diagnostic and interpretive tool for the psychotherapist[6] the case illustration in Chapter Seven is more closely aligned with the tradition of depth psychotherapy where symbolic processes are used to aid the clients themselves in experiencing meaning in their lives. In this chapter, the use of "astro-poetics" is integrated with various psychotherapeutic modalities, some of which are: Gendlin's process of focusing, Jung's process of active imagination, Gestalt therapy, systematic desensitization, and the "reframing" techniques of system's theory.

Various objections commonly held about astrology, possible detrimental effects that the system may have in the therapeutic process and areas of contraindication are considered in Chapter Nine. Questions concerning contraindication are discussed there.

Astrological language is also examined in regards to its propensity to lead to dependency upon the therapist, and its use to make an excuse for the client's neurotic patterns. I discuss how I deal with these problem areas and explore what therapeutic processes might prove viable with each of these. For instance, with clients who use the system to make an excuse for their neurotic patterns, Gendlin's focusing process can move the client away from intellectualizing. I explore which questions might aid people in entering into their experience, and discuss how to deal with clients who are using astrology to justify their neurotic patterns.

Appendix One consists of some of the statistical and scientific data regarding astrology. A discussion of the question of value in psychotherapeutic systems in general and the astro-poetic system in particular takes place in Appendix Two. Since the questions wrestled with in this section are fundamental ones with which all psychotherapeutic systems using symbolic processes must deal, the points discussed may provide impetus for others to apply these thoughts to their own particular areas of interest or to bring new questions to the mat.

---

6. See Dobyns, Z. *The Astrologer's Casebook* , Los Angeles: TIA Publications, 1973.

# CHAPTER ONE

# THE MYSTERY OF PERSONAL IDENTITY AND THE SEARCH FOR ONE'S TRUE NAME

One of the symptoms of alienation in the modern age is the widespread sense of meaninglessness. Many patients seek psychotherapy not for any clearly defined disorder, but because they feel life has no meaning. The thoughtful psychotherapist can scarcely avoid the impression that these people are experiencing the disrupting effects not only of an unsatisfactory childhood experience, but also of an upheaval occasioned by a major cultural transition. We seem to be passing through a collective psychological reorientation equivalent in magnitude to the emergence of Christianity from the ruins of the Roman Empire. Accompanying the decline of traditional religion there is increasing evidence of a general psychic disorientation. We have lost our bearings. Our relation to life has become ambiguous. The great symbol system which is organized Christianity seems no longer able to command the full commitment of men or to fulfill their ultimate needs. The result is a pervasive feeling of meaninglessness and alienation from life. Whether or not a new collective religious symbol will emerge remains to be seen.

Dr. Edward Edinger, 1973[1]

In the beginning was the Word,
and the Word was with God
and the Word was God.

the Gospel According to John[2]

---

1. Edinger, E. *Ego and Archetype*, Baltimore, Md: Penguin Books, 1973, p. 107.
2. *The Bible*, John, New York: Simon & Schuster, 1972, p.1007.

# Introduction

Not only in the teachings of the New Testament but in other traditions as well, the power of the word, God and creation are linked together. Even in the remote regions of Africa this relationship is recognized. The Fulani of West Africa speak of Godlike power which lies in the word, and believe that a creative power is passed on to mankind by our ability to use language. They say, "in bestowing the word upon man, God delegated to him a share of the power of creation," and it is "by the power of the word that man as well creates."[3]

We may never fully comprehend what mysterious creative power lies in the word. Yet we do know that the theme of language's power to create and shape reality has captured the interest of inquiring minds throughout the ages. Perhaps foremost among modern researchers of this theme is Benjamin Whorf, who has inquired into how different linguistic groups perceive and conceive of reality in different ways, and how the language spoken by the group shapes the cognitive structure of the individuals speaking that language.

The focus of this work is upon the role that language plays in shaping a particular kind of reality, that of one's personal identity. Just as the word is linked with creation in general, so do we find it linked with the creation of a human being. For the beginning of an individual's life, and the creation of that separate entity we call a person, is marked with the giving of a word...a name.

Throughout life our experience of identity grows side by side with the words we use to describe ourselves. In fact, the quest for identity is even spoken of as a "coming to terms" with who we are.

So fundamental is the relationship between language and identity that it might be more accurate to change the often quoted aphorism "know thyself" to "know thyself in accordance with the way thou art described." For the words used to describe a person indeed seem to have the power to shape one's experience of self. Ask any child who has been "called a name!"

Even if the child responds "sticks and stones will break my bones, but names will never harm me," we all know that this nursery rhyme was never true. Rather, it testifies to the very power of that which it is used against, serving as a talisman to ward off the awesome power that we feel when we are called a name. Each of

---

3. Whitman, D. "Africa and the Word," *Parabola*, Vol. II, No.2, New York: Tamarack Press, 1977, p.66.

us, I'm sure, can recall times in our childhood when we might have even preferred breaking a bone rather than suffering the humiliation of being called a name by one of our peers.

Any person in any age who has aided the individual in the quest for self discovery has had to be aware of the role that language plays in creating and shaping that reality. This awareness has led a number of modern thinkers[4] to criticize the way the field of psychology describes the person.

Chapter Two discusses in greater detail the criticisms of psychological language, i.e., describing the person's identity through a lens of sickness and thereby coloring it. Although many psychologists are aware of the problems inherent in this type of language, no viable alternative has been suggested. That is the task with which this work will wrestle.

In order to find an alternative to the prevailing nomenclature a radical departure from psychodiagnostic terminology shall be taken. "Radical" means returning to the roots: and so there shall first be a return to the roots of personality theory, to its ancient origins.

To begin there will be a general review of how premodern cosmologies viewed the relationship between the word used to describe the person, and the person's experience of his or her identity. The term "premodern cosmologies" refers to certain earlier cultures which conceived of a person's identity in relation to a cosmological schema conveying to the individual a feeling of his or her life's meaning and place in the universe. (See Chapter Three for further discussion.) This will enable the reader to better appreciate the ancient genealogical tradition from which modern personality theory has grown, i.e., modern personality theory will be viewed as a system of "naming" which carries on an age-old tradition called "name giving."

The terms "naming" or "name giving" refer to the process of people coming to terms with who they are and the word or words used to describe their way of being in terms which give meaning to it. Reviewing this part of psychology's genealogy will create a more historically grounded position from which to examine the problems that modern psychological language has in aiding people in their quests for self discovery.

---

4. Szasz, T. *The Myth of Mental Illness*, New York: Harper and Row, 1961; Torrey, E. *The Mind Game: Witch Doctors and Psychiatrists*, New York: Bantam Books, 1973; Laing, R.D. *The Politics of Experience*, New York: Ballantine Books, 1967.

# "Naming" and Identity in Premodern Cosmologies

The equation between one's name and one's identity may be a difficult one for the modern person to grasp. For in the modern world, the proper name has lost much of the symbolic power that it had in earlier cultures.[5] One American Indian, Lame Deer, offers insight about naming and how strongly premodern peoples felt the connection between their names and their identities.

> Words are symbols and convey great powers, especially names...Each Indian name has a story behind it, a vision, a quest for dreams. We receive great gifts from the source of a name; it links us to nature, to the animal nations. It gives power. You can lean on a name, get strength from it. It is a special name for you and you alone — not a Dick, George, Charles kind of thing.
>
> Take our famous chief Man-Afraid-of-His-Horse. (He) once led the warriors in battle against the enemy who fled before him. The medicine men wanted to honor him and so they bestowed this name on him, which really means: He is so brave, so feared, that his enemies run away when merely seeing his horse, even if he is not on it. That is a powerful name. He had to live up to it.[6]

In premodern cosmologies one's being and the name used to describe that individual are inseparable. Thus in the Akkadian language "to be" and "to name" are synonymous. In general, in premodern cosmologies the name is not only a mark of the person's individuality but it actually constitutes it — for it is the giving of a name which first makes one a person.

This idea is clearly illustrated by the (African) Fulani's words for "thing" (*kintu*), "human being" (*muntu*) and "word" (*nommo*). A newborn baby is a *kintu* (thing) until it has a name conferred upon it, and so it is reported that it is not mourned if it should die in infancy. Only as it receives a name does it become *muntu* (a human being).[7]

In addition to being linked with the creation of one's personality, the name is seen to have the power to destroy that which one is. This idea is illustrated by the Fulani's belief that a witch can take away the *Nommo* (the name, the humanizing creative force) rendering the person a *kintu*, or "zombi." Such a fate, they say, is the worst that can befall a person.

---

5. See Hillman's *Revisioning Psychology*, New York: Harper and Row, 1975, for an excellent perspective on the decline of the mythopoetic power of the word and how it was stripped of its "soul" by the nominalistic tradition.
6. Erdoes, R. *Lame Deer, Seeker of Visions*, New York: Simon and Schuster, 1972.
7. Whitman, D. "Africa."

# The Power of the Name

Because of the great power of the word and the respect with which premodern peoples regarded it, the name was to be spoken with utmost caution. Witness the following example of the legendary fear of revealing one's name. The Egyptian Sun God, Ra, says, "My father and my mother have told me my name, and it has remained hidden in my body since my birth, lest some sorcerer should acquire magic power over me thereby."[8] No wonder early Egyptians had two names — a public one and a private one which was kept secret.

But early legends also speak of a positive cathartic power that can come from sharing one's name with another. Isis's statement to Ra brings this point out, "Tell me your name, father of the Gods . . . that the poison may go out of you; for the man whose name is spoken, he lives." Isis tries to persuade Ra to reveal his name by saying, "It will become a potent spell against every poison."[9]

In these earlier times, finding the right name was often a matter of life or death. In the rite of exorcism the priest first tries to determine by what Name the Devil is taking form in order to get the power needed to deal with this force. Likewise in the Egyptian doctrines of the soul, the traveler in the underworld must know "the names of the gatekeepers in the nether world, for only the knowledge of these names can unlock the doors of Death's kingdom. . . . He must call them by their right names. Only by virtue of this appellation can he render them willing and subservient and cause them to take him to his destination"[10] Interpreting this as a psychological allegory we see here the importance of knowing the names of the forces of our inner world, for through this knowledge we are given a key to aid us in that inner journey.

Our interest, however, is not so much with the names of the forces of the psyche *per se*, but rather with the identity of the individual person in premodern societies. The names derived from premodern cosmologies were different from the Tom, Dick and Harrys of our modern age. They were often enshrouded in mystery and contained deep symbolic meaning. Names embodied the person's very purpose for being.

---

8. Cassirer, E. *Language and Myth*, New York: Dover Publications, 1953.
9. Ibid.
10. Ibid., p.49.

# Naming the Essence of One's Being

According to the Hebrew teaching of the Cabala, for instance, every letter of their alphabet was really an ideogram which symbolized a universal principle. This alpha-number code could be used to explore the meaning of a name. For instance the name Moses (Mosheh in Hebrew) contains the letters Mem (a symbol for the water principle), Sheen (a symbol for the breath of God) and Hay (a symbol for the life principle as it is expressed through one's personal energy).[11]

One can see Moses's name in action when he called upon God in the desert to bring water to his people. In a moment of doubt his name might have given him a feeling of strength and purpose. It might have become a symbol to him of his ability in times of spiritual dryness to tap into that which is of substance in life (as he tapped upon the rock in the desert), and to release the water principle (the well of feeling within) to quench the inner thirst of his people.

According to esoteric teachings, the name of a person was said to carry the very vibration of that which a person was. Thus in Eastern traditions a mantra is chosen which corresponds to the person's "frequency," and in the Western world today we still speak of names as having character, softness or strength.

Hans Jenny's research in cymatics[12] stimulates our imaginations further. Jenny works with a tonoscope, an instrument capable of translating various vibratory patterns into form to demonstrate how physical structure comes into being through vibration. He uses a disc with sand or other material on it and vibrates the disc with various frequencies; even the sound of human words can be translated into a visual representation. (See Appendix One.)

When the sacred Hindu word "*om*" is uttered into the tonoscope it produces the pattern "O" which is then filled in with concentric squares and triangles. A yantra is thereby produced. (Yantras are the geometrical expression of sacred vibration found in many of the world's religions.) One frequency used by Jenny is reported to raise particles of iron on the disc so that they stand on top of each other and then march like an army of soldiers across the disc.

Cymatic research taken together with the aforementioned beliefs about naming gives room for speculation. Does the primal "Word of God" in some way refer to a note which allowed man to stand up

---

11. See Chapter Three for a more extensive discussion of this idea brought out by Carlos Suares in *The Cipher of Genesis*, Berkeley: Shambala, 1973.
12. Jenny, H. *Cymatics*, Switzerland: Basilius Press, 1974.

and walk on the earth? Does the sound of one's name have the capacity to form one's own identity? Could it be that our own forms came into being through some type of vibration?

## Do We Have a Real Name?

A more basic question that underlies the quest for identity is whether any name or vibration could exist which would be capable of describing the essence of that which we are. Objections immediately come to mind — how can any name ever express all that a human being is? After all, each of us seems so complex, we have so many aspects to us, that no single name could ever do us justice.

The literature on the knowledge of how to discover something's real Name parallels the literature on the attempt to discover a language of essence. So, in the occult traditions one hears the statement that "every word in the 'true language' was knowledge and magic, i.e., the revelation of the structure of the things named."[13] In the language of the Gnostic sect, for instance, the magic name *Abraxas* was composed of a numerological base; by adding up the numerical value of its letters we get 365 — the number of days it takes the Earth to revolve around the sun. This number which symbolized the relationship of the earth to a wider whole was the number that was the symbol for *Mithra*, the God of light.

The theme of how to describe the essential qualities of someone or something has fascinated many modern thinkers also. Cassirer states that "the aim of cognition is to reflect and reproduce the essence of things while the aim of language is to reflect and reproduce the essence of cognition."[14] There have been those who have attempted to develop a linguistic structure which was oriented to speak of essences. For instance, John Wilkins' ambition in his seventeenth century publication entitled *An Essay Toward a Real Character and a Philosophical Language* was to create a language which would transmit a complete knowledge of the essential nature of any thing represented. His idea can be illustrated by the word "salmon" which in our language does not really tell us anything about the nature of the fish named. In Wilkins' language "*zana*" tells us that it is a river fish with scales and reddish flesh.[15] Others who have spoken to the need to create a language of essence are Hermann Hesse in *The Glass Bead Game*, and of course Carl Jung, who brought to psychology

---

13. Bergier and Pauwells, *The Eternal Man*, New York: Avon Books, 1973, p.87.
14. Cassirer, E. *Language and Myth*, New York: Dover Publications, 1953, p.92.
15. Bergier. *The Eternal Man*, p.96.

an archetypal language that could speak of qualities underlying life processes.

Let us suspend our judgments about the actual existence of "a name" for each of us and instead accept the questions we have as the very ones which have lain at the heart of the search for self knowledge since ancient times. These questions seem to be a fundamental part of the search, leading the seeker, like Isis attempting to find the many buried limbs of dismembered Osiris, to go in search for a unifying name to bring together one's many buried selves. Whether there is indeed a "true name" that each of us has is a question with which we shall wrestle throughout this work.

The problems involved in finding the name of a person are well illustrated by the ancient tale of Rumplestilskin. In this fairy tale, the queen needs to discover the right name of a mysterious dwarf in order to save her child's life. Like our feeling of being overwhelmed with the many possible names a person could have, the queen almost gives up. Luckily, one of the queen's servants hears the dwarf singing his name (Rumplestilskin) before the fire late one night, and when the queen repeats this name to the dwarf, her child is freed. On the psychological level one might interpret this tale to mean that by discovering our names we can free the child within each of us, i.e., our natural ways of being.

Throughout the ages there have been those who we might call "name givers," whose job it was to aid the individual in obtaining his or her name. Many different types of persons have been in this role including shamans, rabbis, priests and parents.

It seems logical to assume the name given would not always describe the person in such a way that it was an aid to coming to terms with that individual's life's meaning. In fact, there were so many variations in regards to the process of name giving in premodern cosmologies that creating a unified picture of it seems nearly impossible.

For instance, there were different bases for giving names in various premodern cultures.[16] At times names were given in relationship to some quality that the namer or parents hoped the child might possess; other times they were given from a characteristic of the child itself. Sometimes the name was chosen on the basis of some circumstance occurring at the time of birth — such as an animal which was seen.

Also different levels of understanding existed among namers in

---

16. Erdoes, R. *Lame Deer, Seeker of Visions*, New York: Simon & Schuster, 1972.

regards to their choosing of names. In the last case, for instance, perhaps the animal seen at the time of birth was chosen on the basis of its symbolic value or perhaps it was assumed to be psychically drawn to the child by an affinity to his or her basic essence.[17]

Variations existed as to how much individual name givers were respected. Among the Sioux Indians, for example, the most respected namers were Winktes[18] (men who dressed as women). They would only gives names to certain children. The secret name given by a Winkte was said to be especially powerful medicine and the father of the child would give a fine horse or other valuables in return for such a name.

Finally, in many premodern cultures, the person's name changed throughout that individual's lifetime. Sometimes children were renamed in order to balance the personality with a name which was seen as offering other options to the person. For instance among the "dineh" (more commonly referred to as Apache), if a child was perceived to be too serious and had a very serious name, a new, "lighter" sounding name would be chosen.[19]

But my purpose is not an extensive anthropological analysis of the variety of types of naming practices of premodern cosmologies; rather it is to establish that name giving was an important part of earlier cosmologies and that, in at least some instances, it served a meaning-giving function.

Most obvious in this regard was the naming which was part of adolescent initiation rites. The naming that was part of this process was fundamental to the metamorphosis from adolescence to adulthood.

Hyemeyohsts Storm[20] tells us how among the American Plains Indians a youth searches for his name by spending three days and nights in the woods alone, fasting and hoping for a vision of his name. The brave's name is given to him by a medicine man who helps the brave to decipher his experience in the woods and learn his natural name. A painting of it is emblazoned upon his shield for all to see.

---

17. This refers to the belief among certain premodern peoples that each person has an animal which is compatible with his or her personality — referred to as an ally, guardian spirit, or tonal by various different traditions.
18. Erdoes, R. *Lame Deer, Seeker of Visions*, New York, Simon & Schuster, 1972, p.117.
19. From an unpublished interview between the author and Oh Shinnah (Song of the Earth Vibration), a Native American woman who is currently teaching traditional ways. Her name was at one time changed to "She Who is Always in the Trees" from a more serious name for this reason.
20. Storm, H. *Seven Arrows*, New York: Harper and Row, 1972.

This new name then becomes a symbol of the person's identity, orienting him "within the circle of the people and in the circle of all things."

With a taste of the possibilities that lie hidden within the mystery of personal identity, let us return to the question: "Is there a 'true name' for each of us?" We face a question similar to the one that perplexed the queen in the myth of Rumplestilskin. Just as the queen embarked on the seemingly impossible task of finding the right name for the dwarf, so have seekers throughout time embarked on a journey in search of a name for themselves.

Mythological ventures often begin with the search for some particular thing. Jason went in search of the Golden Fleece, the ancient alchemists in search for gold. Mythic traditions teach us that it is not so much "the thing attained" but the process of pursuing it that is the "stuff" of the *Magnum Opus*, the Great Work.

Thus perhaps the search for one's true name also begins as a search for a particular thing — a name capable of describing one's essence. The very questions and doubts one has concerning whether one's true name exists form the horizons against which the search for identity is pursued.

Speaking in terms of a "true name" does not preclude that there may be many names that speak truly to that which a person is. The dialogue between the part in people which says that there are many names (or that they change through time) and the part of us that says there is just one true name leads the search onward.

From the search and the way one pursues it, one may discover an individual "way" and a personal answer; it is this that ultimately bespeaks one's true name. Thus one's name is a symbol of a process of self discovery, not a thing isolated from it. The truth of a name is derived from one's life's journey.

# CHAPTER TWO

# MODERN PSYCHOTHERAPISTS AS NAME GIVERS

## Introduction

In our society today, when we seek to discover who we are, we may go to a psychotherapist as people in premodern societies may have gone to the name giver. The quest for meaning, for finding one's place in the world has not lessened in importance. Many psychologists feel that the person's inability to deal adequately with the meaning dimension is a primary root of psychological disease.[1]

Laing describes how "ontological insecurity"[2] (a feeling of meaninglessness based upon the experience of the unreality of the ground of one's being) may lead to feelings of engulfment, implosion or petrification which are present in the experience of psychosis. Frankl recognizes the role of "the existential vacuum of meaninglessness" in neurotic personality disorders.[3] He even suggests adding the term "noogenic neurosis" (a spiritual neurosis based upon an absence of a feeling of meaningfulness in one's life) to the present nomenclature which speaks of psychogenic (arising in the psyche) and somatogenic (originating in the body) neurosis.

Perhaps the most concise statement about the importance of the dimension of meaning is Jung's statement, "A psychoneurosis must

---

1. Frankl, V. *The Will to Meaning*, New York: The New American Library, 1969; Laing, R.D. *The Divided Self*, Baltimore: Penguin Books, 1965; Erikson, E. *Identity, Youth and Crisis*, New York: W.W. Norton and Company, 1968.
2. Laing, R.D. *The Divided Self*.
3. Frankl, V. *The Will to Meaning*.

be understood ultimately as the suffering of a soul which has not discovered its meaning."[4]

The search for a descriptive term to speak of the person's way of being is still greatly emphasized as it was in ancient times. Just as premodern cosmologies functioned to give a name to the seeker, so do psychologists' diagnostic categories serve to give a name to a person. Using a battery of tests as the Plains Indians used the tests of the wilderness, a name is chosen which defines the person's identity. This name, the client's diagnostic label, influences the subsequent treatment.

## Psychotherapeutic Identity Systems

The psychotherapeutic process itself can be viewed as the client's search for a name. Each different psychotherapeutic system has its own descriptive framework for speaking about personality, and the words chosen affect the process of identity formation as they did in earlier times. In the Freudian system, one learns to describe identity as a product of the past. The Gestalt modality stresses describing one's identity in terms of the here and now, while the Adlerian system places the emphasis in terms of future goals. After time spent in Jungian therapy, people describe themselves in terms of universal symbols, while clients of one of the body therapies know themselves through their felt bodily experiences.

After the process of psychotherapy, chances are great that the clients of each of these modalities will continue to experience themselves through the linguistic parameters of that particular identity system. It will become the lens through which the person comes to see his or her identity, and will become the structure through which the individual comes to experience life's meaning.

Since psychological identity systems play such a great part in the formation of identity, one can appreciate the criticism that present psychological systems can lead the therapist to fitting people into a Procrustian bed which forces them into its confines. This may be a natural outcome of the fact that psychotherapists have often become experts in a particular system of psychotherapy and therefore look through the lens of that system when formulating the client's problem.

The system of the therapist's expertise may not be the one that fits the client's individual needs. Boss's classic discussion of how a

---

4. Jung, C.G. *Psychology and Religion*, Princeton: Princeton University Press, 1969.

Freudian and Jungian analysis failed with a client for whom these approaches were not suited bears this out.[5] Certainly many therapists are aware of this problem, and may end up referring clients to another therapist who specializes in a treatment modality better suited to those clients. This however, does not deal with the underlying problem with psychological systems. Despite holistic intentions on the part of the individual therapists, the specialized character of the systems often leads to a systematic myopia. Barton summarizes this problem well when he says:[6]

> While all therapists do at some practical level make individual adjustments in their ongoing relationships with patients . . . the theories allow little space for individual differences, presupposing a fundamental sameness to the patients. Thus in Freudian theory all patients are fundamentally suffering from a repression of sexuality and aggression, in Rogerian therapy all clients suffer from loss of contact with their feelings.

## The Importance of a Psychology that is Oriented to Individual Differences

Leaving aside the orientations of various psychotherapeutic systems for a moment, it seems obvious that, apart from these theoretical systems, each individual had a unique way of being prior to entering therapy. Jung felt that in order to be effective the therapist needed to orient therapy to these individual differences between people. He said that:[7]

> Human beings differ in significant ways, their ways of being involve different psychologies, different ways of theorizing, different ways of apprehending reality — indeed different therapeutic needs. Corresponding to these differences in type, temperament and modes of life are different pathways of help.

Allport also recognizes that a key ingredient of psychological health is the experience of that which is "peculiarly ours." He calls this the "proprium."[8]

The person may sense that there is a relationship between becoming conscious of one's identity and actualizing the energy inherent in one's personality. An analogy may serve to illustrate this

---

5. Boss, M. *Psychoanalysis and daseinalysis*, New York: Basic Books, 1963.
6. Barton, A. *Three Worlds of Therapy: Freud, Jung and Rogers*, Palo Alto, Ca: National Press Books, 1974, p.261.
7. Ibid.
8. Allport, G. *Personality*, New York: Henry Holt and Company, 1937.

point. A track runner who is small and quick, having large calf muscles, knows that his gift is in being a sprinter and not a long distance runner. By developing his body to be in tune with its form, and by operating within and through its constraints, he best actualizes the energy of his body. Perhaps in a similar way, one may feel that by becoming increasingly aware of the structure of one's being, the individual may increase his or her potential on the path of self-actualization.

Many people enter therapy because they feel blocked in actualizing their ways of being in the world. Those with weak ego structures are especially susceptible to the self-doubt that arises from the questioning of their patterns of behavior. The person who spends much time alone is questioned about why he or she is not with others. One who enjoys talking may be reprimanded not to talk so much. A person who fantasizes frequently is often told that this is unreal. Actually, almost every question put to us about ourselves sends reverberations to that place in us which deals with the foundations of our entire life plan. For some, these questions lead to a path of self-doubt where, afraid to be oneself, a person may become less than who he or she could be. For others, these questions are consciously dealt with and provide a route to increased wholeness of personality. The balance between these two possibilities forms the crux of the dilemma of uniqueness. Dr. Edinger emphasizes the importance that he sees in the individual's coming to terms with his or her identity when he says, "In my experience the basis of almost all psychological problems is an unsatisfactory relation to one's urge to individuality."[9]

In order to further understand how people in the psychotherapeutic relationship come to see their identities, one must examine how their personalities are described. The language that each psychotherapeutic system uses sets the dye from which a person's personality is painted.

## A Critique of Psychological Language

In light of the earlier mentioned belief of the Fulani (Chapter One) that the name has the power to guide the person to self discovery or a zombi-like thingness, the criticism that there are severe problems with the way the psychological tradition describes people seems most serious. For the psychological professional often stands at the

---

9. Edinger, E. *Ego and Archetype.*

beginning place of the quest for identity, just as the name giver did in times past, guiding the seeker's way.

## THE MEDICAL MODEL
Modern psychology was born out of a medical model which focused upon the sickness of personality and saw this sickness to be cured through medical treatment. With the mass popularization of psychology, the linguistic framework of the medical model became the most widely used system of personality description. Thus we see today people commonly described in terms of illness.

The culture in general and even many psychologists themselves have strongly criticized the medical model for being skewed towards describing the person in terms which focus on sickness. It is said that within the continuum of neurotic and psychotic disorders there is little room for those who are interested in the unique coloration of the portrait of an individual's personality. Most strongly put, the psychological lexicon has been called "a semantic blackjack capable of crushing the subject's dignity and respectability."[10]

## THE REDUCTIONISTIC CHARACTER OF PSYCHOLOGICAL LANGUAGE
A parallel criticism of present psychological language is that it is reductionistic in character. Illustrating this point, Frankl points out that "in present psychiatric terms Joan of Arc would be nothing but a schizophrenic" because of her hallucinations.[11]

The problem inherent in seeing people through reductive psychological labels which fit people into narrow categories rather than viewing them as whole people was made strikingly apparent in a recent study by Rosenhan. In his experiment, twelve fellow psychologists had themselves admitted to various mental hospitals where they described problem areas of their lives. Eleven of the twelve were diagnosed as schizophrenic, and the remaining one was labeled manic depressive. The only people who suspected that they were not really mentally ill were some of the patients. Members of the hospital staff interpreted actions of the stooges, such as taking notes, from a diagnostic framework whereby it was labeled as "compulsive writing behavior."[12]

---

10. This statement was attributed to Thomas Szasz in a newsletter of the Network Against Psychiatric Assault, January 2, 1975.
11. Frankl, V. *The Will to Meaning*, New York: The New American Library, 1969, p.29.
12. Rosenhan, D. "On being sane in insane places," *Science*, Jan. 1973, 119.

The psychological profession holds a position of name giver in our society, for it aids the individual in coming to terms with who he or she is. Unfortunately, it sets the tone for the identity quest with a language of illness. This may limit the individual's attempt to come to terms with life's meaning as a whole person.

In attempting to give a balanced view of the issue concerning the use of the illness model, Kelly says,[13]

> The therapist needs to know what kind of problem the client is facing to be sure. But he also needs to know what kind of person the client is. This means elaboration of the construction system as a whole, not just those unfortunate constructions which are applied to the problem areas.

A critique of psychological descriptive terminology would be one-sided if it did not take into account that labeling illness does serve a purpose. Torrey[14] for instance, has shown how it has an important role in healing in diverse cultures. It says to the person that someone understands, that the person is not alone with his or her sickness, and it implies that there is a way to get well. It might be added that by naming a client with a certain diagnostic category, a yardstick is created to measure change and to consider appropriate treatment modalities on the basis of what seemed to work with others who have had similar problems.

A forthright perspective also requires dispelling the popular myth which says that mental illness is solely the result of labeling. To say that mental illness has no existence except that which derives from the term used to label it is to commit "the nominalistic or nihilistic fallacy,"[15] i.e., it reduces a phenomenon with reality of its own to being nothing but its name. As Hillman has pointed out, denying the reality of pathology may be to throw away the very meaning that the psyche is attempting to convey through its pathologizing.

The argument against the pervasive focus on terms of illness does not preclude that the therapist (or person in general) needs to describe what kind of problem an individual may be facing, but rather it leads to the need for a language capable of speaking to what kind of person one is as a whole. Psychologists need a language to speak of those negative habit patterns with which the person is dealing. They also need to be as creative and detailed in developing a language capable

---

13. Kelly, G. *The Psychology of Personal Constructs*, Volume I, New York: W.W. Norton and Co., 1955, p.985.
14. Torrey, E. *The Mind Game*.
15. Hillman, J. *Revisioning Psychology*.

of speaking about individual life myths as they have in speaking about life scripts and the illnesses of personality. In this sense a language is needed which is capable of describing in another light the germ of meaning contained in the life path of an individual.

There may well be reasons for expanding the linguistic framework of psychological problems and questioning within which models they can best be explored, i.e., medical, educational, religious, psychological or mythological. But even more in line with this work is the question of what type of language should be used by someone in our culture to frame the quest for self discovery.

## THE ATOMISTIC DESCRIPTION OF PERSONALITY TRAITS

Instead of developing a holistic language, personality researchers have focused most of their efforts on describing atomistic elements of personality (traits) or upon categories into which the person can be placed. The focus upon elements of personality goes along with the desire to make psychology into a science, since from the scientific perspective, one cannot speak of the structure of anything until one knows its constituting elements.

Allport[16] summarizes this insight into the derivation of the modern description of the person when he says,

> The progress of any science, it is said, depends in large part upon its ability to identify elements which in the combination found in nature, constitute the phenomenon that the science has set out to examine. Without its table of elements, chemistry could not exist. . .The suspicion with which many natural scientists view psychology arises in part from their belief (entirely correct) that the elementary processes of mind have not yet been identified . . .

The most obvious example of the division of personality into parts that ignored the nature of the whole personality was the older stimulus-response psychology according to which personality was simply the total of the stimulus-response connections. Although modern personality theorists show more awareness of the complexities of the personality and its larger units, many still act as if they had never heard Allport's recommendation to concentrate on unique organizations of the personality. Instead they generalize.

## THE PROBLEM WITH CATEGORIES

Although every person is like all other people, like no other person,

---

16. Allport, G. *Personality*, p.238.

and like some other people, personality theorists have focused most of their efforts on the last of these. They have focused on elements common to the species (the nomothetic approach). The problem with this approach is, as Allport puts it, that by looking for the elements common to the species one often neglects the individual's uniqueness, his or her "ideographic pattern of becoming" (the ideographic approach). By doing so the elements that are employed in the analysis of personality are not true parts of the original whole; rather they measure how a person fits into a set of preconceived variables. Expounding on this point Allport (1955) says,

> His habits (the psychologist's) lead him to ablate from John's nature some single segment for study. The surgery is accomplished by impressing upon John certain universal cutting instruments. One incision has to do, shall we say, with the "need for achievement", another with the "intelligence quotient." These incisions are not viewed as intersecting one another in John but rather as intersecting corresponding properties in other persons. The result is that we usually view John's personality as a diagram drawn in a set of external coordinates having no interrelation, no duration in time, no motion, no life, no variability, no uniqueness. What is peculiarly Johnian our methods of analysis do not tell . . . The universal dimensions employed in diagnosing John may be irrelevant to his personality. Perhaps he has no need for achievement but only a peculiar and unique need for exhibitionistic domination. The dimension employed seriously misses the precise coloring of his motivation."[17]

Many psychologists have been critical of the use of categorical trait names to describe the person. As Jung (1931) says in regard to the trait of introversion, "The introverted person does not behave just like every other introverted person, but in a way unique to himself."[18] Also, to assume that a trait that seems to be an aspect of one area of the personality is a general aspect of other parts of the personality cannot be supported. As Kelly (1955) has shown, the person who deals abstractly with one kind of problem is as likely as not to deal concretely with another kind of problem. Furthermore, those who are more prone than others to use abstract approaches in one area might be less prone than others to use abstract approaches in another areas.

## LACK OF ORIENTATION TO PSYCHOTHERAPEUTIC ISSUES

Certainly, the focus on categorization has its value. It aids the researcher in comparing one person with another, and the psychotherapist in choosing an appropriate treatment modality.

---

17. Allport, G. *Becoming*, New Haven, Conn.: Yale University Press, 1955, p.20.
18. Jung, C.G. *Psychological Types*, Vol.6, Princeton: Princeton University Press, 1971, p.536.

However, by meeting the personality theorist's needs in certain areas, a language is created which does not meet the person's need for a language which gives the individual a feeling of who he or she is as a whole person. This lack is well illustrated by the fact that personality tests, the backbone of personality research which are often done upon a client's entering therapy, are rarely even discussed with the client. Perhaps this is because therapists sense that the way psychological tests describe people does not meet their psychotherapeutic needs, i.e., to have a language that can give the individual a feeling of his or her unique identity in such a way that it helps that individual experience his or her life as meaningful. Imagine what a categorical name like "obsessive-compulsive" (diagnostic category 300.30 in the *DSMIII*, i.e., *Diagnostic and Statistical Manual of Mental Disorders*) does to one's sense of identity!

## DRAWING A DISTINCTION BETWEEN IDENTITY AND THE MEANING OF ONE'S LIFE

Thus far the reader may have received the impression that there is an equivalence between one's "identity" and the "meaning" of one's life. The areas of overlap and distinction between these two terms needs more careful consideration.

A distinction between these two terms can be made by imagining two overlapping circles: circle #1 being the term "identity" and circle #3 the term "meaning." The area of overlap is enclosed in circle #2. When I speak of "identity" I mean the attributes of one's personality that make him or her unique. When I speak of "meaning" I refer to the significance one experiences when seeing one's way of being, behavior, or life in general in a new way.

The following figure indicates that these terms may overlap or be distinct from each other. The area where "meaning" can be distinguished from "identity" (#3) might be exemplified by a transpersonal orientation. One might say that one's life meaning comes from touching areas of his or her Self that are beyond the ego structure (as, for example, the feelings that some people who are involved in meditation report). When such a man says that this is what gives his life meaning, he is probably not referring to his "identity" in the sense we have defined it. (Unless one wished to argue that this world view gave the man a feeling of his uniqueness as a person. But then we would still need to examine how he came to his transpersonal view in a way different than others who had the same view, in order to fit the above definition of identity. If the person did discuss it in such a way as to speak of the individual differences between his orientation and others then we would be in the area labeled #2, the area of overlap between "meaning" and "identity.")

An example of where the "identity" circle does not overlap the "meaning" circle would be the case of a clinical psychologist who gave a Minnesota Multiphasic Personality Inventory (MMPI) to a client but did not discuss this with the person. Here the psychologist "identified" the person as high on the hypomania scale but if this was not discussed with the person it would have done nothing for aiding the person in experiencing his life's meaning in a new way.

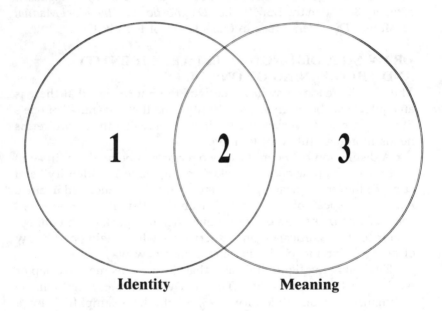

**Identity**                    **Meaning**

An example of the area of overlap (#2) between the two terms could be the Freudian system of identity. If a person saw himself as an anal retentive personality and thereby came to experience the meaning of his stinginess in a new way, we could say that the dimensions of meaning and identity were both present in his insight.

In this work the argument has been made that those identity systems which lie in section #2 of the diagram still have severe problems. Some of these problems that we have considered are that the meaning that they bring forth is oriented toward sickness, and that the terms used to speak of identity are atomistic in character, thereby limiting a holistic view of the person's personality. My intention is to develop a process that deals with the problem area while staying in section #2 of the diagram — i.e., to develop a process through which people can come to terms with who they are as unique individuals and from which they can experience new meaning in their ways of being.

The line of criticism with which we are concerned in this particular section, though, applies to area #1 of the diagram. Current ways of "identifying" psychological patients are criticized for using a linguistic system that is often divorced from giving the person a meaningful view of him or herself — i.e., that it only concerns itself with section #1 of the diagram.

The purpose for which many psychologists study the personality is not to enhance the person's experience of life's meaning, but rather to suit the interests of the researchers of personality. Some of these areas of interest are: the need to identify elements of personality, to diagnose the person, and to compare the person with others for the purpose of measurement or description.

In his book on personality theory, Sanford (1970) discusses how the research on personality is colored by the interests of the researchers. He says,

> Personality research in this country is highly susceptible to trends and fashions. One year values occupy the center of the stage; another year anxiety or cognitive structures or authoritarianism or the achievement motive. This is not to suggest that the fashionable life is bad — on the contrary, it is interesting and in a way productive — but rather that attention to what investigators happen to be doing at a particular time is a poor guide to an understanding of personality.[19]

## SUMMARY OF CRITICISMS OF MODERN PSYCHOLOGICAL LANGUAGE

One can appreciate why an increasing number of psychologists are concerned with the manner in which people are described. In summary, the following are the problems with psychological language:

1. The orientation towards describing people in terms of sickness — the medical model.
2. The reductionistic character of psychological language.
3. The atomistic description of personality traits with subsequent

19. Sanford, N. *Issues in Personality Theory* , San Francisco: Jossey Bass Inc., 1970.

lack of a holistic means of description.

4. A language that boxes people into categories thereby losing the unique flavor of the individual's way of being.
5. The description of personality without proper attention to psychotherapeutic issues.
6. The lack of an orientation towards giving an individual a feeling of life's personal meaning.

## The Holistic Approach: A Historical Perspective

From the above problem areas was born the need for a holistic approach to identity. In its history, the concept of holism has taken on a variety of meanings.

General Jan Smuts, a statesman, philosopher and scientist, first introduced the concept of holism to modern thought. In his book on *Holism and Evolution* (1926) he says that "besides the parts or elements in things there is another factor (the whole) which science does not recognize at all."[20] In order to counter the atomistic trend of the day, Smuts argued that "the whole is more than the sum of its parts."[21] As he developed the concept of holism, Smuts said the following:

> . . . insofar as a whole is consisting of parts or elements they cannot be fixed, constant or unalterable (since) . . . whole and parts mutually and reciprocally influence and modify each other . . . The parts are moulded and adjusted by the whole, just as the whole in turn depends on the cooperation of its parts"[22]

The earliest systematic attempt at developing a holistic conception of personality was the work of the Gestalt psychologists. Like Smuts, they attacked the *weltanschauung* (world view) of the atomists. Kohler (1929) argued that the personality could not be conceived in terms of local stimulus-response connections. Using a musical analogy, he disputed the atomists' idea that a conception of the personality as a whole could be derived by merely adding up its composite atomistic units. Kohler said that when the tones C and G are sounded, they produce a quality which in musical terms is called the Fifth. Fifthness is a Gestalt (a whole) which is different

---

20. Smuts, J. *Holism and Evolution*, New York: McMillan, 1926.
21. Ibid.
22. Rudhyar, D. *The Astrology of Personality*, New York: Doubleday, 1970, p.53.

from either or any of its parts. Kohler concluded that, "The whole is different than the sum of its parts."[23]

The ideas of the Gestalt psychologists had important repercussions in many areas of psychology such as: how the person perceived, how the person learned and how the person could be conceived as a dynamic whole. The latter is closest to our specific area of interest: how the person could be conceived as a dynamic whole.

Lewin (1935) was most instrumental in offering a conceptual model to speak to this last point. His "field theory" approach offered a model of the structure of psychological reality as he saw it. The model emphasized the interconnection between regions of the personality, and its fluid interrelationship with the environment (the person/environment field). He offered to psychology a way of spatially conceptualizing the "life space" of an individual — the name he gave to the person/environment field.

Many psychological theorists have spoken of the need to conceive of **the whole self**.[24] The organismic psychologists (Russell, 1916; Ritter, 1919; and Murray, 1938) believe, as Murray states, that "The organism is from the beginning a whole, . . . the whole being as essential to an understanding of the parts as the parts are to an understanding of the whole."[25] The organismic psychologists aimed their efforts at general psychological problems such as emotional conditioning, sensorimotor learning, perception, and reaction to frustration.

Holism was also the core principle in the views of Lecky (1945), one of the early contributors to the theory of the "phenomenal self."[26]

In his explanation of this concept, Lecky says that all of an individual's ideas are organized into a single system, whose preservation is essential. The nucleus of this system around which the rest of the system revolves is the individual's conception of him or herself. Rogers (1959) has adopted this conception as a cornerstone of his client-centered psychotherapeutic work.

Another important theoretical contribution to the psychology of

---

23. Kohler, W. *The Task of Gestalt Psychology* Princeton: Princeton University Press, 1969.
24. For a more general discussion of how the concept of the whole self is a central concern of humanistic psychology, see Buhler (1967). For a general discussion of this concept in personality theory, Sanford (1970) provides a good review of the literature.
25. Murray, H.A. *Explorations in Personality*, New York: Oxford Press, 1938, p.39.
26. Lecky, P. *Self Consistency*, New York: Island Press Cooperative, 1945.

holism was directed at dealing with the reductionistic way of conceiving of the person. Frankl stands out in this regard. Disturbed that from the psychiatric point of view, Saint Joan of Arc would probably be diagnosed as "nothing but" a schizophrenic, Frankl (1969) developed a conceptual schema called "dimensional ontology"[27] which conceived of the personality in terms of different levels of meaning. As applied to the above example, what Joan of Arc is beyond a schizophrenic may not be perceived within a psychiatric framework; however, as one views her through the "noological dimension" (the dimension of meaning) one can discern other attributes of her way of being. When one can see religious, spiritual, or historical characteristics of her life, Joan of Arc becomes something different than a schizophrenic. Frankl points out that he is not arguing for the elimination of the psychiatric perspective, but rather that the psychiatrists realize that they are seeing a given phenomenon through the dimension of psychiatry.

Angyal (1965) in his holistic theory also makes an argument for including both healthy and unhealthy aspects of self-functioning into a conception of personality.[28] The progression of the personality over time and the inclusion of the person's philosophy of life Angyal also sees as essential to a holistic theory.

**The dimension of meaning** gradually became integrated into the psychology of holism. Frankl (1969) made a most important contribution in arguing for the inclusion of the term "noogenic neurosis" to stress the importance of the frustration of the will to meaning in psychological disorders. Others who played a significant role in speaking to the importance of the dimension of meaning are Maslow (1965), Gendlin (1962), Jung (1960), and Fingarette (1963).

Maslow (1965) added to this subject area by stressing "purposefulness" and "self-actualization."[29] Gendlin spoke of "the felt experience of meaning."[30] The psychotherapeutic insights of Gendlin are used throughout the latter part of this work, particularly his process of "focusing." Jung's contributions to the dimension of meaning are also discussed throughout this work, especially the role of symbols in transforming meaning and the role of Jung's

27. Frankl, V. *The Will to Meaning*, New York: The New American Library, 1969, p.23.
28. See also Hillman (1975) for an excellent discussion of the importance of including the polytheistic possibilities of the self.
29. Maslow, A. *The Farther Reaches of Human Nature*, Baltimore, Md: Penguin Books, 1976.
30. Gendlin, E. *Experiencing and the Creation of Meaning* Toronto, Canada: The Free Press of Glencoe, 1962.

concept of "the Self" in regards to the experience of wholeness.

The distinction that Fingarette (1963) made between "the hidden reality" theory of meaning and "the meaning reorganization" point of view form a central building block of this work.[31] The hidden reality assumes an objective underlying meaning that caused one to be the way one is. For instance, from a Freudian viewpoint a certain past trauma might be seen as having caused one to be shy. The "meaning reorganization" view, on the other hand, emphasizes that when people give meaning to a past event, they use a meaning schema in the present. At another moment in time, another meaning might be attributed to the person's shyness. We perpetually rewrite history in terms of current interpretations and assumptions.

The meaning reorganization view does not preclude that there may be "a meaning" to one's way of being, but rather places the emphasis upon what occurs as the person experiences his or her life's meaning in a new way. The former position is absolutist in nature, assuming a fixed meaning. The later position is phenomenological in nature, emphasizing the experiential shift that occurs in reorganizing one's meaning schema, i.e., changing one's perceptions of meanings and view of reality. Subsequently, we will apply the meaning reorganization view to astrological theory.

Looking back on the holistic psychologists, none has developed a language of identity that could describe the individual differences of people's personalities. For example, the major thrust of Lewin's work was in introducing concepts relating to the structure of the personality and its topography, not on elucidating qualities of the individual's personality. It did not offer a way for the person to experience his or her unique identity or life's meaning. Also, Frankl's system of therapy, logotherapy, which is oriented toward helping the client to deal with life's meaning, never specifically relates meaning to the unique quality of one's personality. Likewise those psychologists who have spoken of the whole self (a concept which is central to a holistic identity system) still have not given us a language capable to speaking of those distinctive characteristics that make an individual's personality what it is.

Many psychologists have doubted their ability to analyze anything so global as the whole personality and thus have scoffed at attempts to do so. Perhaps those who have spoken of a holistic approach to personality have added to this opinion, for often they claim that the personality is an indivisible whole without actually

---

31. Fingarette, H. *The Self in Transformation*. New York: Harper and Row, 1963.

delineating the subtle shades of difference that make the individual's personality unique. Speaking to the problem of nebulous holism, Allport (1937) says:

> This rapturous literature of wholeness does not explore the unity that it apotheosizes; it merely contemplates and admires. Personality, it says, is like a symphony. Granted; but does not the comprehension of symphonic unity come only through an understanding of the articulate weaving of motifs, movements, bridge-passes, modulations, contrasts, and codas? Nothing but empty and vague adjectives can be used to characterize the work as a whole. If a totality is not articulated, it is likely to be an incomprehensible blur; it can then be extolled, but not understood. What is more fatal, the rhapsodic approach seriously oversimplifies the whole problem, underestimating the conflicts and discords in every life. Unity at best is a matter of degree.[32]

And so the dimension of **uniqueness** also became a concern of holistic psychologists. Psychologists have struggled to develop a language that would be capable of describing the uniqueness of each individual's way of being. The dilemma has been that if personality theorists attempt to outline traits of the personality (for example, McClelland, 1951; Guilford, 1959; Cattell, 1970), they are criticized for not being ideographic or not placing enough emphasis on the whole self, whereas if the theorists do not outline the particular personality characteristics of the people they extoll, they are accused of nebulous holism.

There have been some psychologists working with issues important to the creation of a holistic identity system. Jung, for instance, made some important steps in creating a holistic way of viewing the personality that did not sidestep the issue of the development of component traits of personality. He attempted to elucidate the basic structures underlying psychic life, which he called archetypes. These were not traits in the categorical sense, but rather energy potentials which could take form in different personalities in different ways.

Jung's introduction of the concept of the symbol to speak of qualities of personality was particularly useful in dealing with the uniqueness of personality structures. Since symbols are expansive in nature, Jung hoped to provide room for the person to enter into them, to experience how certain symbols applied to one's own self. Jung saw the archetypal symbols as paired polarities — uniqueness came from the interplay of these opposites. For instance, by dealing

---

32. Allport, G. *Personality*. New York: Henry Holt and Company, 1937, pp. 343-44.

with the symbols of the *puer-senex*[33] polarity, people could discover how this archetypal opposition applied to their personalities. Jung's use of polarities led some to think in terms of either-or categories, which would not do justice to Smut's desire to have a means whereby all of the components of a whole can mutually interrelate. Nevertheless, symbols helped to incorporate the experiential dimension into personality. By resolving the tension between the opposites, Jung discovered that new meaning sometimes arose for the person which he called "the transcendent function."[34] Unlike many personality theorists, Jung extended his insights into the therapeutic area by speaking to the dimension of meaning.

Although he contributed significantly to developing the dimension of uniqueness, the typological system of personality that Jung offered was not complex enough to encompass the breadth of his vision. Bringing together the two attitude types and four functions into various combinations such as introverted intuitive thinking type is not adequate to capture the uniqueness of one's personality as a whole.

In other areas of Jung's writing we do find concepts important to laying a foundation for envisioning the personality as a whole. By viewing the personality as a mandala,[35] an image of wholeness can be created. In addition, through his in-depth study of mythology, Jung opened the way to view personality in terms of mythic symbols instead of medical model categories. Equally significant was Jung's definition of the Self, spelled with a capital "S," to speak of a wider center of one's psyche than the ego complex. This was vital to the transcendent aspect of meaning.

Another system of identity that allows for a description of the unique qualities of one's personality and relates it to the individual's own framework of meaning was Kelly's (1955) personal construct method. His framework of personality was composed of adjectives

---

33. The *puer* is a symbol for the eternal youth, ever growing, every dreaming, ever changing, not being held down by anything. The *Senex* is a symbol for the father principle, solid and practical. This polarity centers around the archetypal opposition between the forces of change, innovation and creativity versus stability, structure and conservation of the existing order of things. Von Franz (1970) discusses it extensively in psychological terms in *Puer Aeternus*. See also Hillman, J. *Puer Papers*, New York: Spring Publications, 1979.

34. Jung, C.G. *Psychological Types*, Vol. 6 of Collected Works, Princeton: Princeton University Press, 1971.

35. A mandala is a figure, usually a circle, square or other symmetrical arrangement which is constructed around a center and thereby may aid a person in the internal process of centering. See Chapter Four for a more extensive discussion of the mandala.

taken from the clients' own descriptions of themselves and significant others in their lives. Kelly developed a framework that was
meaningful to the individual person — a most ingenious change from
the usual externally-imposed system which was meaningful to the
psychologist.

However, since the terms that clients choose to describe
themselves have been affected by ways of describing personality in
the culture at large, Kelly's system does not solve such problems
as finding a mode of description that is removed from the current
illness model. Also, although personalizing the description of personality, it does not present a linguistic framework that could serve
as an alternative holistic system of personality structures; it is still
atomistic in approach. Therefore, despite holistic intentions on the
part of therapists who recognize the way the medical model colors
their perspective, it may continue to do so. If one argues that
regardless of the nature of psychological language that the therapist
in particular or people in general can still view identity in a holistic
manner, then one has forgotten the ancient power of the word to
create and its power to color that which one sees.

## The Need for a Holistic Identity System

This chapter covers the background of my search for a holistic identity system. The word "holistic" has been used in a variety of contexts. In personality theory, it refers to various aspects of the
framework of identity that is used to describe the person. For instance, the word "holistic" has been used to speak of the need to
describe the individual's personality as a whole rather than an
atomistic focusing on parts of one's personality. But it has been used,
as well, to speak of what is unique to one's personality.

In the psychotherapeutic process, additional meanings of the
word "holistic" arise. Since the experiential dimension is fundamental here, the psychotherapeutic process requires a system to aid the
person in experiencing life's meaning in a new way. Just as the personality theorist had a variety of factors included in the concept of
a holistic description of identity, so does the psychotherapist have
a variety of factors included in the experiential dimension. Some of
these factors are: the experience of wholeness, the experience of
one's uniqueness, and the relationship of one's life's meaning to a
wider whole. This latter meaning of holistic is connected to the root
word "holy" rather than "whole" (as in adding up all the parts). Finding the connection between one's personality and the wider whole

of which one is a part opens the holy or sacred aspects of a holistic approach to personality.

The integration of these dimensions (descriptive and experiential) forms the basis of a "holistic identity system" as I shall use the term. It is the outgrowth of that area (#2 in Diagram 1, page 20) where meaning and identity overlap.

As I come to the point of summarizing some of the composite attributes of a holistic identity system, I find myself reminded of Lao Tzu. After beginning the *Tao Te Ching* with the statement, "The way that can be spoken of is not the constant way," he goes on to describe aspects of "the way."[36] Similarly it seems that breaking a holistic identity system into its component parts may endanger its wholeness. It seems that the descriptive and experiential aspects of identity, uniqueness, wholeness and meaning all merge together in (risking Allport's criticism) a rhapsody of wholeness. Setting this tone I feel more comfortable in summarizing some of the themes of its composition.

In the following few pages I shall outline those criteria of a holistic identity system used throughout this work to examine the systems being described. For organizational purposes these criteria shall be divided into:

I. Aspects of a descriptive framework of identity and
II. Aspects important to the experience of meaning.

Since these two dimensions are overlapping aspects of a holistic system (Recall #2 of Diagram 1, page 20) certain points listed under the descriptive framework could also be placed in the experiential section. For instance, under the experiential framework, we list "Does the person get a feeling of being reduced by the terminology or does it allow room for an individual to enter into the term and expand beyond its seeming boundaries?" One can see this point might also be included under the descriptive framework section if we wished to emphasize the terminology itself. The former position was chosen in this case because I shall be emphasizing the central role that the expansive character of symbols plays in experiencing meaning.

An additional factor important to a holistic identity system has been separated from the descriptive and experiential points. The experience of a wider whole is discussed under a third (III) heading

---

36. Lao Tzu. *Tao Te Ching*, New York: Penguin Books, 1963, p.57.

because it is a transpersonal aspect of identity, whereas the earlier points refer to the personal dimension of identity and meaning. This third point relates to the experience of self-transcendence that many psychologists deem essential to the individual's experience of meaning (for example, Jung, Jaffe, Assagioli and Maslow).

The criteria that follow under the headings: descriptive framework of identity, experience of new meaning and experience of a wider whole shall be used throughout this work to determine whether a system is a holistic identity system. I shall later examine how certain premodern identity systems, particularly astrology, stand up to these points of concern.

## CRITERIA FOR A HOLISTIC IDENTITY SYSTEM

I. Is there a descriptive framework of identity?
  A. Is the person described in terms of an atomized aspect of personality, or in terms of his or her whole self? Relating to this issue are these subpoints:
    1. Are the elements of one's personality described in such a way that they can relate with the personality as a whole, i.e., that they can mutually and reciprocally influence and modify each other?
    2. Are the elements of the personality described in such a way that they can interrelate with each other?
    3. Is there a dynamic or static conception of the personality? By this, we refer to Kelly's statement that it is important for a personality system to do more than plot differences between individuals as if each person were a fixed body in a galaxy of other fixed bodies and had no rotations, orbits, drifts or other cyclical movements.
  B. Does the system provide a means to speak of the person's unique way of being?
    1. Is the person described in terms of general categories that box the individual with other people, or is there a way to speak of the person's qualities ideographically?
    2. Is there an openness to incorporating new elements into the system that apply to the particular person being described?
    3. Is there a complex framework of elements of personality?
II. Does the system provide a path to experiencing new meaning in one's way of being?
  A. Does the system provide a means to experience oneself as

a whole person? Some words that may convey my meaning in using this phrase are: a feeling of integration of the many facets of one's self, a harmony with oneself, a feeling of being centered in one's way of being, and a feeling of purposefulness (meaningfulness) in one's life. The experience of wholeness includes as well the (Jungian) shadow of the above, i.e., the experience of disintegration, dissonance, uncenteredness and the mystery of one's personality.

B. Does the system provide a way to experience new meaning in relationship to the uniqueness of one's personality? This point refers to both the insight that we have into our unique way of being and the corresponding felt shift (Gendlin, 1962). (The experience of one's unique way of being may be positive or negative, harmonious or dissonant; for one may discover that there are advantages and disadvantages of what one sees as being uniquely his or hers at any moment in time.)

    1. Is the person described in terms of ethics or aesthetics? [37]

C. Does the person get a feeling of being reduced by the terminology of the system, or does it allow room for the individual to enter into the term and expand it beyond its seeming boundaries? This refers to the symbolic mode of description.

D. Is there a dynamic or static conception of one's life meaning? There needs to be room in the system to allow people to reorganize the way they see the meaning of their lives over time. This refers to Fingarette's (1963) "meaning reorganization point of view" which does not preclude that there may be "a hidden meaning" to one's life (this is "the hidden reality viewpoint"), but rather places the emphasis upon what occurs as the person experiences life's meaning in a new way.[38]

---

37. In speaking of an aesthetic mode of personality description, we are referring to a conception of Dane Rudhyar's (1936), i.e., that personality needs a language that leads to an aesthetic appreciation of the various hues of personality rather than a language that describes it in such a way that it is tinged with negative value judgments.

    I wish to extend Rudhyar's idea here to be in line with Angyal's (1965) concept of universal ambiguity. This means that personality qualities are ambiguous in that they take on different forms (positive or negative) depending upon whether they are part of a healthy or neurotic personality structure.

38. Fingarette *Self in Transformation*.

III. The experience of a wider whole
   A.  Does the system offer a way to relate one's way of being
       to a wider whole? This can be important in the transcen-
       dent experience of one's life meaning.

# CHAPTER THREE

# PREMODERN PERSONALITY SYSTEMS: AN ALTERNATIVE TO THE MEDICAL MODEL

## Introduction

Given the importance of describing one's identity in terms which allow the person to experience life as meaningful, and given that modern psychological language seems to be lacking in its ability to do so, what is the alternative? It seems presumptuous indeed to think that only modern man has something valuable to say about the age-old issues of meaning and identity. And yet in the modern literature on personality, earlier systems of personality are often given short shrift. Rarely does one hear positive statements made in relation to what our ancient psychological colleagues have to offer. It is as if modern personality theory has made a genealogical break.

There were reasons for this break. At the time modern theories of personality were born, the prevailing language of personality was often used to validate the maltreatment of the mentally ill. Labels of illness were embedded in a social fabric that gave members of the citizenry an opportunity to attack instinctuality, idleness or other qualities juxtaposed to the prevailing ethic. With humors, curses or stars seen to be at the root of personality formation, there is no doubt that superstition was rampant in the labeling of people. The repercussions of these labeling systems often took on terrifying proportions — such as the burning of the Salem "witches." No wonder an objective psychology was sought after.

The birth of modern personality theory can be viewed as an inflated hero myth. The earlier traditions of personality description are remembered for their negative, superstitious elements or are simply written off as being archaic. From the tales told of the dragons that Western psychology defeated, one is left with the impression that little can be gained from earlier personality theories.

Let us now return to reviving some of these dragons and see what life they may breathe into our modern views. These earlier personality systems will here be called "premodern." The term "premodern" was chosen after careful consideration, for it seems to lend a focus on those identity systems which shall be explored in a way that other terms might not. For instance, the term "ancient" implies a time in the far distant past; and certain identity systems examined, such as that of the Plains Indians of the late 1800s, existed in close to present times. The term "primitive" also does not fit our meaning for the early cultures in which the astrological system thrived. They were certainly not unsophisticated or replete with "concrete thinking"[1] as might be inferred from the term primitive — witness Egypt and Babylon.

The term premodern does not specifically connote a time in the ancient past or an unsophisticated or concrete awareness. Yet there are still certain problems with this term. The criteria for making a culture modern are multi-faceted and the dividing line between modern and premodern cultures is ambiguous.

It would make things easy if we could take a time in history and say that before this or that year, the description of personality was not seen through the lens of an illness model. However, the medical model was **not** born in the 18th or 19th centuries in Western Industrial Europe. Menninger (1963) has shown how in the Western world as far back as Hippocrates (around 400 B.C.), attempts were made to describe psychiatric illnesses of personality. In other areas of the world, such as ancient India, various forms of mental illness were ordered in the *Ayur Veda* (1400 BC). These were not isolated examples, for many classificatory schemas of mental illness have existed since these times.[2]

It is not that any orientation to dis-eased aspects of personality will be excluded in the definition of premodern identity systems, but there will be a focus on those identity systems which saw illness through a lens of a wider perspective rather than the other way

1. Diamond, S. *Primitive views of the world*. New York: Columbia University Press, 1960.
2. See Allport (1937), Menninger (1963), Foucault (1965) and Illich (1975).

around. In other words, when illness was included in one of these systems, it was part of a larger cosmological framework meant to give the person an experience of how this symptom fit into the larger order of the life process, or how the symptom was part of the psyche's journey to heal itself. My interest lies not in categories of mental illness *per se*, but in those cultures which gave Names to be used as living tools with which one could explore the meaning of life.

To attempt to discern where such cultures may have existed geographically and temporally is a task we leave to the cultural anthropologist. To this author, it does not seem that categories such as the rise of technology, a unified cosmological world view, or homogeneity of culture serve as an adequate yardstick to delineate the area of inquiry. It cannot be assumed that cultures falling within any of these categories necessarily yield a language of asset to the psychologist's interest in holism. The nature of my inquiry is not an extensive historical investigation of earlier systems of personality. I shall intensively explore certain premodern identity systems for the purpose of integrating their holistic aspects into modern psychological thought.

The term "premodern systems of identity" refers to certain earlier societies which conceived of a person's identity in relation to a cosmological schema meant to convey to the individual a feeling of life's meaning and his or her place in the universe. Attention shall be directed to those developed identity systems which had a system of typology infused with symbolic language.

One psychologist who speaks to this subject area is Hillman (1975), who shows how one's identity in these earlier times was made alive, "ensouled," with the the use of symbolic language.[3] Hillman differentiates this from what he sees as characteristic of naming in the modern age — "empty nomina." His work serves as a landmark to those who wish entry into how the tradition of metaphorical Naming (called "mythic consciousness" by Cassirer, 1953) differs from ours.[4]

In this chapter, we shall see how the descriptive term with which the person was identified (the Name) helped the individual come to terms with life's meaning, and how the cosmological framework within which the Name was located allowed the person to envision how his or her life interconnected with a wider whole.

---

3. Hillman, *Revisioning Psychology*.
4. Cassirer,E., *The Philosophy of Symbolic Forms*, vol. 2, New Haven, Connecticut: Yale University Press, 1955, p.29.

# The Plains Indians' Identity System[5]

In the American Plains Indians', culture, a young person's name was discovered as part of a cosmological system.

The central unifying symbol of this culture was the Great Medicine Wheel which, it was said, could be thought of as "a mirror in which everything is reflected. The Universe is the Mirror of the People and each person is a mirror to every other person. Any idea, person or object can be a medicine wheel, a mirror for man."[6] When explaining the Medicine Wheel to their children, a circle of stones was made upon the ground. It would then be said,

> Each one of these tiny stones within the Medicine Wheel represents one of the many things of the universe. One of them represents me. Others hold within them our mothers, fathers, sisters, brothers, and our friends. Still others symbolize hawks, buffalo, elks, and wolves. There are also stones which represent religions, governments, philosophies and even entire nations. All things are contained within the Medicine Wheel, and all things are equal within it. The Medicine Wheel is the total universe.[7]

Each individual person, the youth is told, starts off at a different beginning place on the wheel. The brave discovers what this place is by going on a Vision Quest, spending days alone in the woods seeking a vision. After returning and relating his experiences to the religious leader(s) of the tribe, his Name is given to him — being derived from the brave's way of being.[8]

The four directions of the Plains Indians' Medicine Wheel are said to be directions of perceiving. The direction North is a symbol for wisdom, along with the color white; it derives its meaning from the cool north wind of the intellect. The direction South is a symbol

---

5. The discussion on the Plains Indians' identity system comes from Hyemeyoshsts Storm's (1972) *Seven Arrows*. Other books on the Plains Indians' cosmology are Mails' (1972) *The Mystic Warriors of the Plains*, and Erdoes' (1972) *The Sun Dance People*. Whether Storm's account is a literally true description of the process of Naming in the Plains Indians' culture does not affect the object of this inquiry. For this work does not intend to examine premodern cultures as an anthropologist might, but rather to determine whether certain premodern identity systems may have potential as a holistic language of personality for psychology today.

6. Storm, H. *Seven Arrows*.

7. Storm, H. *Seven Arrows*.

8. From Storm's account, it is unclear whether the name in the Plains Indian tradition is chosen in a logical, analytical manner by determining the person's personality qualities and then transposing them into the language of the Medicine Wheel, or whether the name actually comes to the person in a vision while in the woods.

   During the course of writing this work, the author did a forty day Vision Quest where a Name did come through a vision. This does not prove, however, that the Plains Indians received their names this way.

for trust and innocence, along with the color green; its meaning derives from the warmth of the South. East stands for illumination, yellow in color; its meaning derives from the rising Sun. West is the direction of introspection, along with the color black; its meaning derives from the setting Sun. From one's place on the Medicine Wheel, the individual would find his or her place of orientation "in the circle of the people and in the circle of all things."[9] The brave's Name is usually composed of an animal, a direction of the Medicine Wheel compass, and a color. It is emblazoned upon his shield for all to see. To his tribe members, it becomes a symbol of that person's identity, imbuing his particular quality of being with meaning.[10]

As an example, in the book *Seven Arrows*, the personal shield of the great chief Thunder Bow is illustrated. The symbolic structure of his shield tells of a man who is interested in wisdom more than impulsive action, in peace rather than war. This can be seen from a bow changed to a rainbow, and a war axe transformed into a peace pipe. When the white man came, Thunder Bow spoke for peace, when others spoke for war. He said at one point, "Many of our People wish to see this same Power reflection that the white man perceives," as he attempted to convey that identifying with the white man's power objects and throwing away their medicine shields, taking instead shields of war, was as serious as the loss of their lands. Thunder Bow saw his brothers losing their souls. His answer was, "We must grow and seek the four directions and the Brotherhood."[11]

# Does the Plains Indians' Cosmology Meet Our Criteria for a Holistic Identity System?

In order to examine how the Plains Indians' Naming system measures up to those requirements that were earlier listed as criteria for a holistic identity system, let us take a fictitious example of the brave White Turtle of the North. The symbolic structure of this Name

9. Storm, H. *Seven Arrows*.
10. To the best of the author's knowledge, women did not generally go on Vision Quests in Native American tribes. Name giving varied from tribe to tribe. In some tribes, women might receive a name from a tribal elder. In another tribe, a shaman might give a name. Elsewhere, the parents were the name givers. This would be a good subject for further research.
11. Storm, H. *Seven Arrows*, p.327.

reveals that this person, like the turtle, looks within. The color white, the color of wisdom, and the direction north, the direction of wisdom, further tell us that this brave would deeply consider the teachings of his own inner world.

If this brave met the woman Yellow Eagle of the East, he could gather from her Name that she was outgoing and viewed things from above and from a wide perspective. Although White Turtle's introverted manner and Yellow Eagle's extraverted manner might create conflicts at times, their cosmology would remind them that their styles of being were two different places on the Medicine Wheel which they both shared. It would further remind them that their meeting might allow both to grow if they allowed themselves to turn on their Medicine Wheels. In our culture, the conflicts that might arise between these two different types of people could be from one person saying, "You are too talkative," while the others might say, "I don't know what is wrong with you! Why don't you enjoy going to parties like the rest of the gang?" In the Plains Indians' culture, an interesting design is provided that allows for a transformation of their differences. For the Medicine Wheel conveys that theirs are two different aspects of the wheel they share.

To relate this cosmology to the criteria in Chapter One, an experience of one's self as a whole person (Point II, A) can emerge from this way of seeing one's self. White Turtle's Name could permit him to feel many facets of himself integrated, as well as feeling a harmony with himself, a feeling of being centered in his way of being, and feeling a purposefulness in his life. The system provides a structure that might enable White Turtle to feel confident in telling Yellow Eagle that he did not want to go to a party, rather than to feel doubt about his worth as a human being for not being a party person.

The Plains Indians' naming system, therefore, provides a way to experience the value of one's way of being in a manner which transcends a medical model orientation. Yet, it does not oversimplify the matter by precluding a negative view of one's way of being. For example, in pensive moments around the campfire at night, White Turtle might enter into the disadvantages of being "turtle like."

He might feel sad about how he keeps certain people away with his hard outer shell, and he might breathe deeply at the thought of his inner sensitivity. But unlike the medical model perspective which might lead one to ask of a person labeled "introverted psychoneurotic," "What is wrong with you that you are shy?" or "What traumatic experience caused you to be this way?" or "How can this be cured?" the questions White Turtle would ask would probably tend to be asked within the context of the meaning embodied by his name — such as "What do you see when your head is turned inward?" The point being emphasized here is that from such considerations, new meanings might arise to White Turtle about his unique way of being (Point II, B).

### Criteria for a Holistic Identity System

I. Is there a descriptive framework of identity?
   A. Is the person described in terms of an atomized aspect of personality, or in terms of his or her whole self?
      1. Are the elements of one's personality described in such a way that they can relate with the personality as a whole?
      2. Are the elements of the personality described in such a way that they can interrelate with each other?
      3. Is there a dynamic or static conception of the personality?
   B. Does the system provide a means to speak of the person's unique way of being?
      1. Is the person described in terms of general categories that box the individual with other people, or is there a way to speak of the person's qualities ideographically?
      2. Is there an openness to incorporating new elements into the system that apply to the particular person being described?
      3. Is there a complex framework of elements of personality?
II. Does the system provide a path to experiencing new meaning in one's way of being?
   A. Does the system provide a means to experience oneself as a whole person?
   B. Does the system provide a way to experience new meaning in relationship to the uniqueness of one's personality?
      1. Is the person described in terms of ethics or aesthetics?
   C. Does the person get a feeling of being reduced by the terminology of the system, or does it allow room for the individual to enter into the term and expand it beyond its seeming boundaries?
   D. Is there a dynamic or static conception of one's life meaning?
III. The experience of a wider whole
   A. Does the system offer a way to relate one's way of being to a wider whole?

It seems that the system is also oriented to a dynamic conception of meaning (II, D), for it is said that in order for a person to be whole, the individual must turn on the wheel and experience different ways of being which the other people in the tribe represent. In turning on his wheel, White Turtle might open up to what kind of party person he could most easily become. Aided by the symbolic character of his Name (Point II, C), he might reframe his problem into a talent, i.e., that his gift, like the turtle's, lies in turning his gaze inward. So this brave might work on sharing the insights of his inner world, perhaps in the form of storytelling. He might find that by so doing, he even becomes the life of the party.[12]

   In relationship to meeting criteria for the descriptive framework of identity, it seems that this system meets the requirements for

---

12. This parallels the idea in Jungian psychology of meeting one's less developed functions in order to be whole.

describing the person in terms of a whole self (Point I, A). However, it might be criticized for not meeting certain aspects of Point I, B (that the system provide a means to speak of the person's unique way of being). To be more specific, even though the system allows the parts of White Turtle of the North's Name to interrelate (Point I, A-2), allows the elements of his personality to relate to his personality as a whole (Point I, A-1), and is dynamic in nature (Point I, A-3), one might argue that this three-part name could be categorical (Point I, B-1) in that it might box him in with others who have the Name Turtle. However, from an experiential perspective, it seems that due to the symbolic character of his Name (Point II, C), even if we as psychologists were not satisfied that his Name was ideographic, it seems that White Turtle would probably insist that his name captured his unique essence.

Another criticism that might be leveled in relationship to Point I, B is that the system might not be complex enough (Point I, B-3) for the modern personality theorist who would want included information about other aspects of a person. For example, the Name White Turtle does not give any data on his intelligence quotient or his need for achievement.

The system does seem to offer much in relationship to Point III. Since the very components of the person's Name are attributes of a wider whole (nature), the possibility is opened for the person to feel a connection to this wider whole. For the name is an embodiment of it.

This system has some weaknesses from the modern psychologist's perspective, but meets most of the criteria necessary for a holistic identity system. My point is not to say that it did or does produce a holistic experience for all people, but rather that inherent in its structure is this potential.

By introducing the Plains Indians' conception of naming, I am not necessarily calling for a return to Indian naming. Rather in a broader sense, I am suggesting that the tradition of metaphorical description may be able to aid the person in coming to terms with life's meaning and help each individual feel how he or she fits into the universal order of things.

## The Cabalistic Identity System

The Cabala of the Hebrews (mentioned in Chapter One) provides insight into another system of identity. In the book of Moses, it is said that the knowledge of the Name was one of the two keys to the mystery of Israel that was given to Moses. The Cabala, according to Suares (1973), reveals how to use this key. It shows that "every letter (of the Hebrew alphabet) is in fact an ideogram which symbolizes one aspect of cosmic energy."[13]

The Cabala is far more complicated than the Plains Indians' system, therefore I will not explain in depth here. The Cabala shows the meaning of one's personal Name by equating each letter of one's Name with a number which is a symbol for a certain universal principle.

This alpha-number code divides the Hebrew alphabet into three levels of expression. The archetypes in their unmanifested cosmic state are represented by numbers followed by two zeros. Thus, there are nine of these from 100 through 900. The rest of the alphabet is divided into letters which correspond to the various spheres of manifestation into which the archetypes are manifested. The first nine letters correspond to the numbers one through nine, and the second nine letters correspond to the numbers that are followed by one zero, i.e., ten through ninety.

To explicate, let us take the letters zayn, ayn, noun which correspond to the numbers 7, 70 and 700 respectively. To understand the symbolism of this sequence, it may be helpful to note that seven is the only number from one through nine that does not divide the 360 degrees of a circle evenly. According to Suares, Noun (700) represents the universal principle of indetermination in which the interplay of energies throughout the universe is at stake. Manifested in our everyday lives, Zayn (7) represents an opening to all possible possibilities which has its source and its vision in Ayn (70), the word for "eye" in Hebrew.[14]

For an everyday example, let us take a person who has the letter "z" Zayn (70) in her name. Fritzi might keep her eyes open for all the possible combinations of shopping possibilities. She might see that steak is of better quality at this store, baking products are less expensive at that. In relationships, when someone is blocked from working through an area of disagreement, Fritzi might explore every possible way to open the person up to communicating. Likewise, someone with the letter "n" in his Name, as in Einstein, might be more interested in exploring the possibilities of the universe.

Obviously the above are superficial examples that serve to explicate an idea; they are not meant to imply that every person who has an "n" or a "z" in their Name will be this way. For, to be more

13. Suares, C. *Cipher of Genesis.*
14. Suares, C. *Cipher of Genesis*, p.13.

complete, we need to mention that one's Name, in the cabalistic system, is a combination of all the letters of one's Name. As mentioned in Chapter One, the Name Moses (Mosheh) contains the letters Mem (40), the originator of existence which stands for water, Sheen (300) a symbol of spirit or the breath of God, and Hay (5), the life principle as expressed through one's personal life energy.[15] The Name of Moses is expressed when he brought water to his people in the desert by calling upon God. This restored life to his people.

An implication in the cabalist's system is that one's Name as a whole is capable of structuring one's personality, i.e., if one's Name is Baruch (Bruce in English), the Name would itself lead one to being "Baruch-like." Although certain Eastern beliefs concerning the power of mantras and Chaldni's experiments (See Appendix 1) may give some support to this notion, my interest does not center on the objective validity of this claim, but on whether the system fulfills certain requirements of a holistic identity system. Therefore, it is not so important whether the system is used in a nonholistic way, but whether it can be adapted to be holistic. For instance, if the system usually is taken to mean that a person has a static Name that reveals the hidden reality of his or her life's meaning, we could still use the system in a dynamic way by incorporating a meaning reorganization point of view (Point II, D) which does not preclude a hidden reality viewpoint, but has a wider frame of reference. For instance, as far as the Name Moses is concerned, one could conceivably use this Name as a symbol (Point II, C) and allow Moses to enter into it to focus on his life's meaning. He might realize that in times of spiritual dryness, he restores life to those around him by tapping upon that which is of substance in them, thereby aiding the releasing of the river of life within these people. All of the interesting questions that might be posed, such as whether his Name structured him to be this way, if there are other ways that he could interpret his Name, etc., would be part of his coming to terms with his identity. The focus would be shifted to how these insights aided Moses in reorganizing the way he experienced his life's meaning.

## Does the Cabala Meet Our Criteria for a Holistic Identity System?

Although there may be room in the cabalistic system to meet some

---

15. Ibid.

of the experiential criterion listed under Point II, and relate the individual's identity to a wider whole (due to its use of the letters of one's Name as symbols for universal energy potentials), other factors limit it as a holistic identity system.

In regards to Point I (the descriptive framework of identity), the system might tend to categorize people and therefore not meet the ideographic criterion (Point I, B-1). The system might give the same description to two people who were named Baruch. Another limitation relates to the framework of elements *per se*, which due to being designed for Hebrew Names would present difficulties in application to English ones.

In summary, the cabalistic system is most promising in its focus on the dimension of meaning (Point II) and its relationship to a wider whole (Point III) and least useful to us in its descriptive framework.

# CHAPTER FOUR

# THE ASTROLOGICAL IDENTITY SYSTEM

The fault, dear Brutus, lies not in the stars...but in ourselves.[1]

## Introduction

One of the most intricate metaphoric/symbolic systems ever developed to speak of human personality is astrology. Here a language exists which transforms aspects of the universe into symbols to speak of personality.

Mapping out the astrological system presents more difficulties than the preceding systems did. First, to speak of **the** astrological system is misleading. Since astrology has been used in such ancient countries as Chaldea, Babylon, Egypt, India, Greece, and in modern countries the world over, it has an extremely diverse geographical and temporal range. Each of these countries has had different conceptions of the system.

Second, individuals in each culture conceive of the relationship between extraterrestrial factors and their identities based on current levels of psychological development and states of consciousness.[2]

---

1. Shakespeare, W. *Julius Caesar*, Baltimore, Md: Penguin Books, 1960, p.59 — Act 1, Scene 2, Line 140.
2. The relationship between a human's state of consciousness and that person's conception of his or her relationship to the stars has been discussed by Rudhyar (1936) in *Astrology of Personality*, p.3-32. He examines how its meaning changed through the animistic, vitalistic and individualistic stages of psychological development.

Some have looked at the stars as being responsible for causing them to be the way they are. Others have argued that the stars predispose the person to be a certain way, while still others choose to use the celestial bodies as symbols to aid in the process of self-realization.[3] (These viewpoints are not necessarily mutually exclusive.)

Third, it is difficult to present a discussion of astrology without meeting certain adamant prejudices that arise whenever the word "astrology" is mentioned. For "astrology" is usually associated with popular magazines and newspaper columns that present it as a predictive, deterministic way of viewing the world.

My interest is in disentangling certain useful aspects of the system from the web of popular associations surrounding it, so it can be of use as a holistic identity system. Let us begin by exploring how the system applies to the process of Naming. In its most simple form, astrology was used to Name a person after the star rising on the eastern horizon at the time of that individual's birth. In its more complex forms, astrology contains an extremely complicated language to speak of the uniqueness of an individual's personality. As Rudhyar (1970) puts it,

> If one links all the planets of a birthchart by intercrossing lines, one obtains a geometrical pattern on the background of the twelve-fold sectioning of the circle. In a sense, it is the 'star' of the person's individuality — the original word (or logos) of the individual, his celestial name.[4 and 5]

Jesus, as well, may have been suggesting something similar when he said, "Rejoice, that your name is written in heaven."[6]

Such statements evoke questions about the relationship between the pattern of the heavens and one's identity. "Can our names

---

3. Metzner, R. (1971) discusses these different positions in *Maps of Consciousness*. In Chapter 6 (Objection 1) of this work, the reader can also find a discussion of the causal, synchronistic and symbolic perspectives on astrology.

   The general approach of this work could be characterized as using astrology as a symbolic system. By using it in such a way, the existence or nonexistence of a celestial cause-and-effect mechanism is not a subject of debate, but rather the emphasis is placed upon using the system to help the individual give meaning to his or her way of being. More on this topic will follow at the end of this chapter and throughout the work.

4. Rudhyar, D. "Form in Astrological Time and Space," *Humanistic Astrology Series*, Vol.3, p.11.

5. This quote illustrates Rudhyar's synchronistic orientation to the relationship between cosmos and personality. From the meaning reorganization point of view, "is the star of the person's individuality" would be changed to "can become the star of the person's individuality."

6. *The Bible*, Luke 10:20. *A Modern Concordance in the New Testament*, New York: Doubleday, 1976, p.479.

actually be written in some way in the heavens?" From a psychotherapeutic point of view, one need not necessarily address the question of whether it is "actually" there, just as we need not ask whether a person's identity is actually contained within the Rorschach cards.[7] The essential point is whether one can learn something about one's identity from the stars. Is a person aided in discovering who he or she is, by using the cosmos as a mirror to see the self?

Therefore, even if one doubts the scientific correspondence between the pattern of the cosmos at the moment of birth, and one's personality, one can still appreciate that one's celestial Name might enhance a person's feeling of life's purpose. Further, there is no need to determine the external validity of astrology in order to explore the way that the complex symbolic language of the cosmos can be used to speak of the person's identity. In other words, the task becomes the exploration of astrology's use in aiding the person in a search for meaning and identity, thereby separating astrology from the popularized conceptions of it as a predictive, deterministic system.

I was first introduced to the possibility of converting astrology along these lines from the work of Dane Rudhyar, the founder of the humanistic astrology movement. Rudhyar (1970) expresses the meaning orientation of astrology this way: "The function of astrology is not to tell us what will or rather what may happen in the future, but what significance there is in every moment or cycle lived or about to be lived."[8]

Various psychologists and psychiatrists have even come to recognize that astrology may have worth as a symbolic language to speak of identity. (For instance, Jung, 1954; Darling, 1968; Whitmont, 1970; Metzner, 1971; Dobyns, 1973).[9] Metzner (1971) explains that one can regard the planets and signs as symbols for psychological processes just as the alchemists took sulphur and salt as symbols for internal energy processes. Jung (1954) said that, "Astrology consists of configurations symbolic of the collective unconscious which

---

7. An important difference between the current way the Rorschach technique is used and our use of the astrological system is that we use the astrological system to provide a means for the individual to experience his or her identity through its use. Our interest is not merely to provide a means for a clinical tester to discover it for the person, as is true with the diagnostic orientation of the Rorschach.

8. Rudhyar, D. *The Astrology of Personality*, Garden City, New York: Doubleday, 1970, p.88.

9. Arroyo, S. *Astrology, Psychology and the Four Elements*, Davis, CA: CRCS Publications, 1975, p.33 quotes Jung's interview with Andre Barbault in *Astrologie Moderne*, May 26, 1954.

is the subject matter of psychology: the planets are the Gods, symbols of the powers of the unconscious."[10]

# The Problem with Astrological Theory Today

The potential for using astrology as a symbolic language, though, has not been tapped by mainstream psychology. One reason for this is that even the most far reaching astrological theorists muddy the distinction between using astrology as a symbolic language to speak about personality (the symbolic point of view), and proclaiming that there is in fact an objective correspondence between the way the universe is at the moment of birth and one's personality (the correspondence point of view). This derives from Jung's combination of the two stances under his theory of synchronicity where he says that there is not a causal relationship between extraterrestrial factors and personality, but rather an acausal relationship. Jung, in his theory of synchronicity states, "Whatever is born or done this moment of time has the qualities of this moment in time."[11] Although in his theory Jung moves away from saying that the stars cause personality to be in a certain way, he still implies that whatever is happening in one medium (the stars) is also happening within the human psyche. Even though Jung says that the connecting link is meaning, by stating that "whatever is born or done this moment of time has the qualities of this moment in time," it seems that more than a connection through meaning is postulated. A case is made for an actual correspondence between the two realms beyond the meaning one might derive from using the celestial configurations at one's birth time as a symbolic language.

Rudhyar and other humanistic astrologers perhaps inherited confusion about this issue from Jung. Basic to the thrust of the humanistic or transpersonal astrology movement, is the use of astrology as a symbolic language. Yet we still find statements like

---

10. Jung says of the collective unconscious: "But over and above that (the personal unconscious) we also find in the unconscious qualities that are not individually acquired but are inherited...In this deeper stratum we also find the archetypes. The instincts and archetypes together form the collective unconscious. I call it collective because unlike the personal unconscious, it is not made up of individual and more or less unique contents, but of those which are universal...The deeper layers of the psyche lose their individual uniqueness as they retreat father and farther into darkness...Hence at bottom, the psyche is simply — world."
    Jung, C.G., *Memories, Dreams and Reflections*, New York: Vintage Books, 1961, pp.401-2.
11. Jung's commentary on Wilhelm, R., *The Secret of the Golden Flower*, New York: Harcourt, Brace & Yovonovich, 1962, p.142.

the following one in their writings, which rest on a pseudo-scientific presumption of correspondence. "Generally speaking, any person with a natal Moon near her node is likely to be strongly influenced by his or her mother, or by a substitute "Mother Image."[12]

Rudhyar took the important first step in shifting astrology away from a chart-centered to a person-centered approach to emphasize the power of the astrological symbols themselves as a transformative language. However, he still stays tied to that aspect of the Jungian synchronistic stance which posits an actual relationship between cosmos and personality. By taking such a stance, Rudhyar and other astrological theorists have contributed to the continued unwillingness by the greater part of the psychological community to consider using astrological symbols in the naming of persons.

## Revisioning Astrological Theory

In this work, astrology shall be developed as a theoretical system with the following distinction in mind. Since our task is to explore how the astrological language can be used to aid the person in coming to terms with his or her identity, our path will lead away from the question of whether the celestial patterns actually reflect any established patterns of the individual's personality.[13] When the question is addressed, the focus shall be directed to that which is of primary relevance to the therapist attempting to aid the individual in coming to terms with life's meaning.

In this sense, the system will be used in a manner analogous to the Plains Indians' system. There we did not question whether the person was predestined or even predisposed to be turtle-like. We know not. The important thing is that the person felt a sense of who he was from his name. Our position in dealing with astrology is not to preclude that there may be an objective relationship between extraterrestrial factors and personality. This is not our focus. Our initial answer to the question, "Is one's Name written in the heavens at the moment of one's birth?" is that it is to the extent that one discovers it there. This answer follows the phenomenological approach which views a system in relationship to the experience of its user.[14] Therefore, my interest is in using the symbolic language of the cosmos at the time of one's birth or at another time, to explore

---

12. Rudhyar, D. "The Planetary and Lunar Nodes," *Humanistic Astrology Series, No. 5*, CSA Press, 1971.
13. See Appendix 1 for a discussion of some scientific studies of astrology.
14. See Appendix 2 for a discussion of the question of value.

how it affects a person's experience of him or herself.

The greatest negative consequence of astrologers taking a correspondence point of view is that their orientation shifts from valuing the mythological process of the quest for meaning to valuing **the** answer.[15] Taking a definitive stance on questions concerning the actual relationship between the extra-terrestrial sphere and personality reflects humanity's need to have a concrete answer to questions concerning human existence. The alternative to literalism, as Hillman (1975) has pointed out, is mystery.

Perhaps this has not been allowed in rational/linear thinking because there is an assumed equivalence between mystery and the absence of knowledge. It is assumed that when we have adequate knowledge, mystery will give way to clarity. Such a view equates mystery and ignorance. But as Keen has rightly stated, there is a positive relationship that can be seen existing between mystery and knowledge.[16] For instance, the more we know about childbirth, the more questions we find unanswered, and the **more** mysterious it becomes. The most knowledgeable among us realize that the more we learn, the more questions remain unanswered.

Every concept has its shadow side. Perhaps the shadow of mystery lies in the mystification of an idea. Mystification leads to obscurantism when one proclaims something like, "The universe is so big, such a mystery, that we can never really understand it." This type of mystification stops exploration as distinguished from the positive light of mystery which leads people to explore further.

Our rationalistic tradition has denied mystery a place in the multifaceted quest for identity, and has instead committed "the literalistic fallacy."[17] Our need to say, "Yes, this is definitely what my personality is," and "No, it is definitely not that." has destroyed the heart of the mythic quest for one's Name and has prevented deeper penetration into the mystery of personal identity by our imagination.

Hillman captures the concept well when he says, "Literalism prevents mystery by narrowing the multiple ambiguity of meanings into one definition. Literalism is the natural concomitant of monotheistic consciousness...which demands singleness of

---

15. There are a very few astrologers who do use a dynamic approach to the field, not locking the individual into **one** answer, or **one** meaning. See Dobyns, Z., *Expanding Astrology's Universe*, San Diego, CA: ACS Publications, 1983 and Pottenger, M., *Healing With the Horoscope*, San Diego, CA: ACS Publications, 1982.
16. Keen, S. *Apology for Wonder*, New York: Harper and Row, 1969.
17. See Hillman, J. *Revisioning Psychology*, 1975, p.149

meaning.''[18] (But unlike Hillman's call for a return to polycentrism, the astrological system's thrust when taken in the light of mystery, leads to valuing the monocentric versus polycentric dialectic. The question ''Is there a single name underlying one's personality, or are there many?'' is valued for its ability to lead the search for identity onward).

The function of mystery is to lead the person deeper into exploration of the roots of his or her identity, unlike the literalistic tradition's emphasis on fixed answers. The point is not whether heredity or environment or even a desacralized synthesis of the two positions (called ''interactionism'') forms the basis of the generalized human being's existence. ''Isms'' do not lead the individual to explore, and ''isms'' do not allow wonder to live. Wonder is fundamental to the psychotherapeutic journey. How the person meets that within the self, which says ''You are unrelated to the cosmos.'' or ''Your personality has cosmic connections.'' is the stuff of psychotherapy.

When people look at their astrological charts, wonder is evoked. They come face to face with the awe-filled experience which emerges from considering whether there may be a relationship between the cosmos and one's personality. Behind everyone's questioning lie their hopes and doubts as they endeavor to discern whether there may be some cosmic purpose with which their own being is imbued. It is this experience that must be honored!

Questions may indeed arise as to whether it is proper to speak of purpose existing outside oneself as an attribute of the universe, or whether purpose is something we give. One person might say, ''At the moment of my birth, the configurations present in the universe may have set a tone which is related to my life's purpose.'' Another might say, ''By using the language of the cosmos, I can give new meaning to my life.''[19] Even the impartial judge who listens to these people dialogue may begin to wonder.

The very beauty of astrology is that we are not sure how much the system is composed of our projections, or we of its! Perhaps the most important point is that the system be allowed to serve the

---

18. Ibid., p.149.
19. These points of view have been discussed by Fingarette, under ''the hidden reality point of view'' which posits that there is a definite meaning underlying personality and the ''meaning reorganization point of view'' which sees meaning as something given by the person. This later point of view brackets the question of whether there is a meaning behind one's personality.

   See this author's earlier cited work for a discussion of how these points of view apply to astrology.

purpose of leading one into closer relationship to the *"mysterium tremendum,"* the Great Mystery that has lain throughout the ages behind the enigma of human existence. "Enigma," as Ricoeur (1970) points out, "does not block understanding, but provokes it."[20]

There are those who have attempted to demonstrate through statistical research that an objective correspondence exists between extraterrestrial factors and personality. Most notable is the work of the French statistician Michel Gauquelin and psychologist Francoise Gauquelin. Their research serves to lead the question onward regarding whether the relationship between cosmos and personality is real or imagined. (See Appendix One and *The Psychology of the Planets* by Francoise Gauquelin.)

From the Gauquelin data and from other studies like theirs, a beginning attempt is being made to discern what the nature of the relationship between cosmos and personality might be. Since there is so much cultural bias against astrology it is difficult at this time for researchers to obtain support for the kind of intensive research which would be necessary to gain a substantial data base from which more definitive conclusions could be drawn. Until examination of present research by the academic community is undertaken in a substantial way, and new research begun, the studies of such people as the Gauquelins may serve at least to raise questions in the minds of those who would discount any possibility of a correspondence between the two realms.[21]

# The Holistic Structure
## of the Astrological System

The astrological system will now be examined in light of the criteria of a holistic identity system. To do this, the form of the astrological chart will be divided into two major parts: a discussion of the

---

20. Ricoeur, P. *The Symbolism of Evil.*
21. From a recent study at the University of London, Mayo, J., White, O. and Eysenck, H.J., "An Empirical Study of the Relation Between Astrological Factors and Personality," 1977, some interesting new data has emerged. The EPI (Eysenck Personality Inventory) was used with 2323 subjects. Neuroticism scores and extraversion/introversion scores were tabulated. These were then respectively compared with water sign emphasis, and with odd versus even sun sign placements in the subjects' charts. According to Eysenck, significant correlations were discovered — i.e. elevated N scores correlated with water sign emphasis, and odd/even sun signs correlated with extraversion/ introversion scores respectively.

　　Perhaps the most interesting aspect of this study is that a psychologist of Eysenck's stature is interested in pursuing astrological research.

elements of the astrological chart — the symbols, and a discussion of the overall shape of the chart, which will be shown to be a mandala.[22]

The first section of the chapter discusses the meanings of the astrological symbols and shows their use to speak of the qualities of one's personality. This meets criteria for a descriptive framework of identity (Point I), and for the experience of new meaning (Point II). In the second section, the mandalic shape of the astrological chart is examined in terms of criteria for these two areas. The mandalic shape of the chart, however, mainly meets those criteria referring to descriptive (I, A) and experiential (II, A) wholeness, whereas the symbols mainly meet the requirements for descriptive (I, B) and experiential (II, B) uniqueness.

This is not to imply that there is a rigid separation between the criteria met by the astrological symbols and those met by the astrological mandala. There is overlap. For, in a holistic system, the elements and the whole are continuously interrelating, and at times it seems that their respective functions also merge. Thus there may be instances when the structure of wholeness (the mandala) can be seen as meeting criteria of uniqueness, and the elements (the symbols) can be seen as applying to certain criteria listed under wholeness.

In the third section of this chapter we will explore the conception of the wider whole and how the astrological system provides a means to meet this third criterion of a holistic identity system. The astrological mandala and the symbols within it will be shown to play a significant role in allowing the unfolding of the transpersonal aspect of meaning and identity.

The language of personality that our ancient psychological colleagues developed is a symbolic language. The words used to convey the meaning of its terms are more like a hint than a definition. They are symbols and therefore expansive in nature. The words one person uses to describe them will differ from those another uses.

The tradition of symbolic Naming differs from that in which names are used to identify or describe, categorize or organize. This meaning of "the Name" is well put by Needleman (1975) when he says,

> ...there are ideas that are meant to be something more than explanation — ideas that help us to discover the truth for ourselves as opposed to concepts that organize what has already been discovered by ourselves or others. Such

---

22. See page 75 for a definition of a mandala.

ideas are what we have been calling Sacred or Esoteric.[23]

The following attempts to elucidate the symbolic nature of each of the astrological symbols should be taken in this light. They are meant to stimulate the reader's imagination, to lead the person to discovering how each relates to him or her personally.

# The Astrological Alphabet of Symbols (The Descriptive Framework of Identity)

The astrological system can be used as a language which transforms aspects of the universe around us into symbols to speak of the human personality. The system is composed of an interlocking alphabet of three dimensions of description — the zodiac, the houses, and the planets. Dividing the space that the Earth travels in its journey around the sun into twelve parts, the zodiac symbolizes the transpersonal realm of archetypal energy potentials.[24] The meaning of the houses is derived from the daily rotation of the earth upon its own axis. The houses symbolize particular areas of the individual's life as that person, so to speak, turns on his or her axis and actualizes him or herself as an individual person. Rudhyar sees houses as "fields of experience"[25] The sun is a symbol for our life energy, our inner light. How that energy functions is represented by the planets.

Using the signs of the zodiac, the astrologer has a means of symbolizing the way archetypal energy potentials come together to form the individual's personality in terms that relate to the larger cycle of the year. Our yearly cycle of seasons is composed of alternating degrees of the light/dark principle. This basic primordial duality has been expressed in terms such as yang and yin, outer and inner, objective and subjective, and collective and individual. From the interaction of these two principles, four qualities of manifestation arise

23. Needleman, J. A Sense of the Cosmos, New York: E.P. Dutton and Co., 1976, p.12
24. They are archetypes in the Jungian sense of the word. Jung sees archetypes as "energy potentials," which can be compared to "the axial system of a crystal which, as it were, performs the crystalline structure in the mother liquid, although it has no material existence of its own." He sees the archetypes in themselves being a "facultas praeformandi, a possibility of representation which is given a priori." By this statement, Jung is attempting to make clear that they are not images as is often mistakenly assumed. Their content is only determined when they become conscious and are filled out by the material of the conscious experience. (See The Archetypes and the Collective Unconscious, Vol. 9, p.79.)
25. Rudhyar, D. The Astrological Houses, New York: Doubleday, 1972.

which are called "elements" — fire, earth, air and water. According to astrology, the four elements exist in every person, although each person may be more consciously attuned to one than another. Basically, fire is associated with enthusiasm, radiating energy, perception, and drive; air with thought, and intellectual movement; water with feeling and sensitivity; and earth with practicality, groundedness and solidity. The four elements manifest in three modalities — cardinal, fixed and mutable. Each expresses a way of releasing the energy of the element. The cardinal mode represents the generation or impetus of the element, the fixed mode the concentration of it, and the mutable mode, the distribution and transmutation of it which prepares for a new beginning. When we combine the four elements with the three modalities, the twelve primary energy patterns called the signs of the zodiac are constellated. When the meanings of each of the 360 degree symbols[26] plus the relationships among all of the combined aspects[27] are multiplied together there are probably more possibilities to speak of qualities of human beings than in any personality system thus far developed.

The meaning of the various symbols in this alphabet derive in part from mythology, in part from astronomical factors and in part from astrologers' experiences and intuitions encompassing a period of well over three thousand years. Each element of the system does not have a fixed meaning, but neither does it have all possible meaning. Rather the symbolic character of the elements establishes parameters within which the person's imagination operates to discover how a given configuration applies to him or her.

For example, take a Saturn/Pluto conjunction (an aspect where two planets are close together) whose meaning might correlate with a high scale 300.30 in the *DSM III* (obsessive-compulsive disorder). Saturn, the Greek god Chronos, being the last planet visible by the naked eye is an apt symbol for the capacity to form and delimit our experience. Pluto, god of the underworld in Greek mythology, and the last planet of our solar system, is a symbol for the process of going deep into the interior regions of the Self. Although compulsive rigidity can be an aspect of the meaning of the Saturn/Pluto combination, its meaning can also be intensity, tenacity, or the capacity for endurance depending upon what comes to the person looking

---

26. See Rudhyar, D. on the Sabian symbols in *An Astrological Mandala*, New York: Random House, 1973.
27. A wide variety of astrologers have discussed aspects: the relationships between planets. See, Rael, L., *Astrological Aspects*, New York: ASI Publishers, 1980.

at the configuration's placement within the chart as a whole.

Unlike the *DSMIII*, the person is not labelled a thing (300.30 obsessive-compulsive) to be compared categorically with others; but rather the descriptive term chosen is one which applies uniquely to the given person. Saturn/Pluto in air signs might come to signify the person's relentless tenacity as an intellectual debater, in earth signs it might become a vehicle through which the person can explore an enduring capacity for long hours of sustained work.

An important difference between this system and most psychological typologies lies in the fact that the astrological system can function to permit one to explore the advantages and disadvantages of one's way of being, symbolically within the context of his or her unique life's meaning.

Untapped therapeutic implications exist here.[28] Suppose someone has been criticized as a youth for obsessive delving into things "too deeply." A new perspective might emerge by this quality being named with the symbol Pluto. This Plutonic delver might receive a "permission" to be him or herself by having that way of being placed within the universal order of things, i.e., the god Pluto does it too. The unique way the person carries the intensity of the Plutonic way forth, can be explored with the vast number of possibilities within the astrological alphabet. Pluto in an earth sign might lead to a focus on abilities as an investigator, in air signs, abilities as a researcher.

The "permission" here is expanded beyond the current psychological usage of the term where a therapist conveys to clients that it is "okay" to be the way they are. The permission that comes from this mythic tradition is more like a permit to travel in the realm of the gods — to see how one's own world is a microcosm of theirs.

By describing one's self with an astrological symbol from the celestial sphere (the abode of the gods of ancient mythology), one's personality becomes more than a mere word. Now it is a name which brings the person into relationship with the sphere of the divine, where beings of light have enacted mythological dramas throughout the ages. How does my life carry forth their work? How do my problems relate to theirs? What can I learn from examining how the gods dealt with this one?

Describing the positive and negative aspects of one's personality

---

28. The therapeutic implications of the use of astrology have been discussed in this author's earlier work, "A Holistic Perspective of Meaning and Identity: Astrological Metaphor as a Language of Personality in Psychotherapy," Ann Arbor, Michigan: University Microfilms International LD 00166, Vol.3, Issue 1, March 1978.

in these terms can transform one's experience of one's way of being. The characteristics with which one has struggled throughout one's lifetime may be just as painful, but now they have meaning. Instead of feeling alone in our suffering, we can feel ourselves participants in the painful evolution of consciousness which is symbolically represented by the age old struggles of the gods themselves. Mercury/*Hermes*, Venus/*Aphrodite*, Mars/*Ares*, Jupiter/*Zeus*, Saturn/*Chronos*, Uranus/*Ouranos*, Neptune/*Poseidon*, and Pluto/*Hades* become vehicles through which one can explore the character of one's own existence.

Following is a discussion of the cyclical and symbolic character of the astrological alphabet.[29] Keep in mind that all twelve exist in every person, although each person is more consciously attuned to certain ones and manifests the energy of each in his or her own unique way.

# The Signs of the Zodiac

**Aries:** Cardinal fire. The Ram. At the spring equinox the light principle once again equals and becomes greater than the dark principle.

Archetypal qualities and psychological attributes with which it is associated: the spark, emergence, creating life for the purpose of feeling the self create life, initiatory force. Dynamic, assertive, independent, and hasty, impatient, impulsive.

**Taurus:** Fixed earth. The Bull. With the mounting day force, there is an attempt to establish and to feel the substance of what has emerged in Aries.

Archetypal qualities and psychological attributes: the fertility of the Earth as is evidenced in sensuousness, appreciation of nature. Steadfast, aesthetically appreciative, a positive emphasis on possessions; and cautious, hesitant, stubborn, needing security, indulgent.

**Gemini:** Mutable air. The Twins. After establishing a base in

---

29. The cyclic interpretation of the astrological signs was presented in Rudhyar's (1963) *The Pulse of Life*. The following outline derives from there, from study with various astrologers, and from my own interpretation of the meaning of the symbols.

Taurus, there is born the need to explore.

Archetypal qualities and psychological attributes: the moving winds of intelligence, the searching mind, communication. Inquisitive, concrete understanding; and indecisive, scattered, flighty, two-faced, ambivalent, manipulative.

**Cancer:**   Cardinal water. The Crab. At the summer solstice, the light force reaches its summit. After exploring and increasing one's knowledge in Gemini, there needs to be an incorporation of the experience of the self-actualizing light force by feeling the experiences of life in the depths of our being — to bring it home, so to speak.

Archetypal qualities and psychological attributes: the fountainhead which springs from the well within. Sensitive, warm, empathic, nurturing, able to be emotionally vulnerable, and possessive, "clutchy," self-absorbed.

**Leo:**   Fixed fire. The Lion. After feeling in Cancer, there is born the need to express those feelings.

Archetypal qualities and psychological attributes: the glowing coal, expression, dramatic exteriorization of the personality. Expressive, strong character, artistic; and histrionic, "bully-ish." Pride in both "negative" and "positive" senses. Creative in sales, teaching, fields where one pours out from one's own center.

**Virgo:**   Mutable earth. The Virgin. Before the fall equinox there is a need to reform and perfect the personality before entering into the realm of relationships.

Archetypal qualities and psychological attributes: the stone used to sharpen one's knife, discrimination, the quest for perfection. Attentive to detail, practical; and perfectionistic, critical, nit-picking.

**Libra:**   Cardinal air. The Scales. The dark principle is now equal to and becoming greater than the light force. Here, opposite Aries, where the creation of self is born, emerges the relationship to other.

Archetypal qualities and psychological attributes:

exhalation into others, relationship, balance of individual and social aspects of experience. (In Aries, one feels the spark of individuality ignite as the breath comes in. In Libra, the emphasis is more like artificial respiration and giving to others.) Socially sensitive, considerate; and wishy-washy, unstable. Emphasis is on a **peer** relationship — on same level. Does **not** necessarily have to be sweetness and light.

**Scorpio:**    Fixed water. The Scorpion or the Eagle. Further penetration into the depths of relationship leads to union with others. Halloween is that time of year when people try on another personality. The symbol of the jack-o-lantern with the candle inside tells us that Scorpio represents the quest for finding the light behind the masks (persona) we wear.

Archetypal qualities and psychological attributes: like acid delving deeper and deeper. Penetrating, intense; and manipulative, toxic. Watch for issues involving projection and shadow.

**Sagittarius:** Mutable fire. The Archer. With the night force reaching for its summit, this sign symbolizes the reaching for an understanding of the collective realms of existence and of an understanding of one's place in the universe.

Archetypal qualities and psychological attributes: the leaping flame that ascends, symbolic understanding, abstract knowledge. Philosophic, wise, intellectual, gregarious and sometimes repetitive, overly extensive, superficially social, righteous, unrealistic expectations.

**Capricorn:** Cardinal earth. The Goat. At the winter solstice the realm of the collective is given form. Christmas.

Archetypal qualities and psychological attributes: the high peaks of mountains, concrete foundations and structure, orientation towards doing (opposite to Cancer's orientation toward being). Pragmatic, faithful, determined, solid; and materialistic, withholding (anal-retentive). Can be driven to achieve, and feel totally blocked from achievement; dealings with laws on all levels, from cultural regulations to cosmic laws, like gravity.

**Aquarius:**   Fixed Air. The Water Bearer. After establishing structures in Capricorn, they need to be continually transformed and revitalized with new ideas that may arise.
For those who wonder why an air sign is pictured as
a Water Bearer, an ancient Hebrew zodiac may provide an answer. On one synagogue's mosaic floor in
Bet Alfa is an image of Aquarius with what appears
to be a person holding a divining rod.[30] Perhaps the
sense of knowing that is Aquarian can be likened to
the age-old dowsers search for water. What an image
for the Aquarian quest for the answers to the illusive
mysteries of life!

Archetypal qualities and psychological attributes:
the held breath, the whirlwind, and the waves of
transformation, strong opinions, emphasis on
knowledge one holds, reorienting the world in relationship to one's ideas and what one perceives as righteous
for humanity as a whole. Searching, ability to transform
others through one's ideas, innovative; and uncertain,
intellectually rigid, chaotic, rebellious for rebellion's
sake.

**Pisces:**   Mutable water. The Fish. Before the spring equinox,
one feels the whole cycle.

Archetypal qualities and psychological attributes:
the mists of feeling, unboundedness. Intuitive, com-
passionate, spiritual, flowing, porous; and nebulous,
moody, impressionable, dependent, undifferentiated.

# The Planets

When the lay person asks, "What is your sign?" he or she is asking
in what zodiacal sign was the sun at the time of your birth. The
astrologer's alphabet also includes the positions of all the planets and
in what signs they are. The symbolic meaning of the signs is then
combined with that of the planets to obtain a more complete
understanding of the qualities of the person's personality.

**The Sun:**   Symbol of our life energy, the place where one shines,
creative outpouring of energy.

---

30. Bird, C. *The Divining Hand*, New York: Dutton, 1979, p.70

**The Moon**:    Symbol for our reflective capacities — the ability to go into our subjective worlds (the realm of night) and bring light there. Symbol for the "soul." The word "soul" has fallen into disrepute in modern psychological thought, although the very word "psychology" has its roots there. For the word "psyche" in Greek meant soul. Psychology, then, originally promised to be the study of the soul.

Hillman (1975) points out how the word "soul" is often confused with the word "spirit," "*pneuma*" in Greek which has to do with light, ascension and transcendence. He sees soul on the other hand originally being associated with the realm of imagination, passion, fantasy and reflection. It has a connection with the night world, the Moon.

Ideas about the nature of the soul are varied, such as that it is born in sin, that it has to do with the quest for meaning or self-knowledge, that it is an element like air or water or a vaporous mixture of them, that it is divine and immortal. Hillman comments that "the very richness of ideas about the soul tells us how rich is its phenomenology."[31] He comments that this reflection which turns ideas back upon themselves in order to see through to their soul import, makes soul. Another symbolic meaning for the Moon stems from its pull on the tides and its association with the female menstrual cycle. The Moon thereby is a symbol for feminine rhythms, the tides of our emotions.

**Mercury**:    The planet closest to the sun communicating its energies outward is fittingly represented in mythology as the messenger. It is a symbol for the expression of one's life energy, communication. Mind.

In Greek mythology, he is Hermes who serves as messenger of the gods, and the guide of souls. With his golden wand "he charms the eyes of men and wakens who he wills."[32] Like the two-sided sign of Gemini he rules, he was symbolized by a "stone heap" which marked the boundaries between geographical

---

31. Hillman, J. *Revisioning Psychology*, New York: Harper & Row, 1975, p.127.
32. From the last book of *The Odyssey*. See Kerenyi, C., *Hermes Guide of Souls*, New York: Spring Publications, 1976, p.10.

territories. These same stones were placed along the road to mark the way. So Hermes is the guide who leads us into new territory and marks our psychological roads and boundaries.[33]

**Venus**: The planet on the receiving side of the earth in relation to the sun is the goddess of love. It symbolizes the receptive principle. In Jungian psychology, it is analogous to the feeling function which is a principle of valuing, i.e., how one feels about what enters into one's being. Thus we can see why Venus rules music, the arts and aesthetic appreciation.

Venus is Aphrodite in Greek mythology. She rose from the foam of the sea that gathered around Uranus' severed genitals.[34] With Venus/Aphrodite we have the water principle, not the intellectual sky. She has to do with the emotions, passion and desire. When one loses one's detached intellectual stance in life and suffers a wound to one's virility, the vast array of feelings are born.

Aphrodite rules the wounds of love. When she sleeps with the mortal Anchises he is lamed by a lightning stroke in one story, has his eyes stung out by bees in another version. She rules infertility. When the women on the Island of Lesbos bathed in the river Aphrodisios[35] they became unable to bear children. As well, she rules adultery — seen in the story of her marriage to Hephaistos and subsequent affair with Ares. She was caught in Haephaistos's net and was humiliated.

One of her strongest negative qualities is vengeance. She turned Hippomenes into a lion after he neglected to thank her for helping him to win the race with Atlanta.[36] Her love can be possessive and lead to death, as in the story of Adonis.

Anyone who has suffered the pains of Aphrodite's

33. Pedraza, R.L. *Hermes and His Children*, New York: Spring Publications, 1977, p.31.
34. See Graves, R. *The Greek Myths*, New York: Penguin Books, 1960, Vol. I, p.39.
35. Kerenyi, C. *Goddesses of Sun and Moon*, New York: Spring Publications, 1979, p. 57.
36. Tripp, E. *The Meridian Handbook of Classical Mythology*, New York: The New American Library, 1970.

style of love can understand why she is called "An-
drophonos" (Killer of Men).[37]

Out of the pain that Aphrodite brings, though,
comes growth. Despite the fact that she seems to op-
pose Psyche in the tale of Amor and Psyche, it is by
accomplishing and by moving through Aphrodite's
tasks that Psyche is initiated into womanhood. Though
on the surface it seems that Aphrodite is simply jealous
of Psyche, it is the trials that Aphrodite sets up which
lead Psyche to marry Eros and give birth to pleasure.

Out of meeting Aphrodite can come a wide variety of good and bad, pleasure and pain. For instance,
when Aphrodite has children with Ares, they are
Deimos (Fear), Phobos (Panic) and Harmonia
(Harmony).[38]

For those who only speak of Aphrodite's negative
side, they should remember that she also has the
capacity for caring feelings. For instance, she felt pity
when Ino jumped into the sea with her infant son,
Melicertes in her arms. Aphrodite is benevolent on occasion (when she adopted the orphaned daughters of
Pandareus). Aphrodite helps mortals win their beloved
(as she helped Hippomenes win Atlanta)[39] and she
even helps the gods. She lent Hera her magic belt to
win Zeus.[40] Certainly Aphrodite chains us in awful
ways, but she also can release one from chains (as
when she rescued Aeneas's first wife Creusa from
slavery).[41]

With Aphrodite we see contained the dark and light
sides of erotic love. She is called Melainis ("the black
one") but also as "chruse" (or golden).[42] She in-
fatuates, loves laughter, beguiles and "steals the heart
away even from the thoughtful."[43]

Through meeting Aphrodite, one's psyche is indeed
compelled to walk the path of Initiation. One can look

37. Kerenyi, C. *The Gods of the Greeks*, London, England: Thames and Hudson, 1951,
    p.81.
38. Tripp, E. *Meridian Handbook of Classical Mythology*, p.57.
39. Tripp, E. *Meridian Handbook of Classical Mythology*, p.59.
40. Kerenyi, C. *Goddesses of....*, p.55.
41. Tripp, *Meridian Handbook of Classical Mythology*, p.59.
42. Kerenyi, C. *The Gods of...* p.80.
43. Kerenyi, C. *The Goddesses of...* p.52.

at Venus's movement through the astrological houses and signs as such an initiation. Actually, this is true of all the planets, i.e., their movements through the signs and houses express a journey of initiation.

**Earth:** Our planet can be seen as a symbol of the consciousness of the ego complex. It is that center of activity which organizes our perceptions, feelings, thoughts, etc. Our ground.

**Mars:** The planet outside of the Earth in relation to the sun represents the outgoing force of the psyche. On a mundane level, one can see why it has been called the god of war, for this is one way which mankind has expressed outgoing impulses. Assertive energy, aggression, anger.

Ares, in Greek myths, loved battle for its own sake. Showing that aggression does not always win out, Athene (goddess of wisdom) twice defeated Ares in battle.[44] His instincts get Ares in trouble. While having an illicit affair with Aphrodite, he got caught and entangled in a net that Hephaistos set for them.[45]

**Jupiter:** The planet which gives off more energy than it receives, the largest of planets symbolizes the overflowing expansion of our energy. Its quality can be felt when one opens the Self in relating to a large group of people. Mythologically, Zeus was the king of gods. Expansiveness. Faith to move mountains.

**Saturn:** The last planet capable of being seen by the naked eye, forming the boundary of our sight, bounded itself by its rings is fittingly a symbol for the principle of boundaries, limitation and form of our conscious experience. Restrictiveness. Form, pragmatism, working realistically within what is possible. Mythologically, Chronos, father time. Like those fathers everywhere who attempt to control their children and incorporate them into the father's world, Chronos — afraid that his

---

44. Graves, R. *The Greek Myths*, New York: Penguin Books, 1960, Vol. I, p.73.
45. Graves, R. *Greek Myths*, p.68.

children would dethrone him — tried to swallow all of the children Rhea bore him. Only Zeus escaped.[46]

**Uranus:**  The first trans-Saturnian planet. Planets up to and including Saturn represent aspects of the conscious self, while planets past Saturn symbolize aspects of what Jung would call the collective unconscious. Discovered around the time of the American and French revolutions, Uranus represents those forces which come from outside the set boundaries of present conceptions and introduce new ways of seeing. In mythology, Uranus stands above the clouds with a lightning bolt which symbolically can represent the awakening of the mind through the lightning bolt of intuition. Its qualities are the mind open to new possibilities, and the experience of being outside of set boundaries. Explosive. The Observer. Imagination, intuitive flashes. Symbolic thought. Mythologically, Uranus was a sky god of the Greeks.

**Neptune:**  The second planet of the collective unconscious is mythologically the god of the sea. It symbolizes the undifferentiated aspect of the collective psyche, the void. Like the sea, it manifests as a liquid feeling of unity with all things, as in a state of intoxication with certain drugs or alcohol, in a mystical experience or more generally a lack of differentiation of the ego. Compassion. Confusion.

Mythologically, Poseidon, god of the sea. Like humans who are ruled by the sea of emotions, Poseidon revenged himself by sending huge waves to flood the Thrassian Plains. A very instinctual god, he raped Demeter in the form of a horse.[47]

**Pluto:**  The last known planet of the solar system represents the deepest reaches of the psyche. Discovered around the time of the 1929 stock market crash, people were forced to reach a deeper center within themselves beyond their material possessions. Some who could not do so jumped off buildings. Mythologically,

---

46. Graves, R. *Greek Myths*, p.39.
47. Graves, R. *Greek Myths*, p.61.

Hades/Pluto, god of the underworld, symbolizes that deep journey which one embarks upon after everything that one has identified with has been lost. Often there is much pain in the process. In the story where Pluto raped Persephone, this naive maiden picking a narcissus flower became through her painful journey to the underworld a mature woman and queen of the underworld. Psychologically, Pluto can be seen as obsessiveness, intensity of character and shadow issues.

# The Dial of Houses

The third dimension of the alphabet is the dial of houses which is formed by dividing the sphere of the axial rotation of the Earth into twelve parts. Paralleling the zodiacal symbolism, they represent areas of the individual's life or fields of experience. They can be seen as gateways into the initiation process of life. As Heracles went through his tasks, so do we go through ours as we attempt to master the tasks indicated by the astrological houses. Allowing for the interrelationship of all three levels of the system, any one of the zodiacal signs can be on the cusp of a given house, and, depending upon the position of the planets at the time of birth, a certain planet(s) may occupy a house.[48]

**First House:** On the eastern horizon, rising at birth, at the horizontal line of awareness, it symbolizes the awareness of one's self, one's personality.

**Second House:** The life substance used by the self. Possessions. Inner resources.

**Third House:** Relationship of the personal self to substance. The environment, short journeys, communication, the early learning process.

**Fourth House:** On the depths of the vertical axis of power, this symbolizes the power that issues forth from our inner world. The home, the grounding of our feeling self.

---

48. For those wishing more on the basics of astrology, such as house cusps, see Meyer, M., *A Handbook for the Humanistic Astrologer*, New York: Doubleday, 1974.

**Fifth House:** Expression of self. Offspring. Children, creations, speculations and amusements. Any way in which we pour out into the world, doing more than we have done before, hoping for feedback.

**Sixth House:** Further perfection of the manifestation of self. Service, work, health. Efficient functioning.

**Seventh House:** On the opposite end of the axis of consciousness, this is the house representative of awareness of relationship to others. Marriage, partnerships, relationships. On the subjective level, it can be seen as leading toward a realization of how those with whom we form relationships represent other aspects of ourselves.

**Eighth House:** Destruction of personal limitation as a result of human interchange. Metaphysics, study of the occult, business, legacies.

**Ninth House:** The abstract mind, philosophy, belief systems, religion, symbols, long journeys.

**Tenth House:** At the top of the vertical axis of power, this house refers to one's life work, occupation, social position, reaping what we have sown.

**Eleventh house:** Sharing of collective ideals with those who share those ideas. Friendships, hopes. Going beyond limits (psychologically, physically, etc.), "unbonded relationships" in Lois Rodden's terms.

**Twelfth House:** Social transformation (The twelfth house completes the social cycle of houses, as the sixth houses completes the individual cycle of houses.) Bringing any cycle to a creative conclusion, unfinished business, "skeletons in the closet," imprisonment, searching for union with something Higher.

# CHAPTER FIVE

# HOW ASTROLOGICAL SYMBOLS MEET HOLISTIC CRITERIA

How do astrological symbols satisfy those criteria presented earlier as essential to a descriptive framework of identity? Although the order here will be different from that in Chapter 2, to keep with the flow of the additional material introduced in this section, astrological symbols will be shown to:

— provide a complex framework of elements (Point I, B-3),
— allow for the interrelationship among the elements (I, A-2),
— provide an ideographic language (I, B-1),
— allow new ways of describing one's personality to enter into the system (I, B-2),
— aid in a dynamic conception of personality.

This covers all criteria except for wholeness (I, A-1). Although astrological symbols will be shown to combine to give a picture of the personality as a whole, the main discussion of wholeness will be reserved until astrology is presented as a mandalic system. For it is the overall shape of the astrological chart as a mandala that satisfies this criteria.

In the previous section, the basic structure of the astrological alphabet was delineated. If the twelve signs are combined with the twelve houses and the ten planets (including Sun and Moon), 1440 possible combinations result (12 x 12 x 10). The system is actually even more complex. The zodiac can be further divided into 360 degree symbols.[1] This greatly increases the number of descriptive terms. Quantitatively speaking, this number of personality qualities should be quite impressive to psychologists, for it provides more possibilities to speak of aspects of being than any modern personality system. Although this helps to satisfy the criterion of complexity (Point I, B-3), quantity of variables by itself does not assure a descriptive framework of identity that is holistic.

The astrological system also provides room for an interrelationship among the complex system of elements (Point I, A-2). For instance, the planetary symbols can combine with each other and with other levels of the system, thereby changing their meaning to apply to the person's individual personality structure (Point I, B-1). If Mercury (planet of communication) is in relationship to Jupiter (planet of expansion and social outpouring), and Mars (planet of assertion) is midway between them,[2] we might imagine the quality of oratory (the ability to express oneself in large groups) to synthesize these three qualities. If we also analyze the signs that the planets are in, we enhance our description of the unique way this person communicates in a group. If the three planets were in air signs, the mental quality of expression of ideas in groups might be characterized, whereas occurring in earth signs (practical action), the meaning might change to qualities such as execution of group plans.

The intricacy of the interrelationship among elements is also brought out by the cyclical relationship between the various aspects of the system. In addition to the cyclic unfolding of the signs and houses, the relationship of any two planets to each other on the 360 degree circle of the chart has significance.

For instance, there is a difference in meaning if two planets are next to each other (in conjunction) or opposite to each other (in opposition or 180 degrees apart). When two elements are in conjunction, the astrologer speaks of them as if two people had just come together. The relationship begins and there is a need to explore and create something out of the meeting. Applying this to the Mercury-Jupiter conjunction, this might describe the need to initiate social communication, to get things going in a group process. The opposition aspect is analogous to two people sitting across from each other

1. See Rudhyar's (1973) *An Astrological Mandala* where he outlines the cycle of transformations and its 360 symbolic phases. Another astrologer, Marc Edmund Jones, first outlined the 360 degree symbols in his discussion of Sabian symbols.
2. Ebertin's school of cosmobiology stands out in outlining the meaning of planetary midpoints. For further information, see Ebertin's (1940) *The Combination of Stellar Influences* where he presents over a thousand examples of the meanings of planetary midpoints.

at a conference table. There is awareness of one another. The Mercury-Jupiter opposition aspect, then, represents an awareness of social communication processes. The awareness could be of a negative type if the person felt stymied by his or her perceptions, or of a positive type, if the person used his or her ability to be aware of the pattern of communication in the group, perhaps by sharing these perceptions with the group. Actually, in a more complex analysis, there are 360 stages in the cyclic relationship between every two planets, or, as Rudhyar sees it, eight major turning points in the cycle.[3]

One can make an analogy between the cycle of aspects and the cycle of the zodiac. For instance, a waxing square (90°) would be analogous to a Cancer aspect whereas a waning square (270°) would be analogous to a Capricorn aspect. So every two planets go through a cycle of development and unfoldment. This is an initiation journey with regards to different aspects of one's self. For instance, with the Mercury/Jupiter relationship at the conjunction phase, some social idea may need to be expressed but is not quite formed. As it evolves through the formative stages (crescent sextile, waxing square, etc.) it finally reaches it fullness of awareness in the opposition (full moon) phase. The waning cycle is a more reflective time when that which was reached at the full moon aspect can be gathered into one's awareness and then perhaps be more consciously applied socially. (Rael, L. *Astrological Aspects: A Process Oriented Approach* goes into this kind of understanding more extensively).

A most important point is that each element, or each interrelationship among elements, does not have a fixed meaning, but at the same time, does not have all possible meanings. The symbolic character of the elements establishes parameters within which the person's imagination operates to describe how a given configuration applies to that individual. This factor is fundamental to an ideographic descriptive framework (Point I, B-1) and allows new ways of describing the person to continually enter into the descriptive framework (I, B-2).

Another criterion (Point I, A-3) concerns the need for a dynamic conception of the personality. Through the use of progressions (an astrological term referring to the movement of the planets in the chart through time), the astrologer does have the ability to speak of the

---

3. For an extended discussion of the meanings of various cyclic relationships, see Busteed, Tiffany and Wergin (1974) *Phases of the Moon* and Rudhyar's (1970) *Form in Astrological Time and Space*. Also, Rudhyar, D. and Rael, L. *Astrological Aspects: A Process Oriented Approach*, New York: ASI Publishers, 1980.

personality qualities of the individual and their movement and transformation throughout the life of an individual. The earlier discussion concerning the symbolic nature of the system also relates to the dynamic character of the system, for it leads away from fixed interpretations.

Having a way to speak of the personality progressing and evolving through time protects the user of the astrological system from falling into the problems associated with systems that emphasize a fixed, essential self. Harvey Cox, in *Turning East*, puts this well:

> For the individual person, the trouble with basing one's life on the quest for an essential self is that the self, instead of enlarging and deepening its capacities, becomes more and more like itself...;If the "real self" I am uncovering progressively becomes the determinant of my behavior, rigidity and sclerosis set in early. My actions become predictable and my perception of alternative modes of life narrows. I lose my vulnerability, my capacity to be shattered, or even to catch myself by surprise...The self is not an inner essence to be discovered but an unfinished and unfinishable poem...[4]

Progressions in the astrological language give a way for the person to have his or her "name" continue to evolve in a poetic manner. Just as the universe is in continuous flux, so the alchemical mixture that makes an individual is continually changing its composition.

Fundamental to a holistic descriptive framework is the need for the elements to be viewed in relationship to the personality as a whole (Point I, A-1). The symbolic elements in the astrological chart do combine into an overall shape which provides a means to focus on the personality as a whole. Various astrological writers (Jones, 1960; Rudhyar, 1971) have spoken of these Gestalt patterns[5] and feel, as psychologists do, that viewing the personality as a Gestalt is important in moving away from an atomistic preoccupation on parts of the personality. A more extensive discussion of the shape of the astrological chart as a whole will follow when I examine the role of the astrological mandala in producing wholeness and demonstrate how an image of wholeness can be constellated from the Gestalt patterns of the astrological mandala.

---

4. Cox, H. *Turning East*, New York: Simon and Schuster, 1979.
5. See Jones (1960) *Essentials of Astrological Analysis* and Rudhyar's (1970) *First Steps in the Study of Birth Charts*. Jones sees the Gestalt shapes as providing a clue to the "psychological totality" of the personality. The shapes he mentions are the bowl, bucket, seesaw, splash, splay and locomotive. To illustrate, a bowl chart with all of the planets above the horizon has the form of an overturned bowl and symbolizes a personality pouring the contents of the self outward (depending, of course, upon other factors of the personality).

Rudhyar's discussion of Gestalt patterns contains slight variations to Jones' analysis.

# Meeting Criteria for the Experience of New Meaning

One can see that the astrological system has an astronomical ability to speak of elements of the personality. It is no wonder that the psychologist Ralph Metzner (1970) made the following comment about its system of elements:

> We have a psychological typology... far exceeding in complexity and sophistication of analysis any existing system.... The framework of the three interlocking symbolic alphabets of Zodiac signs, houses and planetary aspects is probably better adapted to the complex varieties of human natures than existing systems of types, traits, motives, needs, factors or scales.[6]

Articulating the intricate weaving of the tapestry of an individual's personality is not adequate in itself to meet the criteria for a holistic identity system. An experiential counterpart is also needed. Without this, the astrological system would be liable to the earlier criticisms made of those systems which did not provide a means whereby a person could have a felt experience of identity meaningful to that individual.

The use of symbols in the astrological system provides a way for this to occur. This can be seen by reviewing the distinction between symbols and signs. A sign is a token of meaning that stands for a known entity. Our flag represents the United States. A symbol is an image or representation that points beyond itself to something unknown. Our flag connotes different things to different people — patriotism, imperialism, etc. A sign communicates objective meaning while a symbol conveys living subjective meaning. It is this subjective dynamism which allows the individual to enter into and explore the personal meaning of the symbol. For these reasons, many psychologists (Jung, 1953; Edinger, 1973) have said that symbols are expansive and experiential in nature, not reductive and descriptive.

Most personality systems are composed of signs which stand for known factors. For instance, on the MMPI, if a person has an elevated Pt scale (Psychoasthenia, scale #7), an objective measure is given which the clinician can compare to known populations of people. The astrological system, being composed of expansive symbols, may be better oriented to provide a means whereby the person can enter into the element and experience how it applies to his or her own unique personality. (This satisfies criterion II, C.)

---

6. Metzner, R. "Potential Science and Intuitive Art," *The Journal of Astrological Studies*, 1970, 1, pp.164-77.

Each astrological symbol can become a vehicle leading one to experience new meanings in relation to one's identity. The relationship between symbols and the experience of meaning has been recognized by many psychologists.

Gendlin (1962) in his in-depth study, *Experiencing and the Creation of Meaning*, recognizes the relationship between symbols and meaning when he says, "Meaning is formed in the interaction of experiencing and something that functions as a symbol."[7] Gendlin's work accentuates the felt experience of meaning which he is careful to distinguish from mere intellectualizing of meaning. Gendlin sees symbols as being fundamental to changing feelings to felt meanings. In his words, "Feelings are felt meanings only insofar as they function in relationship with symbols."[8]

The role of symbols in creating a transformation of meaning was extensively discussed by Jung (1954, 1958, 1960) in relationship to depth psychology. Whitmont (1969), a modern Jungian therapist, provides an example. He speaks of the use of the "symbolic approach" with a client who was an aggressive man, independent, self-reliant and overly rational. While very successful in business, he was impoverished in terms of feelings and interpersonal relationships, and especially in terms of orientation toward a higher meaning in life. The problem which brought him to seek therapy was that he could only have sexual relations with a woman if he first kissed and licked her feet.[9]

Whitmont points out that a "symptomatic approach" would view this behavior as fetishism, a neurotic compulsion. In pursuing a "symbolic approach" Whitmont discovered in the course of therapy that the client's behavior reflected an urge to humble himself at the feet of the woman. Through this action, the client's one-sided emphasis on the "masculine" will attitude was being compensated by the psyche's insistence upon giving notice to the "feminine" world: the world of gentleness, softness, vulnerability with which the client was out of touch. Thus his behavior symbolized an inner need to bow down and humble himself before the "feminine" world within himself. Seen in this light, the client was able to experience his actions in a new way.

Another Jungian therapist expresses well the idea that a transformation of meaning can take place by understanding the symbolic

7. Gendlin, E. *Experiencing and the Creation of Meaning*, Toronto, Canada: The Free Press of Glencoe, 1962, p.8.
8. Ibid., p.8.
9. Whitmont, E. *The Symbolic Quest*, New York: G.P. Putnam's Sons, 1969, pp.20-23.

roots of a symptom when he says,

> This manner of interpretation (the symbolic mode) if successful can lead the patient toward the symbolic life. A paralyzing guilt-laden symptom can be replaced by a meaningful, life-enriching symbol which is experienced consciously rather than lived out in an unconscious, compulsive, symptomatic way....To see the symbolic image behind the symptom immediately transforms the experience. It may be just as painful, but now it has meaning. Instead of isolating the sufferer from his fellow humans, it unites him with them in a deeper rapport.[10]

When Edinger here mentions that becoming aware of the symbolic image behind a symptom unites the person with other human beings, he is referring to the Jungian concept that symptoms often arise from some archetypal situation common to human beings. For instance, many anxiety symptoms have as their archetypal roots, the hero's fight with the dragon, or the rites of initiation. By becoming aware of the archetypal symbolism behind a symptom, a transformation of meaning can occur.

Jung felt this transformation is important to the therapeutic process because "a transition is created from the previous attitude to a more fully integrated one."[11] and Gendlin emphasizes the role symbols play in "the creation of new meanings"[12] essential to therapy. The previous example of the man with the foot fetish, illustrates how, by working with the symbolism of a symptom, one's experience of one's way of being can take on new meaning.

The elements of the astrological system, being symbols, allow for new meaning to be experienced in relation to one's personality qualities. The case illustration in this volume shows how the use of astrological symbols can allow a client to experience herself in a new way. Astrological symbols can serve to give the client **permission** to be herself, in **crystallizing** what her unique way of being is, in **transforming** how a client views herself as well as helping new behavioral patterns to emerge, and in leading the client to a **new experience of her life's meaning.** A person can apply the astrological symbol to personality in much the same way that Kelly (1955) uses his Personal Construct Method to give the person a feeling of his or her unique personality qualities.

By working with astrological symbols a dynamic modality is created whereby clients can reorganize the way they experience the meaning of their lives (Criterion II, D). In line with this criterion,

10. Edinger, E. *Ego and Archetype*, p.115-116.
11. Jung, C.G. *Psyche and Symbol*, New York: Anchor Books, 1958, p.xxiii.
12. Gendlin, E. *Experiencing and the Creation of Meaning*, p.167

the system is broad enough to encompass both hidden reality and meaning reorganization viewpoints. One client may say "Now I've discovered **why** I have always been so intense — it's because of my Saturn-Pluto conjunction". Another client, using the meaning reorganization veiwpoint, might say that "The Saturn-Pluto conjunction gives me a useful way to get in touch with **how** my intensity manifests." The emphasis has been upon the meaning reorganization viewpoint in this section because the hidden reality viewpoint is seen by this author as one particular way a person organizes his or her view of the world.

Due to its symbolic attributes, astrology has room for people to experience identity in both positive and negative ways (Point II, B-1). By the word negative, I mean that astrological language can crystallize into consciousness dysfunctional aspects of what transactional analysts like Berne (1972) call one's life script (e.g., "poor me," etc.).

The astrological symbols can lead one to experience those negative habit patterns that need to be dealt with before one can freely choose what one's life is to be. However, it seems that if psychologists are to move away from the illness paradigm, there is a need to be as creative and detailed in speaking of positive life myths as in speaking of negative life scripts. Although many psychologists (Jung, 1933, 1954; Keen, 1970; Heuscher, 1974) have done important work in speaking to the concept of life myths, there has not been sufficient work done in providing a language that can speak of a person's unique life myth. This book will demonstrate how astrology can be used to crystallize the disorders of one's life script, and how it can be used to get one in touch with one's shadow. However, the major concentration will be upon how the symbolic language can bring forth an experience of that which is of value in one's unique way of being. Our lens will therefore focus on seeing in this light the germ of meaning contained within the life path of an individual.

It seems that psychology is in a stage analogous to that of chemistry without its periodic table of elements. Perhaps astrology can give to psychology a table of symbolic elements to speak of human personality; for it seems to provide the ingredients necessary for a holistic identity system. Satisfying criteria for a descriptive framework of identity and for the experience of new meaning, the astrological alphabet may contain a solution in hieroglyphic to those inquiries that people put to themselves concerning their identity.

# The Astrological Mandala

If man has alienated himself from the source, the center within, then it is the purpose of a mandala ritual for our time to be used as a primal tool for investigating and opening that center, once again granting the individual an identification with the cosmic forces and their source.[13]

The term "mandala" can be defined as any figure, usually a circle, square or other symmetrical arrangement which is constructed around a center, and thereby may aid a person in his or her own internal process of centering. From its various manifestations three of is basic properties can be derived: it is a figure with a center, symmetry and has cardinal points.[14] The mandala is among the oldest symbols of the human race and is distributed the world over. From Arguelles' extensive investigation he concludes that they have appeared throughout mankind's history as a universal symbol of integration, harmony and transformation, giving form to the most primordial intuition of the nature of reality.[15] Outstanding representations are found in the Aztec Great Calendar Stone, the Lamaic Vajramandala, in paleolithic Rhodesian rock paintings, in the Plains Indians' Medicine Wheel and in the astrological horoscope.[16] The clock that Western people use to orient their daily activities is also a mandala.

Carl Jung is the psychologist associated with revealing the psychological importance of mandalas to the Western world. After seeing their appearance in numerous clients' dreams and art work (Jung, 1974, p. 177), Jung continued an in-depth investigation of their meaning and significance in numerous contexts — alchemy, astrology, Taoism, Buddhism, Lamaism and tantric yoga. Jung grew to see the mandala as "a symbol of the Self," and as "a symbol of psychic totality"[17] He spoke of it as aiding the psychic process of centering and even in aiding in the production of a new center of personality. (Jung, 1974, p. 173). In speaking of how they can help in the process of creating psychic unity, Jung stated:

Mandalas . . . usually appear in situations of psychic confusion and disorientation. The archetype thereby constellated represents a pattern of order which,

13. Arguelles, J. and M. *Mandala*, Berkeley, CA: Shambala Publications, 1972, p.83.
14. Ibid., p.14.
15. Ibid., p.33.
16. A more complete historical analysis of the appearance of the mandala can be found in Jung's (1974) *Dreams*; Arguelles' (1972) *Mandala*; Wheelwright's (1968) *The Reality of the Psyche*.
17. Jung, C.G. *Memories, Dreams, Reflections*, p.396.

like a psychological 'view finder' marked with a cross or circle divided into four, is superimposed on the psychic chaos so that each content falls into place and the weltering confusion is held together by the protective circle. . . . At the same time they are yantras, instruments with whose help the order is brought into being.[18]

That astrology is a mandalic system has been recognized by psychologists and astrologers alike (Rudhyar, 1935; Von Franz 1972; Metzner, 1971; Jung, 1974; Schwartz, 1970). Nathan Schwartz's (1970) article — "On the Coupling of Psychic Entropy and Negentropy" specifically addresses the psychotherapeutic importance of the astrological mandala. He sees the astrological mandala leading to "primitive logic" more than to "directed thinking." He defines primitive logic in a way that can be compared to Piaget's terms "reversibility thinking" or to Freud's "primary process thinking."[19] Jung spoke of "directed thinking" as being characterized by "inner consistency and logical coherence. Because it is directed, everything unsuitable must be excluded. . ."[20] In his discussion, Schwartz shows that directed thinking strives for a closed system by excluding the opposite of the conscious attitude. Primitive thinking, by contrast, maintains opposites in harmony. Primitive thinking orders events along mythical patterns; it imitates an archetypal ordering process.

Using thermodynamic understanding to illustrate a point, Schwartz says that contrary to common sense expectation, directed thinking leads to producing entropy (disorder) in a system while primitive thinking produces negentropy (order). Explaining this in contexts ranging from thermodynamic laws to Platonic philosophy, he refers to the order-disorder paradox: "Increasing order in a system results in disorder in the same or in a connected system."[21] A simple example may help clarify. A common experience is that when someone speaks of how fantastic he is, the other side — doubt, insecurity, etc. — often arises. This relates to the general principle that when people define themselves one-sidedly, the opposite polarity that is excluded emerges. Jung has demonstrated this in his discussion of the compensatory function of the psyche.

The psychotherapeutic significance here is "not only that

18. Jung, C.G. *Memories, Dreams, Reflections* , New York: Pantheon Books, 1961, p.397.
19. Schwartz, N. and S. "On the Coupling of Psychic Entropy and Negentropy," New York: *Spring Publications*, 1970, p.67
20. Schwartz, N. and S. "Coupling of Psychic Entropy and Negentropy", p.75
21. Ibid., p.70.

increasing order results in disorder, but further that this created disorder tends to 'attack', i.e., degrade, the value of the order-creating system."[22] The disorder often appears in the form of physical or psychological symptoms. Schwartz says that the ego that is developed in directed thinking is specifically built upon and conditioned to the repression of disorder. This ego of repression has, however, a negative gain because disorder often can produce a positive disintegration preceding the formation of new symbols and ordering structures. Thus to reject disorder can be to reject personality growth.[23]

After speaking of the importance of the therapist using a form which would allow primitive thinking to occur, Schwartz cites astrology as such a system. He says,

> The horoscope is a mandala structure that can be used as a code or grid superimposed on the flux of events in the unconscious. We do not speak of astrology in its vulgar form of prognostication of the future — this has always been its downfall, because then astrology is used in linear, 'profane time' for the purpose of directed thinking; rather, we speak of the horoscope as an example of primitive or qualitative logic.[24]

Explaining how the astrological mandala allows this to occur, he says that when the horoscope is used as a meditation glyph there are locations for any initial information or fantasy. From here the mandala structure of the horoscope immediately has oppositions and various correlates to the initial information. Schwartz recognizes that the chain of associations is extensive but finite requiring the synthesizing power of the imagination. Unlike a system of directed thinking,

> All the words one thinks up cannot replace the signs of the planets, nor can they explain the so-called square or trine aspect that planets, i.e., psychic qualities, may make with one another.
>     ...in the way we have presented the horoscope (it is) a particular fantasy, a particular metaphorical formulation of the totality as extracted through the multitude of patterns within the basic pattern of the horoscope. The 'solution' is a new way of saying something that was potentially always there, but that required a special combination of patterns to condense into a unifying image or fantasy.
>     The point of these remarks is not to explain astrology but to show that the horoscope is a form into which information enters (by association), through which information is actualized into negentropy.[25]

22. Ibid., p.73.
23. Ibid., p.77.
24. Ibid., p.79.
25. Ibid., pp.79-80.

# Meeting Criteria for a Descriptive Framework of Identity: Wholeness

The astrological mandala can serve as a holistic ordering system by integrating the elements of the astrological system into its structure. Its ability to satisfy criteria for describing the personality as a whole can first be seen in regard to Point I, A-2, which speak to the need for a holistic system to provide a structure in which **all of the elements can interrelate with each other, mutually and reciprocally modifying each other**.

From Schwartz's discussion one can see that the mandalic form of the horoscope can indeed act as a structure which allows this to occur. In his words, ''. . .the mandala structure of the horoscope. . .immediately impresses laws of association and opposition upon any single piece of information. The chain of associations is extensive but finite.''[26] Earlier, this idea was exemplified when we considered the symbolic Mercury opposition Jupiter with Mars at the midpoint between them. These three elements came together and modified each other to symbolize the personality quality of oratory. In an astrological analysis, all of the elements can be seen in their cyclical relationship to each other by viewing their relative positions within the mandala.

The mandala not only provides the structure which allows an interrelationship of elements, but as well it provides a structure which allows **the elements to be described in relationship to the personality as a whole.** The essential nature of the mandala suits it to satisfy this criterion (I, A-1) since its structure leads to integrating parts into a whole. This attribute of the mandala was illustrated by the Plains Indians' Medicine Wheel, which allowed every person in the tribe to be united by this symbol of wholeness. Likewise the astrological mandala integrates all aspects of the personality into a whole.

The overall gestalt shape of the chart was shown to accomplish this function by integrating all of the separate elements of the chart into a holistic patterns. The image of wholeness that the astrological mandala is capable of producing goes beyond what astrologers describe as the gestalt shape of the chart; it is perhaps more accurately depicted by Schwartz's statement that the combinations of patterns in the horoscope ''condense into a unifying image or

---

26. Ibid, p.79

fantasy."[27] The synthesizing function of the person's imagination has been spoken of by many psychotherapists (Jung, 1954; Assagioli, 1965) as having great value in crystallizing aspects of the person's inner world that are important to the process of self realization.

To see how the astrological chart can function in **crystallizing an image of wholeness**, let us take as an example a man who has the sign Libra emphasized in his chart and the planet Uranus in a prominent position. As this person uses his astrological mandala as a meditation glyph, an image might arise of a deer kissing someone's eyes. If he sees the name "Deer Kissing Eyes" as a symbol of his identity, he will have a unified image that crystallizes his ability to stimulate others' perceptions by gently encouraging them to imagine new ways of viewing life.

Although one might attempt to come to an atomistic explanation of the emergence of this image by saying that Libra means gentleness to others and Uranus means stimulating the imagination, actually the image is different from the sum of any of the elements within the chart. For nowhere in the astrological language is either a deer or eyes mentioned. This demonstrates that the astrological mandala is **dynamic** in its ability to **allow new images to enter into the system** that apply to the particular person being described (Points I, A-3 and I, B-2).

# How the Astrological Mandala Meets the Criteria for the Experience of Wholeness

By bringing together the elements of the astrological chart into a whole, the astrological mandala allows for a felt experience of wholeness to emerge. Earlier the experience of wholeness was described as a feeling of integration, a harmony with oneself, a feeling of being centered in one's way of being, and a feeling of purposefulness.

Inherent to the mandalic form is the possibility of leading a person to his or her center. As is said in the book, *Mandala*,

> The principle of the Mandala lies not in the external form which is unique for each situation but in the center, the source through which the form-creating energy flows. To be integrated, to be made whole, means to be able to maintain contact with one's center. Mandala is a centering technique, a process of

27. Schwartz, N. and S. "On the Coupling of Psychic Entropy and Negentropy," *Spring Publications*, Dallas, Texas: University of Dallas, 1970, p.79.

consciously following a path to one's center.[28]

An example of what we mean by feeling centered can be seen in our earlier example of White Turtle who, by viewing his Name within the mandala of the Medicine Wheel, could feel grounded in his ability to look within. Being a mandalic form, the astrological horoscope also provides the possibility for the person to feel his or her center. By concentrating upon its mandalic form, one can literally be structured into a concentric experience, i.e., the organism's energies can be turned inward and focused into the center of the chart which represents the person's own center. The shape of the chart leads the person from the outer circle which represents the movement of the Earth through the zodiacal signs, to the inner circle representative of the rotation of the Earth around its own axis, forming the circle of houses, and finally to the marked center of the chart.

Other aspects of White Turtle's and Deer Kissing Eyes' experience may also be related to the mandalic form. By recognizing that all qualities of being, including one's own, are contained within the mandala, the person can experience his or her way of being as a valid part of the universal whole. This can lead to a feeling of harmony both with one's own self and a harmony with others, as their qualities are seen to be part of the wheel that we all share. The integration that one feels in coming to realize that one's way of being is a unique composite of the universal possibilities contained in the mandala of life can allow one to feel life as meaningful. If people doubted the validity of their ways of being before, such an experience can help them to view themselves in a new way.

When it is stated that the astrological mandala can aid a person in these aspects of feeling one's whole self, we mean that the form of the mandala is oriented to this purpose, not that in all cases it will produce such an experience. It would take a different sort of study to determine how much the form itself is responsible for allowing these experiences to unfold, and how much the presence of other psychological factors is involved.

The astrological mandala allows experiences other than positive feelings of wholeness to emerge. The symbols that are constellated through working with the chart can give one the opportunity to confront nonadaptive aspects of one's way of being. The ability of the astrological chart to aid one in dealing with positive and negative

---

28. Arguelles, J. and M. *Mandala*, p.20.

aspects of one's being will be examined in greater depth in the Case Illustration Section with Case A.

# How the Astrological Mandala Can Constellate the Transpersonal Experience of a Wider Whole

A third criterion important to a holistic identity was earlier described as its ability to provide the possibility of experiencing one's way of being in relationship to a wider whole (Criterion III). The astrological mandala is a tool capable of serving this aim.

The idea that there is a transpersonal aspect to one's identity as a human being is not well received in certain psychological circles. There are those who attempt to explain such experiences by stating that they are representative of an undifferentiated ego state, are correlated with a confused sense of identity and can lead to faulty reality orientation. Even those psychologists who recognize the subtle distinctions between psychopathological states of consciousness and transpersonal experiences have spoken of the dangers of entering into such realms. Carl Jung, for instance, had this to say,

> Anyone who identifies himself with the collective psyche or in symbolic language lets himself be devoured by the monster and becomes absorbed in her, also attains to the treasure defended by the dragon, but he does so in spite of himself and to his own great loss.[29]

In the field of astrology there are as well those who recognize the dangers involved in the experience of expansion of the boundaries of the self. Rudhyar (1968) here amplifies Jung's warning when he says,

> Nevertheless anyone will court serious and in a sense perhaps fatal danger who being fascinated by the end of the process often unwisely seen as the mystical experience, rushes to the path of self transcendence only too ready to surrender what in fact he has not yet built within his total person. To such a one, the illumined road may turn into a very dark pathway filled with obsessions and irremediable devotions and perversions.[30]

Regardless of the position that different persons take on the existence of and the wisdom of exploring transpersonal consciousness, it seems that the field of psychology is being forced to more closely

---

29. Jung, C.G. *Memories, Dreams, Reflections*, p.294.
30. Rudhyar, D. *Tryptych*, Netherlands: Service/Wassenar, 1963, p.6

examine this subject area. What are called transpersonal experiences have been opened to the masses through the rapid proliferation of consciousness-expanding drugs and the spreading of transpersonal techniques from the East. Some psychologists have played an important part in exploring these realms with work done in sensory deprivation tanks (Lilly, 1973), journeys to the East (Ram Dass, 1971), and by investigating the effects of consciousness-expanding drugs (Lilly, 1973; Grof, 1969).

The importance of transpersonal awareness to this work is how such experiences relate to the dimension of meaning. Speaking to this point, Jaffe (1971) says that "the experience of meaning depends on the awareness of a transcendental or spiritual reality that complements the empirical reality of life and together with it forms a whole."[31] Various psychologists have spoken to this subject area in different terms. Maslow speaks of the importance of "peak experiences," and Assagioli speaks of the "higher self" as an integral part of the realization of one's life's meaning.

It seems obvious that any biological unit's meaning must be considered in relationship to the wider whole of which it is a part. For, throughout the various realms of nature, all biological units have both independent properties of wholes and also dependent properties as parts of a wider whole. As Koestler (1972) puts it,

> Every organ has the dual character of being a subordinate part and at the same time an autonomous whole — which will continue to function even if transplanted into another host. The individual himself is an organic whole, but at the same time a part of his family or tribe. Each social group has again the characteristics of a coherent whole but also of a dependent part within the community or nation.[32]

In order to give value to these dual aspects of all living things, Koestler has coined the word "holon." Deriving from the Greek "holos" meaning whole, with the suffix "on" meaning a part, the word incorporates both aspects of an organism's identity. The concept of an organism as a holon suggests that it must preserve and assert its autonomy, otherwise it will lose its articulation and dissolve into an amorphous mass. At the same time, it must remain in tune with the demands of the existing or evolving wider whole of which it is a part.

Among the early psychologists, Jung most clearly developed the idea that the individual's experience of the wider whole was

31. Jaffe, A. *The Myth of Meaning*, New York: G.P. Putnam's Sons, 1971, p.21
32. Koestler, A. *The Roots of Coincidence*, New York: Vintage Books, 1972, p.111

important to the experience of identity. He spoke of the experience of the wider whole as a psychological state which corresponded to a "psychic center of the personality not to be identified with the ego."[33] When Jung discussed the concept of "the Self," he capitalized the "S" to convey that he was speaking of a wider center of the personality that included the ego complex.

The idea that there is a wider center of the personality than the ego complex contains the seed for a concept of the psyche as revolutionary as the vision of the solar system that Copernicus presented centuries ago. Just as Copernicus' theory pointed to a center larger than the Earth, so does the Copernican revolution of the psyche postulate a wider center than the ego complex.

According to Jung, an important aim of the analytic process is to establish a link between the ego complex and the wider Self. Jung saw this link as important to preventing the ego from being swept away by the larger collective psyche.

The mandala was seen by Jung as a symbol of the Self in the above sense of the word. He saw its structure as capable of leading to the production of this wider center of the personality, and as being an important aid in centering the psyche as the contents of the wider Self are integrated.

Long before Jung brought the concept of the mandala to modern psychology, mandala symbolism was used to represent humanity's relationship to a wider whole, augmenting a transpersonal awareness. The physical structures built by premodern mankind, such as houses, churches and cities were often constructed in the form of a mandala. From a central point, the four cardinal directions were projected outward and marked, being a representation of the four cardinal turning points of the Earth's journey around the sun. The structure was thereby transformed into a cosmos giving it the value of an "*imago mundi*" (an image of the world).[34] Thus a structure in the everyday surroundings of premodern humanity was transformed into sacred space.

A fireplace, stone or altar would often be placed in the center of the structure marking not only the center of the structure, but actually representing the center of the entire cosmos. So, through the structure and concept of the mandala, the person was able to experience the unity of everyday space with that of the wider whole.

In addition to the experience of sacred space, the mandala was

---

33. Jung, C.G. *Dreams*, Princeton: Princeton University Press, 1974, p.173
34. Eliade, M. *The Sacred and the Profane*, New York: Harcourt, Brace & World, 1959, p.42.

used to constellate the experience of sacred time. By celebrating the various stages of the Earth's circular journey around the sun, the people would be brought into relationship with this larger cycle. Although the cardinal points of the Earth's journey are still celebrated today (Christmas corresponds, for instance, with the Winter Solstice and Easter corresponds to the Spring Equinox), their transpersonal significance has become desacralized and technology has brought us out of touch with these larger cycles.

Another aspect of the experience of sacred time that the mandala is capable of constellating is called the experience of "the center of time" or "the eternal present."[35] By participating ritually in the end of the world and its re-creation at the time of the new year, the person can experience being born anew. According to Eliade (1959) this annual repetition brings the person in touch with the experience of that sacred time when the world first came into existence.

By the time of the so-called Psychological Mystery Schools[36] in the fifth century B.C., the experience of the wider whole was seen as being fundamental to the consciousness of the deeper meaning of one's life. The Pythagoreans, for instance, taught that the person was a "*kosmos*" which they defined as a "self evolving or self transcending whole."[37] Using a mandala based upon celestial coordinates to describe the person, aids the experience of one's self as a microcosmic embodiment of the wider macrocosm. From the Greek doctrine of "the harmony of the spheres" which taught the underlying harmony between microcosm and macrocosm, to the Hermetic aphorism "as above, so below," and in our Bible's statement "on earth as it is in heaven," a transpersonal perspective has been seen as an integral part of the experience of life's larger meaning.

A symbol of the wider whole often took the form of the "*unus mundus*" which pointed toward a "unitarian aspect of existence which transcends our conscious grasp."[38] In the Hermetic tradition, Marsiglio Ficino used this symbol to represent the whole universe as one living being, and Komarios in the first century AD used the

---

35. Arguelles, J. and M. *Mandala*, p.91.
36. Material on the Psychological Mystery Schools can be found in Schure (1971) *The Ancient Mysteries of Delphi, The Ancient Mysteries of the East, The Mysteries of Ancient Egypt,*and *The Mysteries of Ancient Greece.* Also see Meier's (1967) *Ancient Incubation and Modern Psychotherapy,;* Collins (1954) *The Theory of Celestial Influence,* and Hall's (1971) *The Secret Teachings of All Ages: Masonic, Hermetic, Qabbalistic and Rosicrucian Symbolic Philosophy* for a deeper understanding of our ancient colleagues' approach to psychology.
37. Collins, R. *The Theory of Celestial Influence,* New York: Samuel Wiser, 1973, p.17.
38. Von Franz, M.L. *Number and Time,* Evanston, Il: Northwestern University Press, 1974, p.171.

symbol of the *unus mundus* to represent the transcendental experience of wholeness (Von Franz, 1968). By using these symbols as methods of divination, some people purportedly were able to learn things which could not be known, such as where an escaped slave was hiding or whether a patient would live or die.

Whether it in fact turned its user into an efficient magician is immaterial to how it could be used to reform and reconstellate the inner person. The moot point concerning the "objective reality" of the *unus mundus* leads away from exploring the psychological reality experienced by the person when using such symbols.

In this context, Jung speaks of the mandala as the psychological equivalent of the *unus mundus*, and von Franz (1968) says that the best known symbol of the *unus mundus* is the astrological horoscope.

The astrological horoscope contains a circle of the heavens as the outer circle (the zodiac), an inner circle picturing the axial rotation of the Earth (the astrological houses) and a central point which represents the individual's center. The structure thereby provides an isomorphic representation of the transpersonal and personal aspects of human experience which come together through the center of the person. By using the astrological mandala to center one's self in relation to the wider whole, the person's own center may be transformed into sacred space.

Since the whole horoscope is symbolic of one's Self, a structure is established whereby the possibility is opened to experience the cosmos within one's being. Some see astrology's birth as mankind's projection of humanity's own transcendent nature into the cosmos.[39] The horoscope could also be used to withdraw this projection, allowing the experience of the unification of both aspects of the Self. In Koestler's terms, a perspective of the person as "holon" is represented; a new center of personality is given room to emerge which, in Jungian terms, would correspond to the wider Self.

In relationship to our earlier discussion concerning the dangers that the ego may experience in meeting the contents of the wider collective unconscious, the mandala may be particularly useful. Neumann (1954) recognizes this function of the mandala when he says,

> The genesis, stabilization, configuration, and consolidation of the personality

---

39. A question arises here as to the degree and quality of primitive peoples' consciousness. A classic argument centers around this question with Jung and Levi Bruhl assuming a "participation mystique" of primitive peoples. This is argued against by Radin, Goldstein and Diamond in Diamond's (1960) *Primitive Views of the World.*

> are therefore associated with a symbolism whose ingredients are perfect form, balance, harmony, solidity. The mandala, whether appearing as the circle, sphere, pearl, or symmetrical flower, contains all these elements...representing the indestructibility and permanence of something that can no longer be split apart by the opposites.[40]

So that one does not get the impression of the mandala as a static structure precluding the maturation that evolves from meeting opposites, Neumann goes on to say that accent does not lie so much on indestructibility and permanence, but upon the person as a living organism who grows, develops and renews. The bringing into harmony of the forces of the psyche by the mandala plays an important part in the dynamic process of the development of consciousness according to Neumann (1954). He says,

> Structural wholeness, with the Self as center of the psyche, is symbolized by the mandala, by the circle with a center, and by the hermaphroditic uroboros. But this uroboric circle now has the luminous core of the Self for a center. Whereas in the beginning the uroboros existed at the animal level only, so that the ego germ contained in its midst was almost hidden, in the unfolding flower of the mandala, the animal tension of opposites is overcome, transcended by a Self which blossoms forth into a corolla of opposites. At the beginning of the development, consciousness was all but extinguished by the crushing superiority of the unconscious; at the end it is broadened and strengthened by its connection with the Self. This combination of the Self with the stability of the ego serves to subdue and bind in a magic circle all contents, whether of the world or the unconscious, outside or inside."[41]

There are those who object to the use of the mandala on the grounds that it does not fit with the present conception of the universe. It is said that the ancient image of the cosmos, the mandala with a center and its complementary opposite, the closed circular periphery, is not compatible with modern astronomy which conceptualizes a universe without a center. From this point of view, the mandala seems too static for the idea of the expanding universe which, having no centre, demands particular attention to the periphery. As applied to human psychology, there is concern that this might lead to a focus on a static center rather than movement, expansion, and growth outward. The alternative image of the spiral is suggested as being more in tune with the modern age.

In defense of the continued use of the mandala, one can see from the discussion here, particularly the statements by Neumann, that the mandala need not produce a static conception of the person.

---

40. Neumann, E. *The Origins and History of Consciousness*, Princeton: Princeton University Press, 1954, p.416.
41. Ibid., p.417.

Rather, it allows for a view of a growing, developing organism which transforms itself like an unfolding mandalic flower.

Secondly, regardless of the current state of astronomical understanding, mandalas seem to be spontaneous productions of the human psyche. Whether Jung is correct in his conclusion that they are produced when psychic equilibrium is disturbed, as a centering tool, it at least seems certain that they do appear at certain stages in both phylogenetic and ontogenetic development. (See Kellogg in Wheelwright, 1968.) Just as the Earth needs a center around which to revolve, so does the human organism. This does not preclude movement (witness Tai Chi Chuan — the art of centering in movement), and may even add to a feeling of purpose in movement outward, i.e., in having someplace to move from, and having an organismic center into which one can incorporate one's life experiences.

Thirdly, the astrological (celestial) mandala, is in certain respects much like a spiralling mandala. With the use of astrological progressions, the development of the person through time is given pictorial representation. This allows a comparison to earlier turns on the spiral of one's life path. Further, the actual use of the mandala is not bounded by the circle. Rather it allows the incorporation of new elements coming from outside its so-called boundaries. The astrologer can speak of the entry of comets into the system, galactic motion, chaos and the black holes of life, etc., as symbols relating to the person.

Nonetheless, I felt a need to expand the scope of the astrological system. From the synthesis of astrology and psychology to which I ultimately came, any aspect of the universe can be used to speak symbolically of the person. This wider, metaphoric language allows any symbol helpful to the person, including the spiral, to be incorporated into its form.

## The Symbol as a Missing Link to the Wider Whole

> The man who understands a symbol not only opens himself to the objective world, but at the same time succeeds in emerging from his personal situation. . . reaching a comprehension of the universal. Thanks to the symbol the individual experience is awoken and transmuted into a spiritual act.[42]

In discussing the mandala, the psychological importance of

---

42. Arguelles, J. and M. *Mandala*, p.53, quoting Mircea Eliade.

establishing a connection with the wider whole was emphasized. This quest existed in primitive times where our ancestors sought to experience a link between the sacred and profane in their everyday lives. It is no less significant in this age of the Copernican revolution of the psyche. With the increasing dangers of premature consciousness expansion, many therapists feel a pressing need to investigate the transpersonal. It seems that particularly in this age of mind-expanding drugs and the inner astronaut, there is a need to find a strong connecting cord to aid one on the journey into these realms of experiencing.

Throughout psychological history, the need to find a connecting link between the realms of "the sacred and the profane" (Eliade, 1959) has been seen as important to assure "the possibility of passage from one zone to another."[43] According to Eliade, many symbols have expressed this need: the bridge, the cosmic pillar, the tree, the sacred mountain, and the opening above. A number of Babylonian sanctuaries were specifically named *ur-an-ki* which means "link between heaven and earth."[44]

Some might see this as expressing the importance of a link to the wider dimension of transpersonal experience. Jung might speak of it as establishing a connection between the ego and the wider center of the Self. The psychologist interested in the general dimension of meaning might speak in terms of helping the person bridge the apparent gap between everyday experiencing and the wider world of meaning.

Earlier the experience of meaning was shown to come from a deepening of one's perception of external reality through recognition of its numinous background. In the example of the man with the foot fetish, for instance, the symbolic perspective provided a connecting link to the archetypal meaning of his behavior. Then his foot fetish was no longer "just a foot fetish," but became a symbol of his archetypal need to meet the "feminine" principle.

To make more explicit how a symbol serves the general function of connecting different dimensions of reality, let us first examine its etymological derivation. The word "symbol" derives from the Greek *"symbolon"* which combines two root words, *"sym,"* meaning together or with, and *"bolon,"* meaning that which has been thrown. The basic meaning is "that which has been thrown together."[45] In original Greek, usage, "symbols" referred to the two

---

43. Eliade, M. *Sacred and Profane*, p.181.
44. Ibid., p.41.
45. Edinger, E. *Ego and Archetype*, New York: Penguin Books, 1973, p.130.

halves of an object, such as a stick or a coin, which two parties broke between them as a pledge to later prove the identity of the presenter of one part to the holder of the other. A "symbol" then referred to the missing piece of an object which, when restored, or thrown together with its partner, recreated the whole object.

The use of symbolism in the premodern person's life enabled the individual to establish a connection with the wider whole of which he or she was a part. The fireplace in the center of a lodge, for instance, became a living symbol connecting the warm glow of one's personal center with the mythic center of the universe. By being changed into a representation of transcendent reality, the thing symbolized had its usual limits abolished and instead of being an isolated fragment became connected to the wider system represented. Even further, the thing was experienced as embodying the whole of the system represented.

Symbolism makes it possible to move from one dimension of reality to another, opening the possibility of either unifying or separating different dimensions of existence. As far as the above example is concerned, the symbol of the fireplace is capable of unifying the warmth of the physical center of the home, the warm glow within the person, and the warmth of the mythological center of the universe.

Eliade (1963) puts well the function of symbolic thought when he says,

> What we may call symbolic thought makes it possible for man to move freely from one level of reality to another. Indeed 'to move freely' is an understatement: symbols, as we have seen identify, assimilate, and unify diverse levels and realities that are to all appearances incompatible.... Man no longer feels himself to be an 'air tight' fragment, but a living cosmos open to all the other living cosmoses by which he is surrounded. The experiences of the world-at-large are no longer something outside him and therefore ultimately 'foreign' and 'objective,' they do not alienate him from himself but on the contrary, lead him towards himself and reveal to him his own existence and his own destiny.[46]

As applied to human personality *per se*, the symbolic mode of description provided by certain premodern naming systems can establish a connection between a person's identity and the wider whole. The intricate symbolic system that astrology provides is particularly suited to this purpose, for through describing the person with symbols of the larger cosmos (the macrocosm) one can

---

46. Eliade, M. *Sacred and Profane*, p.455.

experience how the universal possibilities of being came together through his unique personality.

By using this vast universal language, one may be opened to exploring how one's own way of being plays the tune of a cosmic melody. The complexity of the language can enable one to describe the unique way in which he or she improvises upon its theme. Although the notes may be experienced as being played from the keyboard of a wider whole, they take on a unique character as they are arranged in our personalities. Disconnected notes may be transformed into chords. Dissonance and harmony can be brought into new perspective as one becomes aware of their life's composition.

Whitmont (1970) expresses well this use of the astrological chart when he says,

> Applied in this broader sense, astrological techniques can become as valuable to the depth psychologist as dream interpretation. They would inform him, not of future events or even fixed character traits, but of unconscious basic dynamics and form patterns that a given person is 'up against' and to which he continues to react through his own peculiar, individual manner as the characteristic way his particular life is embodied in the cosmic whole. [47]

---

47. Whitmont, E. "Why causality," *Aquarian Agent*, 1970, 1 (13), p.8.

# CHAPTER SIX

# ASTRO-POETIC LANGUAGE

Although the astrological system seems to satisfy the criteria necessary for a holistic identity system, at least one serious limitation remains. The complexity of the language presents a possible barrier to those wishing to have an alternative means of speaking of the personality.[1]

Therefore another step seems necessary to penetrate into that which is essential to the symbolic language and transpose it into a language more easily usable by others. In this chapter, the astrological language is not discarded, but rather is shown to be one end of a continuum stretching to a more simplified metaphorical language at the other end. In this way, a broader communicative framework is established to suit a broader range of needs.

## Astrology as Metaphor

> I would have no quarrel with anyone who asserted that the language of the novelist, poet or musician is closer to the quality of human experience than the language of psychologists.[2]

How can one further expand upon the connection thus far made between celestial referents and personality qualities? As has been

---

1. In this sentence, an inference is made that there may be other limitations than the complexity of the astrological language. Other limitations do exist concerning implementing the astrological system, and shall be discussed in the Case Study Section. (See sections entitled "The Problem of Dependency," and "Considerations of Contraindications.") See also a general review of certain questions concerning astrology in Chapter Nine.
2. Van Deusen, *The Natural Depth in Man*, New York: Swendenborg Press, 1972.

shown, one way that astrological language creates meaning is that its symbols enable people to make a bridge to another dimension of meaning which can lead to experiencing new meaning. How can this process of finding new meaning by moving from one dimension of reality to another be simplified? For the poet this is no problem, for metaphorical language is the epitome of this process. A poet moves from roses to loved ones, from the starry sky above to the starry light within, from waves of the ocean to waves of emotion, with the mere wave of a pen.

In *Experiencing and the Creation of Meaning*, Eugene Gendlin provides a wealth of information on the metaphorical process and its importance to psychotherapy. Explicating how metaphor enables one to make a transition to a new area of experiencing, he says that:

> . . .metaphors differ from ordinary symbols in that they do not simply refer as ordinary symbols do to their habitually felt meaning. Rather, the metaphor applies the symbols and their ordinary felt meaning to a new area of experience and thereby creates a new meaning and a new vehicle of expression.[3]

He uses the metaphor "My love is like a red, red rose" to illustrate how new meaning is created by incorporating another dimension of reality. An undifferentiated experience (of "my love") becomes specified by relating it to a new medium (the metaphorical rose). New meaning emerges as certain likenesses between the woman and the object of nature are assumed. One becomes aware of those characteristics of the woman that are believed to be blooming, eventually passing, beautiful, tender, quietly waiting to be picked, and part of a greater nature.

Thus a metaphor is a device that enables one to see how something in our everyday experience is similar to something in another dimension of reality (in this case nature). New meaning is thereby created. Gendlin is careful to point out that by listing the similarities between the two, we have not stated the metaphoric meaning completely, but have only drawn out some essential aspect of it. For the metaphor can never be exhausted by stating or analyzing the likenesses upon which it is supposed to be based, but which it really is in the act of creation. This echoes Schwartz's (1970) earlier statement that speaks of astrology as a metaphorical system, i.e., that "all the words one thinks up cannot replace the signs of the planets; nor can they explain the so-called square or trine aspects that planets,

---

3. Gendlin, E. *Experiencing and the Creation of Meaning*, Toronto, Canada: The Free Press of Glencoe, 1962, p.113.

i.e., psychic qualities, may make with one another..."[4]

In Cassirer's (1953) discussion of the power of metaphor he likewise recognizes that metaphor creates a "transition to another category" of experiencing. Through the "equivalence principle" of linguistics "entities which appear entirely diverse in direct sense perception or from the standpoint of logical classification may be treated as similar in language, so that every statement made about one of them may be transferred and applied to the other."[5]

Eliade brings out this point further in his discussion of the characteristic of symbolism which he calls "multivalence." He refers to the capacity of symbols to "express simultaneously several meanings, the unity between which is not evident on the plane of immediate experience." For instance, "the symbolism of the moon reveals a correspondence of a(n)...order between the various levels of...reality and certain modalities of human existence."[6] He particularly emphasizes how symbols reveal a multitude of structurally united meanings in which diverse realities can be fitted or integrated into a system. Although Eliade was interested in unifying the realms of "the sacred and the profane" one can see his insight extending into other areas as well, including personality qualities.

From the psychotherapeutic standpoint, metaphors can be particularly useful. Throughout his work, Gendlin (1962) emphasizes the psychotherapeutic importance of processes which allow changes in one's feelings to occur. Other psychologists and psychiatrists are aware of the therapeutic functions that metaphor may serve. From listening to tape recordings of psychotherapeutic interviews, Dr. Rohovit (1960) grew to believe that "a person's selection of metaphor was in some way related to his unique unconscious processes."[7] Using an experimental research design to investigate his hypothesis with a technique of free association to metaphors, his results support his hypothesis. He says, "Many clinical observations suggest that the affect and content of one's past and present life problems may in part be communicated by metaphor."[8] Dr. Krag (1956), a New York analyst, likewise appreciates the use of metaphor when she says, "All these metaphors not only clarify; they give the analyst a subjective emotional understanding of the experiences described, which is helpful since he deals not only with the ideas of others but

4. Schwartz, N. and S. "Coupling of Psychic Entropy and Negentropy", p.79.
5. Cassirer, E. *Language and Myth*, New York: Dover Publications, 1953, p.96.
6. Eliade, M. *The Two and the One*, New York: Harper & Row, 1965, p.203.
7. Rohovit, D. "Metaphor and Mind," *American Imago*, 1960, 17, p.293.
8. Ibid., p.289.

mostly with their feelings."[9] In relation to our previous discussion concerning connecting to the universal dimension of human experience, Dr. Krag makes an interesting statement. She says that:

> The reader or student or psychoanalyst who is attuned to these intuitive subtleties finds in himself an awareness of universals in human experience which the metaphor enables him to confirm or elaborate or they cause him to feel a need to deny or to modify by a compromise.[10]

In these examples, although these psychologists realize the psychotherapeutic importance of metaphor, they do not relate its use to speaking of personality qualities. Asch (1955) has investigated this aspect of metaphor and has discovered that a common cross-cultural property of languages is that words that describe psychological qualities of people also describe physical properties of things. He reports that "all the languages so far examined possess morphemes that simultaneously describe a physical and psychological quality."[11] For instance, terms such as warm and cold describe thermal properties of things, and the same terms also refer to corresponding properties of persons. Asch says that "there is hardly a term in English which while describing some physical aspect of things or events does not also describe some psychological aspect of persons."[12] For people too are deep and shallow, narrow and wide, hard and soft, bright and dull, straight and crooked, he adds.

Asch goes further by questioning what the connecting link that joins the straightness of a line and the honesty of a person, or its crookedness and dishonesty. Whether we call this link a shared essence or a common structural organization, one can feel that which connects the two in meaning. In conclusion, Asch states that

> ...when we describe psychological events in the same terms we employ for the description of the forces of nature — of fire, sea, wind — we are referring to functional properties they share. We see natural events as conductors of the same fundamental forces that we find in the human sphere.[13]

Although Asch was not interested in the psychotherapeutic issue of meaning specifically, one can see how his insight applies here. By using metaphors to see natural events as conductors of the same

---

9. Krag, G. "The Use of Metaphor in Analytic Thinking," *Psychoanalytic Quarterly*, 956, 25, p.69.
10. Ibid., p.70.
11. Asch, S. "On the Use of Metaphor in the Description of Persons" in H. Werner, Editor, *On Expressive Language*, Worcester: Clark University Press, 1955, p.32.
12. Ibid., p.29.
13. Ibid., p.93.

fundamental forces that we find in the human personality, the person described may find a connection between the self and another dimension of experience — a consciousness of the universals of human experience. It seems that this could lead to the use of a metaphorical language to connect the individual's personality to this wider universe of meaning.

The connection between two different dimensions of reality is explicated by the principle of isomorphism used by the Gestalt psychologists (Kohler, 1969; Arnheim, 1949). According to this principle,

> Processes which take place in different media may be nevertheless similar in their structural organization. Applied to body and mind this means that if the forces which determine bodily behavior are structurally similar to those which characterize the corresponding mental states, it may become understandable why psychical meaning can be read off directly from a person's appearance and conduct."[14]

The Gestalt psychologists usually use the term isomorphism to examine similarities in structural organization between states of mind, neural correlates, muscular forces, kinesthetic correlates and shape and movement of the body. Our use of the term shifts the emphasis to shared structural similarities between personality qualities and their representation in the dimension of archetypal patterns, i.e., the realm of energy potentials manifested in different dimensions of reality.

# The Roots of the Astro-isomorphic Perspective

It may help the reader to know how I came upon the isomorphic perspective. Years ago I remember a young woman coiling up to me for warmth on a cold winter night. In a relaxed state, an image came to my mind — it was an electrical coil. Then another image emerged — the coiling spiral of a galaxy. I realized that these images contained what might be called a shared structural similarity, or a common essence. They all can be seen as figures which produce warmth or energy in the process of coiling.

People in many different fields have enhanced the description of something by transposing its structural organization into another

---

14. Arnheim, R. "A Gestalt Theory of Expression," *Psychological Review*, 1949, 56, p.160.

dimension to expand and elucidate its essence. For example, the world of animated films expresses this idea. In the film "*Fantasia*" a musical theme can be seen embodied in the motions of the conductor and given isomorphic representation in the images Walt Disney has chosen. The resultant symphony is played through three different mediums: the music, the bodily structure of the conductor, and the animated images. The result is that all three seem to be connected by a common theme, a common structural organization. Likewise, in the "montage" technique that Eisenstein uses in "*Potemkin*," the dynamic pulsing of the engines parallels the working of its crew. This parallel image of the engines considerably expands one's feeling of the workers' energy by this extension into another dimension of reality.

In the field of literature Hermann Hesse expresses the concept of isomorphism in his culminating work, *The Glass Bead Game*, where he speaks of a universal language which takes a theme in any dimension and translates it through others — such as a musical theme being taken through art, philosophy, mathematics and religion. In the world of art Salvador Dali's (1968) "paranoiac critical method" also takes an image from one dimension and translates it into another to expand its meaning. In his picture on "*The Decay of Time*," for example, one sees the idea of the ephemeral nature of time illustrated in an image of a melting clock which represents the decay of everyday time. This image is then juxtaposed to a picture of a cliff eroded by the sea, which represents the passage of geologic time. The impact of Dali's idea of the ephemeral nature of time is considerably expanded by this isomorphic transposition through mundane and "Great Time."

The ancient roots of the idea of isomorphism can be traced to the birth of philosophy when humanity's consciousness awakened to the unity of being as opposed to the multiplicity of existing things. Many early thinkers searched for a language to speak of the essences of being. These essences were seen as qualities existing in various dimensions of the life process. The Pythagoreans spoke of them in terms of number, and the early philosophers and alchemists sought to discover the root essence of all being which they called the *prima materia*. Perhaps the fullest discussion of the structures of being in early history was Plato's theory of "ideal forms."

In more modern times, the search for the structures of being continued in Kant's discussion of "categories of mind," in Leibnitz's "monadology," and in Jung's exploration of the "archetypes" underlying the life process. In Jung's later writings, he spoke of archetypes as being "psychoid," i.e., that they existed in both physical and psychical modalities.[15]

Fechner attempted to prove the isomorphic hypothesis by showing that all of the objects and events composing the physical world are like the processes of the cortex of the human brain. He wanted to give empirical support to the psychical nature of physical processes, and wished to convey "how pleasing and inspiring the world becomes when thus regarded."[16]

The isomorphic idea has as well been used in various parts of the psychotherapeutic process. In the interpretation of dreams, a person discovers that some essential aspect of life is represented by the dream symbol. The symbol transposes this essential quality into another dimension of reality, which often leads the person to a new awareness of a life pattern (Assagioli, 1965; Jung, 1954). For instance, when a person dreams of an ostrich, he might be asked, "What in your life feels like you're putting your head in the sand?" Here the ostrich serves as a symbolic representation of the archetype of hiding from the world.

Stevens (1971) suggests some useful exercises to develop an isomorphic perspective when he has a person identify with various objects of nature and then feel how these objects convey qualities of his or her personality. One person looking at the thorns on a rosebush comes to a realization of how he is afraid to be intimately touched by others, and how he protects himself from this eventuality by his thorny personality. The theme is thus repeated — by seeing one's self transposed into another structure, new meaning can be constellated.

There has not been a systematic integration of the isomorphic perspective into the field of personality, especially the interest of the depth psychologist in meaning and identity. The use of poetic terms to describe personality could give the psychologist a way to incorporate the perspective that isomorphism brings, without needing to develop proficiency in the astrological frame of reference. This provides a way for the psychologists who are uncomfortable with the use of medical language to expand their linguistic parameters.

Who has not sat by the ocean and seen their Self reflected there? But is it the seaweed with its reaching arms that captures the clinging character of one's emotions, or is it the ocean's pulse that conveys

15. Jung, C.G. *The Structure and Dynamics of the Psyche*, Vol. 8 of Collected Works, Princeton: Princeton University Press, p.176.
16. MacDougall, W. *Body and Mind*, Boston: Beacon Press, 1911, p.138-139.

the way one has been carried by the tides of love?

Our names lie not only in the ocean, but in the birds hovering above. Does one view the plains of human happenstance with the farsightedness of the eagle, sing the tune of sociability as does the robin, or resonate with the deep hoot of the owl as one questions "hoo" one is in the dark night of the soul.

The world can indeed be a mirror for those who wish to explore their identities there. For the universe around us reflects the constellation of the universe within each of us.

Who has not sat under the stars and felt the life process pictured there? The more one speaks this cosmic language, the more one's connection with humanity...with nature...with all creation is revealed. And one's own universe cannot help but expand as does the universe itself.

Anthropomorphism, some may call it....

The experience of the Sacred, some may feel it.

## Applying the Astro-isomorphic Perspective to the Question of Identity: Astro-poetics

Just as metaphor is used by the poet to reorganize meaning and to bridge the gap to another dimension of meaning, so can the astrological language. When one speaks in terms derived from celestial referents, the term astro-isomorphic seems to describe the process. I have coined this term to speak specifically of the shared structural organization between personality qualities and celestial metaphors. It describes the process of extracting the essence which one wishes to describe, and transposing it into the celestial dimension. As has been shown throughout this work, this transposition can lead to meaning reorganization.

Although the word "astro" derives from the Greek word for star, the term is here being used in a psychological sense. We do not wish to emphasize the physical bodies in the heavens, but rather the experience of looking there. The experience of looking at the stars at night can be an illumination of one's place in the universe.

By using an astro-isomorphic perspective, an "astro-poetic" language emerges which uses elements of the cosmos to speak of personality. The term astro-poetics is being substituted for the term astrology to emphasize its function in meaning reorganization.

Astro-poetics is a poetic language that combines the language of the universe above and the language of nature so that a range of terminology exists to speak with varying degrees of complexity about one's way of being. Either the more complex system of celestial metaphors or simple metaphors from nature can be used in a given instance to describe one's personality.

# A Comparison of Poetic and Astro-poetic Imagery

Two systems of metaphors are offered here: from nature and from astrology. The purpose for which I am suggesting the use of metaphors from nature is to enlarge the scope of descriptive terms of personality for those who do not wish to become proficient in the use of astrological imagery.

Both language systems enable the therapist or the lay person to view personality, discover the essence which one wishes to describe and transpose it into another dimension. In both cases meaning reorganization and holism may be possible. But whether other types of metaphor meet the criteria, outlined in Chapter Two, for a holistic identity system, depends upon the particular poetic system used as well as how it is used. Much of this work has dealt with how astrology could be reformed to meet these criteria; the same kind of thorough analysis would be needed to explore how metaphors in general would measure up to these criteria.

Even at the risk of a cursory examination of the everyday used metaphor, some attempt at comparison must be made. The question inevitably arises, "If meaning can be given to a person's way of being through using metaphors from everyday realities, why then do we need astrological symbolism?"

The complicated framework of elements of the astro-poetic language meets the criterion of complexity (Criterion I, B-3) which was earlier shown to be important in speaking of the unique nature of one's personality. Whether a given metaphorical system would be able to do the same is open to question. For instance, in the course of our discussion of the Plains Indians' system, we had serious questions concerning whether a Name such as White Turtle would be complex enough to speak of the multifaceted aspects of a person's personality. But it is not our purpose here to re-explore this identity system, rather it is to state that astrology meets the criterion of complexity, while some poetic frameworks may not.

A key point in discussing the ability of metaphorical language to meet the criterion earlier outlined is how the language is used.

For example, one could imagine a person being described with a metaphor of a tree that would be dynamic or static, intellectually disassociated or experientially moving.

The most obvious difference between the metaphorical language of poetry and astrological language is the different mediums from which they take form. One could perhaps make the strongest case for what astrological language adds beyond what simple metaphor does by saying that the wider the whole from which one's personality is described, the further the dimension of transpersonal meaning may be brought forth.

This viewpoint posits that a progressive expansion of one's relationship to a wider whole may take place as one moves from the poetics of nature to astrological metaphor. To make this point clear, we can first take the example of a therapist who communicates to a person that "it's okay to be idealistic." Even here there is a connection being made to a wider whole, i.e., to other persons who are also idealistic. With a movement to the dimension of natural qualities, such as saying, "you're like a bird," another step may be made. In addition to feeling a relationship with others who have a perceived essence similar to that of a bird, one also may feel a connection with nature herself.

With the movement to the astrological dimension, the opportunity is opened for one to experience a connection with still a wider universe of meaning. For in addition to feeling a kinship with others who share this quality to a certain extent, and in addition to the capacity for an awakened perception of one's unity with nature, the astro-poetic language enables people to see how their personalities reflect qualities of the cosmos.[17]

The wider sense of meaning referred to here can be explicated by using Otto's (1923) concept of "the idea of the holy." In his analysis, he explains one of the attributes of "the holy" as a feeling of "creature consciousness" by which he means a feeling of one's dwarflike relationship to that which is greater than all creatures. This in turn may lead one to experience the *"mysterium tremundum,"* the mystery beyond the limited understanding of our personal selves.[18]

By describing a person in relation to nature, one might expect

---

17. Although the referent in the astrological system seems to be the outer cosmos (the actual stars), one can come to see how the stars act as symbols for universal archetypal qualities existing on multiple levels of reality. Being archetypes, and therefore in Jung's terms "psychoid" qualities, they exist in psychical and in physical modalities.

18. Otto, R., *The Idea of the Holy*, London: Oxford University Press, 1923, p.25.

the person would experience being a creature of nature whereas by describing oneself in relationship to the universe, one might be expected to experience being a creature of the universe. In both cases, the individual might feel a relationship to a wider whole, but in the latter case, the experience of numinosity might be expanded.

By establishing one's connection with this larger numinous sphere, one's sense of personal purposefulness may also be expanded; for one is opened to question — in a medium different from that of nature — the mystery of their existence. When people see that a quality of theirs existed in a larger realm (the cosmos) at the time of their birth, it seems that something often happens in addition to feeling a harmony with even the elements of nature symbolized by the astrological signs. People come to question in a new way how the vessel that is their personality embodies a larger universal purpose. Whether one relates to the *mysterium* by saying "at the time of my birth the configurations present in the universe reflected my seed nature" (hidden reality point of view) or by saying "by using the language of the cosmos at the time of my birth or at any other time, I can give new meaning to my life" (meaning reorganization point of view), still new meaning may emerge regarding the enigma of one's place in the universe.

In summary, an extensive language of personality which provides a continuum of descriptive terms exists. At its most complex end, the astro-poetic language uses astrological terms to speak of personality. At its more simple end, it uses aspects of our everyday surroundings as metaphors for our ways of being. Whether one uses the language of cosmos or of the Earth, the person has a language to speak of life's meaning in a way related to the life process. By using these language systems, one can explore how the elements of existence have come together to enable the individual to flower at a particular time in history. The advantages and disadvantages of one's form can be explored through a particular symbol, and one may grow in new ways to adapt to the purpose called forth by one's environment.

Using poetic terms from the wider whole to describe one's Self can open the sacred experience of one's name. It is by moving through the door of the name into the inner sanctum of the symbol behind it, that a doorway may be opened leading into the poetics of one's soul.

The principle of the Mandala lies not in the external form, which is unique for each situation, but in the center, the source through which the form-creating energy flows. To be integrated, to be made whole means to be able to maintain contact with one's center. Mandala is a centering technique, a process of consciously following a path to one's center.''

In a world that is split, divided by the 'Civil War of Man,' healing is needed to make whole. Mandala is a whole-ing technique; it is the alchemy of opposites reuniting, a blueprint that can be placed upon anything, or any man or being. It is a vision, it is a song, it is a story and a dance — the infinitely renewed seed that contains in its nucleus the collective dream of its kind, the energy of its species.[19]

19. Arguelles, J. and M. *Mandala*.Berkeley: Shambala Books, 1972, p.20.

# CHAPTER SEVEN

# THE ASTROLOGICAL MANDALA AS A PSYCHOTHERAPEUTIC METASYSTEM

Astro-poetics is a capable holistic psychotherapeutic language, but an additional element is lacking. For even if this language were to be incorporated into the psychotherapeutic framework, without this framework itself embodying holistic principles, little movement could be expected towards our goals. The background against which any phenomenon is viewed affects the perception of the phenomenon itself, as the Gestalt psychologists have amply demonstrated (Kohler, 1969).

This chapter views the psychotherapeutic background holistically by using the astrological mandala as an ordering principle. Astro-poetic language is used to view the tapestry of psychotherapeutic systems, demonstrating how it is not just a body of symbols, but a way of thinking.

## The Current State of Psychotherapeutic Systems

In this age of specialized functions, psychologists also have their own specialized ways of looking at the world; these ways of perceiving systems organize their experience. The existence of many different approaches to psychotherapy would be expected at the current stage of our prepardigmatic "science," for, according to Kuhn (1970),

> Every scientific field emerges in a sprawling and uncoordinated manner with the development of disparate lines of investigation and theoretical ideas that preserve their autonomous and competitive positions until a particular set of ideas assumes the status of a paradigm.[1]

Specialized systems in the field of psychotherapy have important repercussions for the course of therapy. Some of these problems were discussed earlier under the title "systematic myopia." The general relationship between the system through which the therapist perceives and its relationship to the emergent psychological problems of the client has also been mentioned.

Most psychological systems, if not excluding altogether the viewpoints of other systems, do not incorporate within themselves these other systems. Dualists call monists undifferentiated, while monists see dualists as splitting the unity of the psyche. Behaviorists laugh smugly at phenomenologists' immeasurable experience, and phenomenologists experience the behaviorists' lack of humanness.

It is indeed strange that the very field which attempts to heal the split of modern mankind is rent with the same kinds of divisions as our segmented society. The danger of this is that the therapist will develop "an approach" which is divorced from a particular client's needs in that client's unique life space. As was mentioned in Chapter Two, the clinical importance of this issue has been addressed in Medard Boss' (1963) classic presentation of the cases of the failure of Freudian and Jungian analysis with a client for whom these approaches were not suited.

While all therapists do at some practical level make individual adjustments in their ongoing relationships with clients, the systems through which they see allow little space for differences, presupposing a fundamental sameness to the patients. The limitations of seeing through a single system are realized by many progressive therapists, yet as with the problem of current psychological language, there is no developed systematic way of dealing with the problem.

Our young field could benefit from a metasystem that includes these various systems and sees their interrelationships with each other — their place on the wheel, so to speak. Although a more comprehensive approach cannot prevent all forms of narrowness in therapy, it may reduce the extraordinary specialization of

---

1. Kuhn, T. *The Structure of Scientific Revolutions*, Chicago, Illinois: University of Chicago Press, 1970.

consciousness and ideologizing so characteristic of traditional orientations to psychotherapy. The metasystem offered here is the astrological mandala. When superimposed upon any realm of experience, it can reveal its wholeness. This chapter applies to organizing therapeutic systems into a whole, as well as centering the therapist in his or her feelings of how to meet the person. As well, this metasystem can be used to reflect upon possible narrowness that may be inherent in the astro-isomorphic approach and approaches to therapy which are meaning-oriented.

# A Holistic Perspective
# on Psychotherapeutic Systems

To list exactly how each system fits into a prearranged place in a schema would involve far greater space than this work allows. More importantly, such a task does not correspond with the tenor of a holistic perspective. The interest is not to see into what box each system fits. Rather the aim is to develop holistic ways of seeing and thereby realize how each system is in itself an expansive perspective if one is conscious of its place in the world.

# An Astrological View of the Birth
# of Psychotherapeutic Systems

The astrological language allows each psychotherapeutic system as a valid place on the therapeutic wheel. Essentially, each system was born from an individual's vision which represented one way of seeing the world. Although the social environment was of great importance in coloring how each system took form, my interest here is in how the system reflected the personality of its conceiver. Metzner (1971) gives a good feel for this idea.[2] Although he examines merely one superficial aspect of the astrological framework, the sun signs of various originators of psychological systems, still he provides valuable insight into the relationship between the personality of the therapist and the system he uses.

Sigmund Freud, for example, was a Taurus, a sign associated with building and constructing foundations, being a fixed earth sign. Upon entering into this symbol, one might see an emphasis on the

---

2. Metzner, R. *Maps of Consciousness*, New York: Collier Books, 1971. See also a series of articles by Rudhyar in the 1930's on this topic.

structural aspect of physical form. Freud spoke of the mechanisms by which energy is bound into structures (cathexes), and how they were channeled from one area of the body to another. He spent a great deal of time constructing the foundations of psychoanalytic theory.

Wilhelm Reich, by contrast, was an Aries, the cardinal fire sign which emphasizes the functional aspect of the movement of energy. Reich was more interested in energy expression and functioning than was Freud. His therapeutic system of bioenergetics certainly reflects this interest, and his most important insights came from his discoveries concerning the streaming of energy in the body.

Carl Jung was a Leo, a fixed fire sign. Through this symbol, one might gain insight into his emphasis on psychic structures, more than on physical structures, as was Freud's emphasis. For the symbol of fixed fire refers to structuring energy. Although Jung eventually came to seeing the archetypes as psychoid (of the body), his emphasis was on the psyche itself. His difference from Reich can be seen through the fixed emphasis of fire in his chart compared to the cardinal emphasis in Reich's. This fixed emphasis is symbolic of an awareness of the structure of energy more than its functioning, and Jung's chief interest was in archetypal symbols (which are energetic structures).

From the above examples one can get a sense of how astrological language can be used to speak of essential aspects of one's way of being.

## Using the Mandala to Order Psychotherapeutic Systems

Psychotherapeutic systems as a whole can also be viewed through the structure of the astrological mandala. The following page will give an idea how one might arrange them. The psychotherapist having a certain orientation not found in this holoscope[3] is not being ignored, for the purpose of this elaboration is not to list all

---

3. The word holoscope is being substituted for the word horoscope to convey the theoretical position of this work. The word holoscope derives from the Greek root words — holos which, according to Oxford Dictionary of English Etymology, means whole or entire, and the word skopos which means observer. Thus, an astrological holoscope provides the possibility of the people observing their personalities holistically. The word horoscope derives from horoscopus which refers to the position of the planets at the time of one's birth. This latter meaning emphasizes objective positions of the celestial bodies whereas the former definition conveys a meaning more in tune with its use holistically.

possibilities. By using astrological symbols, the metasystem can incorporate other therapeutic modes in accordance with that which is seen to be their basic essence.

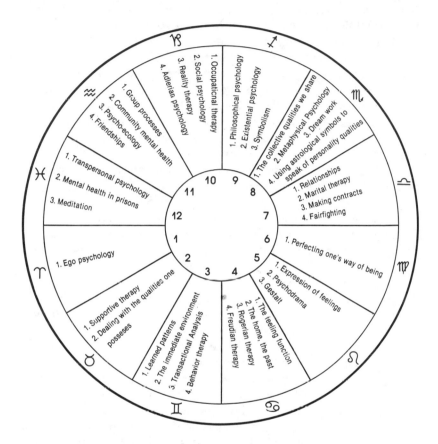

For instance, the basic essence of psychodrama is to act out one's feelings, which those familiar with astrological language recognize as the meaning of the fifth house ruled by Leo. This house of the expression of one's feelings occurs after the fourth house which symbolizes feeling one's inner world. The many systems which speak of getting in touch with one's feelings find their symbolic place here: the Rogerian approach of getting the client in touch with his or her "real feelings," Gendlin's "focusing" method, as well as the Freudian emphasis on the past home life of the individual.

But my interest is not fitting systems into slots, rather in perceiving their interrelationships within the whole and their valid place within it. To see an example of mandalic thinking, one can view the relationship between the second, eighth and fifth houses. Supportive therapies (second house) have in common confirming those qualities that the person possesses as a basic way of being. By looking at the opposite place on the wheel (180°), a new awareness can emerge that makes the perspective more full. (The full moon is that stage in the cycle that is marked by a 180° angle.) Opposite the second house is the eighth house, symbolizing those qualities possessed by others. Realizing the holistic relationship between one's own qualities and those qualities possessed by others may indeed lead to a greater perspective of one's character. Rather than simply "feeling okay" about the qualities one possesses, there can be a fuller awareness of the purpose one fulfills in the myriad possibilities of human being.

In addition to the second/eighth polarity, if we look at a system which is 90° away from each, we have a T-square. This is a configuration which some astrologers compare to a bow and arrow. The base line (in this case, the 180° line) gives the line of awareness from which the symbolic arrow is shot. This 90° point midway between the two is said to release the dynamic action of the configuration. As applied to our example, we could say that once someone sees their way of being and how it relates to others, the person might feel more free to express his or her own way of being. (The fifth house makes a 90° angle with the second and eighth houses.)

Also, a more inclusive framework is established to view schools of thought which have dissonance between their various perspectives. For example, one can examine the conflicts between behaviorism and transpersonal psychology. Instead of the behaviorist only accentuating the negative aspects of the transpersonal way of perceiving, such as saying that it is loose, subjective with little experimental grounding, the behaviorist might grow to see it as part of the same wheel having its particular importance. A recognition may emerge of the importance of the consciousness of a wider whole. Likewise the transpersonal psychologist might more easily be able to see the importance of symptom removal through systematic desensitization and various conditioning procedures. By seeing each system as a valid part of the whole, one may be able to change the way of thinking from the categorical either-or to the nuances of when, where and how. After all, Schwartz showed that this is the function of the mandala. It can lead one from directed thinking to primitive thinking where all possibilities are open. Further, the mandala can point to a cyclical thinking where one realizes that different way of being are called for at different times. From this temporal perspective, the question is not which therapeutic mode is best, but rather which fits this particular person at this particular stage of unfolding.

By giving each system a place on the wheel, we do not mean to imply that this position is fixed and absolute. For depending upon who is looking and in what context, different positions will seem fitting. One person looking at insight therapies will stress its tenth house position at the top of the chart symbolizing a view from above in intellectual awareness. Another might stress its fourth house position relating to exploring and entering into the depths of one's inner world. What is of prime importance is that the system be viewed holistically.

## Beyond Systematic Eclecticism

The metasystematic perspective does not merely see all systems as "okay," for this would obfuscate the important discriminations that need to be made. The mandalic perspective's design allows for focusing on a given element revealing the meaningful place that it plays within the whole. As with the individual client, centering does not preclude taking a stance in a given situation, and can even enhance it by seeing a given part's place in the whole. What may be eliminated is the narrowness that would deny *prima facie* other possibilities on the therapeutic wheel.

The metasystematic perspective need not preclude entering into a given systematic mode. As the astro-isomorphic system has been presented, it is a system for revealing the meaning of any way of being, by elucidating its connection with another dimension of reality. One way of looking at this system is through the Sabian symbol of the rising degree at my birth time, 25° Libra. The rising degree is the exact degree of the zodiac that came over the eastern horizon at the moment of one's birth. Changing about every four minutes with the rotation of the Earth on its axis, it can be seen as a symbol of one's unique way of coming into the world — the sunrise of one's way of being. It is a finer division of the circle than the twelve-fold division of the zodiacal signs since it has 360 degrees symbols whose meanings are derived from the symbolical meaning of the numerology of the particular degree.

The feeling that I had upon reading Rudhyar's analysis of this degree symbol in *An Astrological Mandala* was first one of amazement for it seemed to capture much of my way of coming to the world. The keynote for this degree reads: "The ability to discover in every experience a transcendent or cosmic meaning." Rudhyar goes on to further explicate its meaning:

> The mind open to the multifarious wonders of natural processes, because it sees everything with fresh eyes, not only witnesses simple facts, but pierces through appearances and perceives the great rhythms of universal life. Without such a faculty the aspirant to spiritual realities is always looking for "elsewhere." Yet the spirit, life, God is ever present, here and now....It is a state of CLAIRSEEING, or "seeing through." This world is illusion only to the individual who cannot see through its phenomena and fails to apprehend the reality these phenomena reveal even as they conceal it.[4]

By entering into this symbolic vehicle, I was given permission to develop that system which seems most natural to my way of seeing the world, the astro-isomorphic perspective. My experience of the coiled woman becoming an image of an electrical and galactic coiling spiral seems to exemplify the quality of this Sabian symbol to me. The symbol lets me see in a new light my interest in expanding upon the meaning of phenomena with symbolic vehicles.

The metasystematic mandala can aid the therapist in choosing which system to use, both in terms of one's most natural therapeutic style and in terms of adapting to that which is needed in the individual therapeutic encounter. The mandala gives a visual representation of the way each system fits into the whole, and its importance to it. The therapist, in this sense, can be "given permission" to enter into a given therapeutic mode by seeing it holistically.

One might remark here that the impression is given that therapy involves nothing but the therapist picking the appropriate system. A therapist who merely picks a system does indeed lose a fundamental ingredient of healing encounters — genuineness — which comes from the therapist being centered in his or her way of being and being sensitive to the individual client, not from a mere picking of a system.

Systems are reflective of therapists's natural ways of being. Psychotherapeutic systems can be seen as in-depth explorations of various ways found effective in the healing process — supportive therapy, insight therapy, freeing repressed conflicts, confrontation therapy, getting in touch with the feeling function, etc. Each therapist chooses a system to focus on in accordance with that therapist's natural way of being, and therefore it is genuine.

Each position (the use of and abuse of thinking in terms of

---

4. Rudhyar, D. *An Astrological Mandala*, New York: Random House, 1973, p.188.

psychological systems) reflects a way of perceiving. Perhaps truth is brought forth from an integration of both positions. Although it is helpful to explore in depth a particular therapeutic style, there is a danger of becoming locked into a way of being when one chooses a system within which to operate. A way that goes beyond systems is needed in developing a holistic therapy. For beyond using a system in a formulaic manner, the therapist needs to be centered in his or her way of being. In this light, no system can replace a quality which one might call "being there." A mandalic metasystem can aid the therapist in this quest.

## Centering the Therapist

The question of centering the therapist has two aspects which are in practice two parts of the therapeutic whole: (1) being centered in relationship to the unique therapeutic situation and (2) being centered in the therapist's own way of being.

The first point expresses the belief that in order to be therapeutically effective, the therapist's way of being with a client must relate to the individual person with whom that therapist is relating. In order to be genuine, it cannot be a preestablished technique. This does not mean that therapeutic systems are of no use, but rather that they seem to be more healing if they arise from the individual therapeutic encounter. As indicated, the mandala is oriented to keep one open to many possibilities of being.

The metasystematic mandala can be helpful to the therapist in this regard in allowing the response most appropriate to the situation to unfold. Rather than having a mixed theoretical stance on what is supposed to be therapeutically effective in general, one can see the value in certain situations of feeling warmly sympathetic from the depths of one's heart to a person expressing pain. Other times one may feel detached and questioning of the pain of another person who attempts to drag the therapist into the morass of a never ending script of "poor me." Likewise, the therapist has a framework leading to being in ways not strictly interpreted as psychological — for these can be centered upon in a given situation. At times a political or religious discussion of some issues that emerge may be appropriate. At times a situation calls for a directive approach; other times, a nondirective one. Sometimes clients may be seen in the office, other times outside of it.

Another aspect of the unique situation, which has been a central theme of this work, is the "typology" of the individual client.

From the metasystematic perspective, a framework is opened which includes the possibility of supporting a person's basic way of being or contrasting it with its opposite, which we shall call conjunction therapy and opposition therapy respectively. For instance, in line with the oppositional mode, a client who basically manifests an "air" way of being (hovering above everything) could be shown the beauty of the "earth" path through various sensory awareness techniques which would allow an entering into the textures of everyday experience. With another client the therapist might instead find the conjunctive idea of supporting his intellectual distance more fitting. In accord with the astro-isomorphic perspective, the therapist might not only give the person permission to be the way that person is, but might explore the unique parameters of that individual's way of manifesting the "air" quality, encouraging him or her to be more this way to actualize that air talent.

This does not preclude the opposite emerging. I recall one client who was a very critical person, and with whom I chose to take the conjunctive approach. By using the astrological symbol of Virgo, which can be seen as the interest in polishing the gem of one's being in the quest for perfection, I told him how I enjoyed the fine discriminations he made, and how his attention to detail offered a depth of insight into things that many people usually do not even notice. Caught off guard, he replied that no one had ever told him that his critical faculty was a good thing. However, whenever anyone had told him he was too critical, as people had all of his life, he had always been extremely defensive. His most often used defense mechanism was denial. This led to his inability to "see" this quality, and to attempt to refine it. I noticed in subsequent sessions that the client, for the first time, addressed the negative aspects of this quality, owning that it created distance between himself and others.

In much of the therapeutic literature the differences between conjunctive and opposition therapy are not consciously dealt with, i.e., either one or the other is not addressed. For example, in Barton's (1974) phenomenological elaboration of three different worlds of therapy, he says of the Jungian mode of therapy: "The excessively outwardly directed patient would need to develop inwardness, the overly introverted patient would need to attend to the external world; the overly skeptical patient would need to develop trust and Faith."[5] From the metasystematic perspective, one can see that Barton here emphasizes the oppositional aspect of therapy, where a

---

5. Barton, A. *Three Worlds of Therapy*, Palo Alto, California: National Press Books, 1974, p.261.

certain situation might call for a conjunctive approach. In terms of therapeutic style for a client who is one-sided in development, the therapist might choose in a given situation (as in the above example) to encourage the client to enter even further into his or her way of being. Frankl's technique of "paradoxical intention" emphasizes this idea of further entering into a quality in the conjunctive sense.

We do not mean to imply here that the only possibilities are giving support or bringing into consciousness the opposite. Mandalic thinking goes beyond the linear form. Based on the symbol of the circle, one can view many other possibilities on the wheel, from conjunction (0°) through opposition (180°) and completely through the 360° cycle. Obviously, space does not permit us to explore the meaning of each aspect here,[6] so one brief example will have to suffice.

The holistic therapist might perceive that a man attempts to see both sides of everything (essence of Gemini or Libra) and has difficulty making decisions. Although the therapist might concentrate on any aspect of the cycle helping the person to act spontaneously or to do something which requires instantaneous action (i.e., sports), let us concentrate on the 60° aspect (sextile). The sextile imbibes the essence of the practical application and manipulation of energy by relating to some way of being that is complementary to one's own. This interpretation is derived from the fact that a sextile divides the circle by six, or a trine (which divides it by three) multiplied by two. Three symbolizes synthesizing ease while the two symbolizes the manifestation of this ease. So the therapist might concentrate on aiding the client in spontaneously manifesting his energies, in this case by using the symbol of Leo (60° away). Leo, a fire sign, and Gemini, an air sign, are said to be compatible elements and, in this case, together symbolize the combustion which would represent the igniting and expressing of his energies. If one had the chart of the client, one could look at what house Leo ruled, to give the person a field of activity where he could see its application — for instance, the realm of relationships, or work. Even without a chart, a therapist could aid the person by crystallizing into consciousness this symbol of a glowing coal (Leo) or allow the client to choose a symbol he felt appropriate.

In relation to the second point, centering the therapist in his or her own unique way of being, "there are as many ways as there are

---

6. For more information on the meaning of aspects of the cycle see Rudhyar's (1970) *Form in Astrological Time and Space.*

hearts of men"[7] No system can substitute for the therapist being in his or her own unique way. The astrological system outlined in this work can serve as an aid for the therapist to meditate upon what his or her own style is. Since the system is oriented towards the discovery of uniqueness, it need not be limited to the client. The astrological mandala was an aid to this author in coming to what I see as my most natural therapeutic style.

# An Astrological Perspective on the Counter Transference

It was emphasized by Jung that "analytic psychology requires the counter application to the doctor himself of whatever system is believed in...the doctor is as much 'in the analysis' as the patient."[8] The astro-isomorphic system involves looking at one's way of being and relates to client and therapist alike. "The therapist is equally a part of the psychic process of treatment," continues Jung, and therefore "to the extent that the doctor shows himself impervious to its influence he forfeits influence over the patient."[9]

The counter transference was described by Jung (1954) as "one of the chief occupational hazards of psychotherapy."[10] It seems to be a part of the therapeutic process for the therapist to have personal complexes constellated in the course of therapy. The astrological system can aid in providing a framework to view both persons' ways of being. In addition, it can bring to consciousness the differences in "type" which can be a block in the psychotherapeutic process.

To illustrate, one client came to my office who would notice smells, textures and colors which I had not been aware of. I felt that I should be noticing these things, that I must be unobservant. When dealing with his dreams and in symbolic dimensions in general, the client felt blocked, and felt that he was moving too slowly. The Jungian therapist hearing this might observe that there was here a difference in type, possibly the sensation and intuitive types. Since this client was more familiar with astrological terminology, we spoke of it as a difference between earth and air essences. By bringing into

7. Shah, I. *Tales of the Dervishes*, "The Three Dervishes," New York: E.P. Dutton & Co., 1970, p.103
8. Jung, C.G. *The Practice of Psychotherapy. Collected Works*, Volume 16, New York: Bollingen Foundation, 1954, pp.72-73.
9. Ibid.
10. Ibid.

consciousness our different ways of being, a new phase in our relationship started to emerge. After owning my inadequacy with remembering earthy details to him, he spoke of those instances in his life where he felt inadequate. We then worked on feeling the bodily change that occurred when owning those areas where we felt weak and became more open to exploring each other's realms of proficiency. We were both taking a journey around the wheel.

The issue of difference in "type" between therapist and client has not been given the attention it deserves as an integral part of the therapeutic relationship. It seems that the astrological (astro-isomorphic) system might help by providing a framework through which the differences and similarities between the two people could be addressed in a more holistic manner. The astrological (astro-poetic) language can provide an intricate typological language which may enhance the exploration of individual differences.

# A Metasystematic View of the Orientation to Meaning and Identity

In summary, the general orientation of this work was towards aiding the person in coming to terms with his or her identity and in discovering new meanings thereby. This obviously is not a catch-all for all psychological dis-eases. As discussed earlier, there are cases where the modality is contraindicated. Here we wish to make clear how this orientation is one place on the metasystematic wheel.

From this perspective the focus on identity is merely one stage in development (See Erikson, 1968). Although in one sense the dimension of identity is present in everything a person is and does, from another point of view, it comes in and out of focus depending upon whether it is of primary concern. From Erikson's viewpoint, the focus upon identity would not be warranted, for instance, with a client who was dealing with the trust versus mistrust stage. Furthermore, there are many clients for whom specific problems of their everyday worlds are the main reason for coming to therapy, of which their identities are but a part.

The orientation directed in this work towards the dimension of meaning is also just one place on the metasystematic wheel. In some cases it may prove to be counterproductive, leading the client away from his or her experience. By entering into the tension surrounding a particular complex in ways suggested in Chapters Eight and Nine, some of the negative aspects of this orientation can be averted.

One may even further question the general approach of aiding a person in discovering meaning by saying that it can rob one of the existential experience of meaninglessness which can lead one to recognize the unfathomable depths of the human condition.

But certainly meaninglessness and meaningfulness are both essential constructs arising within the vast panorama of human experience. Although attempting to discern meaning in the human personality may seem like trying to discern order in the multifarious design of the infinitude of space, in both spheres — human and celestial — patterns inevitably reveal themselves to the searching human mind. By exploring these archetypal patterns one may be given pause to contemplate the universal order of things, and how one's own form reflects that order.

# CHAPTER EIGHT

# CASE ILLUSTRATIONS AND DISCUSSION

The following cases are presented to illustrate how the astro-poetic language can be integrated with the psychotherapeutic process. The particular focus shall be upon how this symbolic language aided the individuals discussed here in their process of self-discovery. The use of symbols has been discussed by many psychotherapists (Jung, 1954; Assagioli, 1965; Gendlin, 1962) as being useful in providing a vehicle to aid the transformation of meaning essential to the psychotherapeutic process. The use of astrological symbols, when aligned with this tradition, similarly makes use of the transformative function of symbols.

Since the nature of our mode of inquiry[1] seeks to explore in depth the experience of individuals and the qualities inherent in that experience, the generalizations made from the data may be limited. Whether other individual's experiences would differ from that of these clients is not the purpose of our study. Extensions of the process discussed here may be posited for heuristic purposes but cannot be empirically stated from this approach to the research material. This investigation is but a first step in showing how astro-poetic language may be employed in psychotherapy. The generalizability of the data must await application by others to larger populations.

---

1. See Appendix 2 for a discussion of the subjective, experiential, existential and phenomenological modes of inquiry versus the mode of scientific inquiry.
   For support of the former types of research methodology see Shapiro and Alexander, 1975; Jourard, 1967; and Moustakas, 1967.

From an empirical frame of reference one might also question how much astrological language in itself led to producing the changes discussed, or whether other variables may have influenced the process of change. Unlike a "scientific" research methodology where the principle of Occam's Razor cuts away other variables from the object under study so that the data is not contaminated, the thrust of our mode of inquiry leads us to seek out these very variables to explore how they together, as a whole, aid in the process of meaning reorganization. For example, the integration of psychotherapeutic modalities with the use of astrological language may cloud one's ability to determine whether astrological language *per se* effects a transformation of meaning, but this integration is precisely the point of our study. So, when astrological language is spoken of as an aid to these individuals in their changing experience of their life's meaning, we do not mean astrological language isolated from a multiplicity of variables, but rather as a part of a process.

In the case of "Golden Tooth" a quite extensive exploration shall be made illustrating how astrological symbols aided the client's process of being given permission to be herself, in crystallizing the unique nature of her personality for her, in transforming the quality of her way of being, and in providing a vehicle through which she discovered new meaning in her life.

How one determines whether value exists in a process that is by nature experiential is a most difficult question. For those wishing a more penetrating discussion of the question of value in psychotherapeutic systems in general and the astrological system in particular, turn to Appendix 2. There, such issues as the differences between experimental and experiential models of proof, the differences between criteria of value and the question of solipsism will be explored.

Later in the present chapter, an attempt shall be made to broaden the scope of astrological language to make it more communicable to others in the counseling community. We shall demonstrate with brief vignettes how the language can be transposed into the mediums of history or nature to convey in a more simple manner noogenic insight. Our discussion here shall not be limited to personality qualities; it will extend to giving meaning to life situations.

In this chapter the focus will be upon how the astrological language can be incorporated into the therapeutic process. Although possible problems arising with its use shall be spoken of here, Chapter Nine will focus upon where the modality may be contraindicated and upon general theoretical problems associated with its use.

# Case A: The Case of Golden Tooth

To illustrate how the integration of astrological language into the psychotherapeutic process aided the process of changing a sickness orientation to a meaning orientation, I have chosen a case of a thirty-two year old woman, a native Californian of lower-middle class parents who was employed as a dental technician. She had been married for three years and was divorced for two years prior to entry into therapy. During her marriage she had seen a marriage counselor which was her only other experience with therapy. Her educational background included a degree from a local junior college, and she was a student of various spiritual paths, particularly Eastern religions and Sufism.

A came to me fearing that she was schizophrenic, stating that she had heard that there was no known cure. I asked her what led her to believe that she was schizophrenic, to which she replied that many people had told her so on the basis of the way she communicated.

In Sessions 1-5 of therapy I learned that she did indeed have a unique way of communicating. She often stopped conversations in the middle of a sentence preoccupied with the sound and the meaning of a word that was mentioned. For instance, in a discussion we were having about a T.V. program, when the word "television" was mentioned the client stopped and started to enter into each separate sound: "t" — seemingly tasting the letter in her palate, "v" then associations came to the word such as "tunnel vision." She then went on to describe how "tele-vision" was a vehicle for "tunnel vision." I could certainly see how it could be disconcerting to someone trying to discuss a subject to experience this apparent drifting from the topic of conversation.

The rhyming quality of the client's associations and her drifting to associations with similar sounding words might lead one to see an example of "associative drifting" which can be a characteristic of schizophrenia. It can also, however, be a characteristic of the poetic experience. One distinction seems to lie in the fact that the schizophrenic person ends the associative chain losing the connection with the original word. For instance, in associating to the word "wood" the person might say "tree, teak India, Gandhi, poverty," and in speaking of poverty forget that the beginning of the exploration started questioning the nature of wood. In **A**'s case, however, the associations were more closely connected to the original word by her search for the deeper meaning of the word. Although the participant in the discussion would often get lost in her associations to foreign languages, or feelings unique to her about the meanings of the sounds of the word in her own linguistic schema, I noticed that there was a link maintained with the original word.

The important factor from the therapeutic point of view was that the client herself felt that there was something wrong with her way of thinking. As **A** put it in our second session, "Eventually I felt bad about doing it in public because people think you're crazy. I tried to shut it off, but I couldn't stop the ideas from coming into my head."

Although it was the client's desire to learn how to get rid of this quality (an egodystonic disidentification with her thoughts), in the following few sessions I encouraged her to explore with me her feelings about her way of thinking, hoping to lead her to an identification with her own thought process. Using Gendlin's (1969) "focusing" modality, I directed **A** to simply accept and report what her "felt sense" was at a given moment, and watch to see what images arose out of her bodily feelings. Through focusing on the tension she felt about her way of thinking, an image came to consciousness which was the precipitating event leading the client to seek therapy. This image was of her ex-boyfriend who had ended his relationship with her, calling her crazy. She explained how this was the reason for her depression in the last few weeks.

Through dialoguing (in the Gestalt mode) with her boyfriend, she was able to turn her depression into anger. I was left, though, with the feeling that she still doubted that there was anything of value in her way of thinking. However, after the initial four sessions, instead of being obsessed with how to get rid of her way of thinking, the client seemed more willing to question whether there might be something of value in it. Because of her precarious mental condition at this time, it seemed unproductive to go further into the stuff of the complex. I felt it was important to provide a means whereby she might be able to discover a deeper strength from feeling the worth of her way of being.

As **A** questioned what value might lie in her manner of thinking, she mentioned that she had heard from the person who had recommended me as a therapist that I sometimes use astrological charts in therapy. She questioned whether a horoscope could tell her anything about **why** she was the way she was. After explaining to her the way that I used the astrological horoscope to explore **how** we are the way we are, rather than why we are the way we are, we decided that we would explore this dimension.[2]

A's knowledge of astrology was somewhat beyond popular conceptions. She had one astrological reading done earlier in her life, and had read two elementary books on the subject. I would not, however, characterize her knowledge as extensive. She did have a feeling of comfort dealing with the symbolic dimension which I surmised from a discussion we had about a particular Tarot image. Her symbolic abilities proved to be an aid in her relative ease at entering into astrological symbols.[3]

## SESSION 6

At the beginning of this session, **A** excitedly inquired whether I had drawn up her chart. A copy of the chart I showed her can be seen on the following page. I reminded her that when we discussed a particular symbol that she should feel free to explore the symbol with me, since our aim was to see how the symbols applied to her. To lower the threshold of resistance I engaged her in a discussion of how she felt about exploring this relatively new language with me. After we both shared examples from our lives about learning a new language in our school days and how learning to do many new things brings out the child in us, I felt she was more relaxed. She agreed to tell me when she felt her "child" coming up.

Since my initial aim was to help to give her a sense of what meaning there might be in her way of being, I chose to start with a broad symbol from the chart which could give her a feeling of entering into and exploring how her life energy (the Sun) was generally expressed. I proceeded to tell her that one outstanding aspect of her birthchart was her Sun/Neptune conjunction: that astrologers said that when the Sun was in conjunction with a planet this colored the way the person's energies were expressed. I asked her then if she saw the symbol of Neptune in relation to the way she generally expressed herself, as I added that Neptune was the god of the sea, which was sometimes seen to symbolize the liquification and

---

2. The causal world view that is often projected upon the astrological system is a major problem to be dealt with in integrating this language into the therapeutic milieu. Various ways of dealing with this problem are discussed in Chapter Nine as well as throughout this case.

3. The ability to enter into astrological symbols does not necessarily seem to correlate with knowledge of the language *per se*. For there are those who have an extensive knowledge of the language on the descriptive level, but find difficulty in entering into the symbolic dimension.

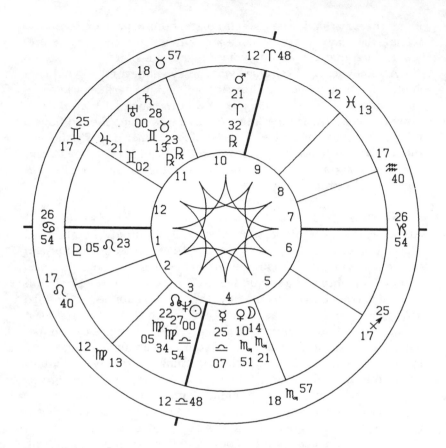

| | | ⊙ | | | | | | Occupied Signs | | | Occupied Houses | | |
|---|---|---|---|---|---|---|---|---|---|---|---|---|---|
| | | | | | | | | Cardinal | Fixed | Mutable | Cardinal | Fixed | Mutable |
| ☽ | ∠ 1°33 | ☽ | | | | | Fire | 1 | 1 | 0 | 1 | 0 | 0 |
| ☿ | | | ☿ | | | | Earth | 0 | 1 | 1 | 1 | 0 | 0 |
| ♀ | | ♂ 3°30 | | ♀ | | | Air | 2 | 0 | 2 | 0 | 3 | 2 |
| ♂ | | | ☍ 3°35 | | ♂ | | Water | 0 | 2 | 0 | 3 | 0 | 0 |
| ♃ | | | △ 4°05 | | ✳ 0°30 | ♃ | | | | | | | |
| ♄ | △ 2°31 | | | | | | ♄ | | | | | | |
| ♅ | △ 0°41 | | | | | ♂ 1°50 | ♅ | | | | | | |
| ♆ | ♂ 3°21 | ∠ 1°47 | ⅄ 2°27 | ∠ 1°43 | | □ 6°32 | △ 0°49 | △ 2°39 | ♆ | | | | |
| ♇ | ✳ 4°29 | | □ 5°28 | | ∠ 0°39 | | | | | | | | |

expansion of boundaries that is felt in various states of intoxication or in mystical experiences. She replied that expanding boundaries was an important part of her life; that her experiences with marijuana were important in opening her boundaries and in experiencing another kind of awareness. She went on to explain how her interest in altered states of consciousness had extended to investigating various spiritual paths — Sufism, mind dynamics (a form of developing ESP), etc.

To guide A in her exploration, I added that I wondered how she saw her Neptune as being in Virgo. I explained to her how I saw the sign Virgo and she picked up on the keywords "specifics" and "details." At first she nervously said, "Maybe it's a symbol of how I space out on details," but after I questioned whether she could see anything of value in this quality, she said that she did enjoy expanding the boundaries of specific things around her and communicating these observations to others. In response to my request for an example, she replied that many people passed over details in their environments and that she enjoyed "expanding and expounding" upon these things. After looking away a little nervously after her play upon the words expand and expound, she continued. She recalled how she would communicate to people about her plants' awareness of their surroundings and would enjoy opening up their assumptions about the level of consciousness of the plants. When I added that her liking to look at and expand upon the meaning of various components of words could be seen as another example of this quality, she replied that this was a new way to look at it. In response to my questioning "how so" she somewhat nervously yet smilingly replied that it made her feel like there "might be something to my way of thinking."

At the end of the session, she asked if she could have the chart so that she could meditate on it at home. I gave her the original colored chart that I had drawn and kept a copy that I had made for my records.

## SESSION 7
At the beginning of this session A said that she had been wondering about what the meaning of the conjunction's specific position in the chart was. I said that her Sun was on the autumn equinox point, which I saw as that point where relationship to others is born, and that the third house traditionally symbolized communication, and exploration of the immediate environment. I asked her what meaning this had to her to which she replied that she was starting to realize

how important it was to her that she be able to communicate her observations to others.

I also brought up at this point the fact that this configuration was in conjunction with the North Node of the Moon. We spoke about how the nodal axis had to do with the destiny line of the chart which "tells the 'why' of an individual's life."[4] Due to the client's interest in Eastern religions, she translated this as being "the *dharma* point" of her chart. She said that when she first heard the Eastern idea that each person has a purpose (their *dharma*) that they are actualizing, that she had wondered what her *dharma* was. From the way she spoke about *dharma*, though, it became apparent that she had always seen it as something far removed from anything she could attain. I hoped that through the therapeutic process she would grow to see that her *dharma* was who she was.[5]

In the course of this session we explored how looking at her way of thinking through the Sun/Neptune conjunction in the third house had brought about a new way to look at herself. We now had a commonly shared definition which was: the ability to explore and to expand the boundaries of specific things around her and to communicate these observations to others. These words, however, do not fully capture what was included in the symbols. As we discussed the Sun/Neptune conjunction, it grew to encompass for us such things as using her intuitive feeling for teeth as she did the detailed work of a dental technician, noting specifics of her environment and communicating about their larger significance to others, and her love for expanding the meaning of words. But it was particularly the emphasis on communication to others (which we now both saw in the placement of the conjunction in the third house) which occupied our attention during much of the session. I shared with her that I had noticed a change in what our therapeutic goal was, for it now seemed that she no longer wanted to stop these thoughts from coming into her head, but instead to learn how to communicate her thoughts to others. She agreed, and said that she had noticed that lately she had not been fighting these thoughts "as much" as they came into her mind.

## SUMMARY OF SESSIONS 6 AND 7

At this point in the therapeutic process I felt that the client had made

---

4. Rudhyar, D. *The Astrology of Personality*, New York: Doubleday Press, 1970, p.293.

5. See page 153 of the Case Illustration Section to see the client's changed relationship to this idea.

progress in feeling that there were positive aspects to her way of being due to her realization (in the sixth session) that there "might be" meaning in her way of thinking. I was seeing a gradual change from her disidentification with her thinking process to a gradual yet hesitant movement towards reclaiming this alienated aspect of herself. It is difficult to make assumptions about the cause of her process of change. This growth may have been due in part to my interest and support for her way of thinking (giving permission), in part to her entry into the astrological symbols which seemed to be an important factor in helping her to see that there was meaning in her behavior, and in part due to catharsis and the movement of the therapeutic process in general. The astrological language seemed to be of particular aid in reframing the way she experienced her way of thinking, and crystallizing what value there was in her way of being.

I would not, however, characterize her feeling of meaningfulness as going very deep at this point (based upon her saying that there "might be" meaning in it during the sixth session), and her statement in the seventh session that she had not been fighting these thoughts "as much." Also my feeling was that some of her "realizations" were not deeply experienced, and it seemed that there was probably some positive transference which at times led her to trying to please me. Still it seemed that her precarious mental state had been sufficiently strengthened so that I felt more comfortable about her ability to enter more deeply into exploring her way of being.

It seemed that the meaning orientation was helpful in strengthening her view of herself. In this case particularly, due to her depression and her possibly unstable condition, this modality seemed to add to her ego strength which I felt was important before entering more deeply into the stuff of the complex. This might seem to go against Reich's (1949) therapeutic axiom that it is important to enter into the stuff of the complex before exploring the meaning dimension. With the particular client I saw this issue as a continuum moving from experiential work to reflecting upon meaning as the therapeutic process unfolded.

## SESSION 8

Apparently during the week **A** had been thinking about our discussion during the last session of how the therapeutic goal had changed from altering her thought process to examining the way she communicated her thoughts to others. At the beginning of this session **A** said that she had been questioning why, if she had all of these planets in the house of communication and her Sun in Libra, did she have such a hard time in communicating to others and in being understood by them? I asked her what she felt the answer to this question was to lead her to examining her communication process herself.[6]

She replied that in reflecting upon our discussion she had been questioning whether the problem might lie in her way of thinking about herself; and that while she was feeling all this out, she had been drawn to the symbol of Mars in Aries.[7] She continued, saying that she had heard that Mars in its ruling sign was "supposed to have to do with a strong way of asserting yourself," that perhaps it was because she was coming on too strong that made it hard for others to understand her. I asked her to explore the way she saw her unique Martian nature (assertion and expression) while "focusing" on this planet.[8] I asked her to be aware of any bodily feelings and to watch if any images came to her. In response to her asking me to tell her more about what Aries is about, I said that it was the sign of the spring equinox where the light principle was just becoming greater than the darkness principle. I again asked her to enter into her "felt sense," "focus," and wait to see if an image came to her of how her assertive nature was captured by the symbol of Aries. She closed her eyes and noticed that she felt strength in her arms and around her body, but fear in her belly. Out of this felt sense, she pictured "a young girl walking through a cave deep beneath the surface of the earth. She is carrying a candle and trying to prevent the darkness from overpowering it. Instead of giving in she blows on the candle, sort of like a dragon, and the flame increases in size so that she can find her way out."

From working with this image in conjunction with the astrological symbol we were able to explore this life theme of hers. She saw how people had often accused her of asserting herself too

---

6. Here we see illustrated an example of the question of dependency. Various ways that may prove helpful in dealing with this issue are considered in Chapter Nine in a section discussing the issue of dependency.

   Whether the astrological system, due to its complex language may be particularly prone to increase the dependency upon the therapist is discussed in the last section of Chapter Nine under "Consideration of Contraindications."

7. As one can see from the way the chart was drawn, the planet Mars was emphasized. But apparently the meaning of the planet itself, with which A was familiar, contributed to her movement towards exploring this symbol.

8. This refers to Gendlin's focusing process, which I had introduced in the beginning sessions of therapy. For those wishing more details on the focusing process, the most updated source is Gendlin, E., *Focusing*, New York: Bantam Books, 1981. This work includes a nationwide list of coordinators for this process, one of whom is the author.

strongly, but that she did not really feel this strength. I mentioned that a characteristic of the symbol of Aries was that of being over-powered in the creation of new light, which could be correlated with overcompensating to confirm the reality that one is seeking to create. This seemed to be an important insight to her, and she then alluded to a previous session where she had been talking to me and went off on a stream of associations (having to do with the Indian word *"vasana"* meaning desires — she had been talking about how desires cause one to vacillate). She remembered how in her desire to assert her associative chain, she had not stayed in touch with whether I (and also others in her life) were following her. After I asked her how she felt in these kinds of situations, she paused for a moment and was then able to tell me that she felt blocked.

I asked her to allow herself to "focus" on the block. She said that she felt fear — that it was "a sort of queasy feeling in my stomach." I asked her to stick with the feeling and watch what im-age came out of it. An image emerged of a situation where she would be associating to her boyfriend and she wouldn't be watching to see if he was listening. I asked her to go back to her felt sense of what this was all about and again check to see what came to her. An im-age arose of her father not listening to her at the dinner table when she was a child. After I asked her to refer back to her bodily feeling again, she reported that it was "the same kind of queasy feeling but more like a gripping, a tightness." As she stayed with this feeling for quite some time in apparently deeply felt exploration she replied quietly, "I'm afraid that no one will ever understand me." I asked if she could allow herself to enter into this feeling, and she cried.

For the rest of this session we explored this feeling. She saw how her fear of not being understood blocked "just about all of my con-versations with people." We then started to explore how the presence of this fear might play a part in preventing her from being understood by others. I felt she was starting to come to the realization that her fear of not being understood was a self-fulfilling prophecy; but I did not share this thought with her for I hoped that she herself would come to see how this was the case. I concluded the session asking her to focus during the week on how this fear affected her way of expressing herself.

On the way out of my office I gave A support for the work she did in this session. She then expressed some uneasiness about waiting a week for our next appointment, stating that she felt that she was in the middle of something very important. We together explored how to balance this need of hers with the variable of time to assimilate the insights she had gained in this session and to explore further on her own the question I had put to her. We agreed on a compromise of three days until our next appointment. I mention this discussion because her ability to engage in this decision-making process in the adult way she had was an important indicator of therapeutic movement to me. For up until this time, although after most sessions I asked her when she wanted to see me next, a covertly accepted routine of once a week had become an established pattern. Now, she was expressing her needs and taking the initiative to break this routine.

## SESSION 9
Early in the following session **A** said that she had been thinking about her fear of not being understood, and that she had realized that earlier in her life, "when speaking in my Neptunian way (It is interesting to note that the client has incorporated this astrological word into her vocabulary) I hoped that someone would ask me what I was talking about . . . I guess I was testing to see if they cared enough to ask me. Later in my life I just gave up." At this point I discussed with her the difference between a childlike giving up and an adultlike taking responsibility for reaching out for what she needed. **A** seemed to be affected strongly by our discussion and wanted to explore this more fully.

I asked her if she could picture one of these situations so that she could see her process at work. From this exercise in active imagination she saw that when she was talking to her boyfriend (and to others) and they would look away in discomfort, she would "become even more like an Aries" (asserting herself even more strongly, she became even further lost in her own associative patterns) due to her fear of not being understood. At this point I felt comfortable in crystallizing the pattern that she had outlined, giving it the label of a "self-fulfilling prophecy" so she could have a term which would express how she caused the "not being understood" herself. This would hopefully lead her to taking responsibility for her not being understood.

We then examined the outline of the process:

1. She would see an association to a particular word or idea.
2. She would notice that the other person was having difficulty following her.
3. This would trigger her fear of being misunderstood which
   a. led to an initial feeling of withdrawing, with the accompanying

bodily feeling of queasiness in her stomach.
b. led to an even stronger assertion of her associative chain, with a subsequent loss of contact with whether the person was listening to her.
4. This led to an even further lack of understanding on the part of the person with whom she was communicating. (It was at this point that her boyfriend had angrily responded that she was crazy.)
5. The conclusion of the interchange was exactly what she had been afraid of — that she was not understood.

We then discussed how she could take responsibility for making sure that she was understood. I suggested that a particularly good point to break the pattern was at the point where she had the feeling which she described as a queasiness in her stomach (3a). For here she could allow herself to feel the fear and take responsibility for doing something about it. In response to my questioning what she could do about it, she saw that she could ask the person where he was getting lost to make sure there was communication — if this was what she really wanted.

## SUMMARY OF SESSIONS 8 AND 9
In these two sessions there was movement from her earlier preoccupation with how to get rid of her way of thinking to an increased desire to focus on her way of communicating her thoughts. Using the symbol of her Mars in Aries, she focused on the way she asserted herself. A became aware that her fear of not being understood led to certain communication patterns that indeed stopped her from being understood. She learned how she could begin taking responsibility for her way of communicating.

## SESSIONS 10, 11, 12, 13
Although A seemed to accept the principle of taking responsibility for her way of communicating, she reported that she was having trouble implementing the idea of confronting people when she felt that they were not listening. In order to give her practice dealing with this situation I introduced her to a process somewhat analogous to **"systematic desensitization."** We worked in these sessions on establishing the connection between her queasy feeling accompanying her fear of not being understood. She practiced expressing her feelings in an appropriate way to the person with whom she was communicating. We worked on this in the interaction that was going on between us, and in guided fantasies where she would imagine

herself in situations of not being understood.

During these sessions I cannot recall any use of astrological material. By the end of this process **A** reported being more able to own her feelings of not being understood to others, and reported that she was beginning to question people as to whether they were following her. However, in the 13th session **A** mentioned that although she could now call people on whether they were listening, she was starting to doubt again that "there is that much worthwhile in my way of thinking."

Although I feel that there was value gained by the client in this work on systematically desensitizing her fear, the fact that at the end of this process she made the above statement shows that in this case Weitzman's (1967) insight seems to be correct. In his article he points out the deficiency in using the systematic desensitization process without an accompanying meaning orientation. Weitzman is careful to point out that in certain cases the client wants to just get rid of a symptom, and that in these cases and others systematic desensitization can be useful in accomplishing certain short-term goals. As applied to the present case, the work on the level of symptom removal can be seen as a pendulum swaying to the meaning dimension as the client's development unfolds.

Therefore at this point, although there was evidence of progress in the client's ability to confront people with her feelings of not being understood, it seemed that a return to the meaning dimension was important since the client was again doubting the value of her way of thinking. In response to my questioning how she wanted to deal with this, **A** said that she would like to do some more work with her chart, remarking that she had found our previous work with it helpful.

Although from a psychoanalytic point of view one might see this as a dependency developing upon the chart rather than upon the client's own resources, one might also look at this in a different way. From a process orientation, even if one were to see evidence for dependency, perhaps at this point she needed this support. Further, it seemed that since **A** sensed that her chart helped her to further crystallize her value as a person, her request to return to the chart then might show a willingness to further enter into exploring her way of being.

Exactly what the client's conscious or unconscious motivation was here is impossible to surmise since I did not discuss this question with her. However, from subsequent sessions the reader will see how the return to the meaning orientation did lead to a further spiraling into her self.

At the end of this session I suggested that the client might focus on her chart during the week and see what emerged.

## SESSION 14

At the beginning of this session **A** mentioned that it seemed that we had only dealt with a small part of the chart and that she couldn't help but notice the triangular structure encompassing the whole middle section. She said that this was what she wanted to explore.

To give us a common starting place from which to work, I outlined for her how I saw this structure (which is shown on the following page). It is a triangular structure whose base is formed by a novile aspect (40°) between the Sun in Libra and Venus in Scorpio. Both of these two planets are in (quadra) novile aspect (160 = 40 x 4) to Mars at the apex of the triangle. I remarked to **A** that this configuration was a rare one, and was amazing to me because of its exactness; all of the planets in the structure were exact within 1° of orb. I further explained that the novile aspect of 40° symbolizes gestation, for from Moses' 40 years in the desert to the human 40-week pregnancy we have a symbol of the attempt to give birth to something. The question I then posed to her was, "What are you trying to give birth to by your way of being?"

We then reviewed the meaning that we had come to about the two points of the structure with which we had already worked. The Sun/Neptune conjunction signified her gift of expanding the boundaries of details of her surrounding environment, and Mars signified the way she expressed and asserted her insights. There had been additional factors adding to these symbols since the last time we had spoken about them, for **A** proceeded to tell me how a recent acquaintance of hers had used the words "very interesting" to describe how he felt about one of her "Neptunian associations."

The symbol of Mars had taken on a positive significance for her since our examination of it in relationship to her overly assertive manner of communication. She mentioned how since we had worked on her style of communicating she had been feeling better about her active assertion of her perceptions especially when she could stay in touch with the person she was talking to. She had apparently, on her own, gone even further in thinking about the symbol of Mars for she now mentioned a contrasting example to her mode of asserting herself. She spoke with added strength of a girlfriend of hers who "never speaks her mind."

The changing meaning of this symbol is a good example of the

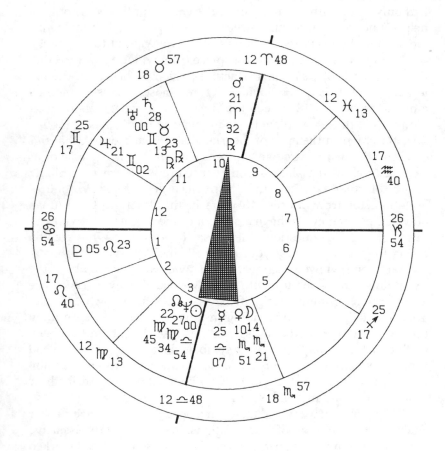

nonstatic quality of astrological symbols. In Angyal's (1965) terms it demonstrates how the astrological language can be useful in crystallizing the dual nature of personality qualities; he speaks of how personality qualities are "universally ambiguous" — any personality trait can function as part of the organization of health or of neurosis.

An additional factor seemed to help her to further crystallize the new meaning she now saw in her way of asserting herself. I mentioned that Mars in her chart was retrograde, which I explained occurs when a planet appears to move back and forth over a certain area of the zodiac due to its position relative to the Earth. In response to my questioning what this meant to her she replied that, "It's like it's trying to get itself together before moving on." Applying this idea to herself, **A** went on to say that she could see how her way of asserting herself was being refined by going over and over it to make sure she "had it together."

During this session **A** brought up the fact that she was still having problems staying in touch with others when communicating with them. Although I had noticed a certain amount of improvement had occurred in regards to **A's** staying in touch with me (increased eye contact, etc.) after our systematic desensitization work, we had not actually concentrated on this during earlier sessions. For since increasing ego strength seemed most important, the focus on giving her permission to assert herself and to call people on whether they were following her had assumed a foreground position. Retrieving her projection that others didn't listen to her, the client now was examining her own lack in listening to others. As we explored this we went back to our earlier discussion about how, due to her fear of not being understood, she had shut off her receptivity to others in order to prevent the dreaded experience of feeling others are not listening. **A** then expressed a lack of confidence in her ability to listen to others. I commented that it was interesting that the other point of the structure that we had not yet examined was Venus. Its position on the receptive side of the earth in relation to the Sun makes it a symbol for the receptive function, I added. I asked her what its position in Scorpio meant to her, as I commented that Scorpio was a fixed water sign, a symbol for the penetration into the depths of others' inner worlds through one's feeling function. After **A** expressed that she was having difficulty getting in touch with this symbol, I suggested that she might go back to the active imagination exercise that we had done a few sessions earlier (Session 9), and instead of "focusing" on her way of asserting herself (Mars) as we had done then, to "focus" this time on being receptive to how her boyfriend might be feeling (Venus).

By asking the client to do this I was hoping that she would start to explore how her receptive function operated in an actual life situation. Generally speaking, this approach seems particularly useful when a person has trouble getting in touch with a particular symbol due to difficulty in understanding it or lack of clarity on the part of the therapist presenting the symbol's meaning.

In order to lead the client to seeing her receptive function in a new way I suggested that while reentering into the active imagination process she could imagine how her way of communicating looked from his point of view by identifying with him. Through this exercise the client did come to a deeper understanding of how her way of communicating (specifically her associative process) looked to others. A eventually saw how others might have difficulty following her train of thought. Her exact words here were, "You know, I can really see how he (her boyfriend) had trouble understanding me." A further realized that she had taken this "looking away in discomfort" as a confirmation of her worst fears that she was crazy and that she would never be understood; but now she saw that it was "**just** that he couldn't understand me."

## SUMMARY OF SESSION 14

We did not specifically crystallize the nature of the client's receptive function in this session as we were to do in the following session. However, by using her receptivity, A was able to come to a deeper understanding of her way of being. With her comment that it was "**just** that he couldn't understand me," A was saying that what had earlier been her deepest fear was not so bad. . . It was something that could be met and worked with.

By the introduction of the symbol of Venus here, a common language was being developed to speak of what being receptive meant to A. The following session carries the exploration of the nature of this quality — to her — further.

## SESSION 15

Early in this session A mentioned rather confidently that she was starting to feel that when she was not afraid of being misunderstood or ignored by others that she was a good listener. To move her into further exploring the unique way that she listened, I asked A how she saw her way of listening as different from other people's.

Smiling, she replied, "I bet you want me to do that focusing thing again." **A** then told me that she had been focusing on the symbol of Venus at home and had noticed a red line coming off it and going to Pluto. Pluto, she added, was always the planet that she related to most. From recent reading that she had been doing, Pluto seemed to be doubly emphasized in her chart. It was both her rising planet and a ruler of the configuration with which we had been working (Pluto rules Scorpio, where Venus is located). **A** added that she had never connected it with her way of listening, but had seen it as a symbol of her liking to "take things out to the end of their existence" since Pluto is the last of the planets. She added, "I've always liked music that takes you out to the end of existence . . . 'cause when you come back you're peaceful. It's healing to take something out to its limits." **A** then saw a connection between listening to music in this way and how she was tuned into the sounds of people's words, saying "What I love to do is to take the sounds of people's words out to their limits!" I added that Venus ruled music and aesthetic appreciation.

In response to **A's** questioning me as to how I saw what Venus in a fixed sign symbolized, I shared with her some of my thoughts on this configuration. (Note — it is important for the therapist to be sensitive to how the client asks for interpretations from the therapist. Requests can come from a dependency or a desire for information. If the therapist acquiesces in the former case, dependency is increased; if a therapist refuses in the later case, genuine human interaction is lost and all that is increased is the feeling on the client's part that a therapeutic game is being played. In this situation **A** had already told me how she felt about the configuration and was obviously asking for increased information.) I proceeded to draw a diagram of the meaning of fixed signs as I had grown to understand them. Since they are midway between the generating points of the equinoxes, they can symbolize a search for values removed from their relationship to life circumstances, in other words for things in themselves. However, I added, constellating two different viewpoints, the symbol of the fixed sign of Scorpio also contains the meaning "deep relationship from penetration into and union with others." I reminded her that we had seen how she did this when she rose above her fear of not being understood. I said that it seemed that the depth that was reached from this second path was a merging with another in shared communication, while the first path led to exploring words without reference to the person with whom she was talking. I added that I saw value in each way: one was useful for the student of linguistics, the other for deep listening and sharing with others. One led to entering into the deeper meaning of the words that were used; the other led to moving deeper into **the person's meaning**. A responded that she felt both were important aspects of who she was, and that she could see them both contained in the symbol of Venus in Scorpio.

At the end of this session we came up with a definition of her Venus/Moon conjunction in the fourth house. It became a symbol for her deep penetration into the meaning of what others were saying and feeling, with particular emphasis on the textures and sounds of their words. Through her ability to listen she could enter into their inner worlds (fourth house) or into the depths of words in themselves.

## SESSION 16

Due to schedule conflicts, two weeks passed before our next meeting. A came to this session smiling and obviously quite happy with herself. She proceeded to share with me an encounter with a male friend. He had used the word "smart" to characterize a female friend of theirs. A then told me how she had tasted the word "in my usual Venusian way," as she demonstrated to me, saying the word "smart" — "s" — wrinkling her nose at the coarseness she felt in the sound. . . "t" — snapping her hand down, emphasizing the hardness of the word. A then related to me how she had told her friend that "the word 'smart' is like when you are hit sharply by something and it hurts," i.e., it smarts. She then told him how "that's what a lot of people's intellect is like, but not hers (referring to her friend's). She's brilliant." A then demonstrated for me, as she had for her friend, her view of the word "brilliant," tasting its letters especially the "l's," and then making reference to its connection with light. I then told her, feeling quite genuinely, that that was a very interesting observation. To my surprise, I noticed that for the first time in the course of therapy she did not seem to be interested in my support. Previously when I had given her support A would first look away with a tinge of embarrassment, and then she would give a somewhat hesitant yet sparkling smile, and often she would reply, "Do you really think so?" (asking for increased confirmation that her way of being was really okay).

I could not be sure at this time whether this signalled a breaking down of her need for my approval or whether she merely felt it more important to continue with her story. I did not feel that it was appropriate to get an answer to my question in this session, for I usually allow (although sometimes lead) the client to bring up the transference question herself. (Two sessions later the client did do so.)

Pausing for an instant, after my support, **A** immediately went into what she had been leading up to. She proceeded to tell me how she had noticed her friend looking away while she was "expanding the boundaries of the word 'smart' in my Neptunian way." What followed illustrates well the transformative function of astrological symbology when combined with Gendlin's (1969) direct referent technique of "focusing." I will therefore quote at some length this portion of her story.

> I at first felt that queasy feeling (after he had looked away), then I remembered that focusing exercise that we did. I flashed on my Venus in Scorpio (being receptive to what others are feeling) and I realized that I wasn't tight anymore... (Pause, intently trying to express something) It was like I was relaxing or something. In any event the next thing I noticed was that I was really tuned into where he was at. I saw that he was feeling put down. He wasn't thinking I was crazy or anything, he was just having a hard time listening **to me** (emphasizing "to me" as if to contrast it with how she had a hard time listening to others).
>
> Then I asked him if he was feeling put down, and you know that's just what was going on. I could see it in his eyes, even though he first answered my question by telling me that I came on too strong. I was amazed that I could just answer him without, you know, feeling defensive. I think what helped was that I could see how he was just reacting out of his own space of being afraid... (pause)... You know, I think this was the first time I've gone through one of those circles with someone and come out feeling closer with the person than I felt before.

I said, "That's what being centered is all about."

## SUMMARY OF SESSION 16

Of interest at this point is that the client is actualizing her sensitivity to others in her everyday life. Although we can see various stages in her growth in relationship to this quality, I would consider this experience a major breakthrough.

From the astrological point of view it is significant that **A** used the words "Venus in Scorpio" when she was proudly telling me that she was really able to feel where others' discomfort was coming from. I should also mention that in the course of this session **A** realized that when her old boyfriend had called her crazy after their big fight (the precipitating event leading her to therapy) "that he might have just been reacting to his feeling of inadequacy in understanding me." It seems that through **A's** entering into her receptivity to others, she is coming to the realization that other people have as hard a time dealing with their discomforts as she has.

## SUMMARY OF SESSION 17

This session began with **A** wanting to explore "the line running down the center of the structure" we had been working on. This line introduces a fourth element to the triangular configuration. The concept of transforming the trinity into a quaternity to give form and to produce wholeness has been spoken of extensively by Jung (1969), and von Franz (1974). Astrologically, the number "three" also symbolizes synthesizing ease from duality being brought into perspective from the third point. By bringing in the fourth element, form and structure is added; this can be seen in the square. In the astrological system, through structural analysis there is an ability to symbolically represent three aspects of the personality and then to constellate the fourth element of wholeness by looking to the point opposite the apex of the triangular structure. It is here that one finds a symbolic vehicle representing a place where the energies of the triangle can be discharged thereby bringing the qualities of the personality into a further embodied whole. Darling (1968) in his analysis of the use of the fourth element in structural analysis of the personality gives the name **"tetradic thought"** to this procedure. We see the client herself moving to this fourth element in line with Jung's observations about how the psyche itself has a tendency to move towards wholeness.

At the fourth point opposite the apex of the triangle is the planet Mercury in 25° Libra.[9] Mercury, I then said to her, is a symbol for communication emphasizing the more concrete aspects of thought and speech. **A** added that was a fitting symbol for her interest in specific letters and details of people's speech. To further explore its meaning I suggested looking in Rudhyar's analysis of the Sabian Symbols.[10] The keynote for 25° Libra reads, "The ability to discover in every experience a transcendent or cosmic meaning." **A** was awestruck at this, exclaiming, "I can't believe it, that's exactly what I do." Particularly moving to her was the sentence in the analysis which reads, "This world is illusion only to the individual who cannot see through its phenomena and fails to apprehend the reality these phenomena reveal even as they conceal it."

**A** emphasized that this symbol was the most potent one we had looked at for seeing the importance of her examination of specific

---

9. It is an interesting synchronicity that I have my rising degree (25° Libra) in the exact same degree as the client's Mercury.
10. See Rudhyar's (1973) *An Astrological Mandala* where he presents an analysis of the 360° symbols.

words and details of people's speech. She mentioned how the symbol of Neptune had helped her see the importance of expanding the
boundaries of words, but that the symbol of Mercury captured for
her even more clearly the meaning of this quality of hers, i.e., looking for transcendent meanings.

After stating that she now saw her way of thinking in a whole
new way, **A** wanted to know whether Mercury's position in Libra
(sign of relationship to others) and in the fourth house (symbolic of
the inner world — the home) meant that she should think about the
meaning of words themselves or about the meanings that others were
attempting to convey.[11]

I reminded her how we had worked with such questions before,
and that I didn't have an answer for how she was supposed to be;
that the symbol would reveal its meaning as she focused on it. I suggested that she might dialogue with the two voices since this seemed
to be an important issue for her. Through the meeting of the voice
which said that she wanted to be tuned into others' inner worlds,
and the voice that wanted to enter into the transcendent meaning
of words in themselves, a synthesis took place where **A** realized the
importance of both. One important outcome of this dialogue was
a more strongly felt commitment to enhance her knowledge of words
by taking up the study of a foreign language that "really gets into
what words are about."

At the end of this session we summarized the meaning of the
structure which we had been working on for some time. We saw
how her ability to expand the boundaries of specific things in her
environment (Sun conjunct Neptune) and her ability to tune into the
depths of people's inner worlds through her receptivity (Venus conjunct Moon in Scorpio) formed a baseline from which she asserted
her perceptions (Mars in Aries). Her unique way of perceiving
culminated in her ability to examine specific qualities of words and
thereby discover hidden transcendent meanings (Mercury in 25°
Libra). By remaining in touch with the whole of herself this could
lead to expanding the boundaries of both people involved so that
there would be a feeling of togetherness. It was this that I told her

---

11. This again brings out clearly a possible detrimental potential of the astrological
system — the possibility of looking to the therapist for the answer rather than
looking within. A therapist can deal with this in a similar manner to the way
he answers dependent questions while using other modalities. For example, the
therapist may simply ask what the clients feel the answer to be, why they feel
that the therapist knows better than they, or have a person dialogue with each
of the voices that express the conflict that is being questioned.

I saw her trying to give birth to through the novile structure.

## SESSION 18

During the course of this session, I asked **A** how she felt about her mode of thinking during her life. Although we had discussed this to a certain extent in earlier sessions, I wanted to give her a feeling of looking at her past from the new perspective that she had established. (It was around this time that I was developing the idea of "the symbolic quality time trace," a method whereby a person takes the "felt sense" of a personality quality from their chart and traces how it manifested throughout their life.) While she looked back at this quality I felt her talking with an increased strength, and a certain detachment colored by a touch of humor. **A** recalled how in her childhood she continuously expanded the boundaries of things around her in her search for the deeper meanings hidden there. She had wondered what purpose each tooth served and how it got formed in the course of human development. Also she played with the sounds of words and questioned their meanings. **A** recalled how she had even developed her own system of spelling which corresponded with what words meant to her, and explained how it was a combination of a phonetic alphabet and pictures that corresponded to her associations to certain letters which were particularly pleasing to her. **A** recalled how on one occasion her schoolmates ridiculed her, and how embarrassed she had felt as a young boy she liked looked nervously away. I asked her how she saw this quality of hers now. She replied, "It's all different. Now I know it has meaning."

## SESSION 19

**A** had called me up and had cancelled our weekly appointment, asking for one the following week because of her full schedule. During the course of this session **A** owned that during the course of therapy she had been afraid of me and that she realized that she had really been trying to please me . . . "so that I would think she was brilliant" (smiling when emphasizing the word "brilliant" in obvious reference to the earlier session where we had discussed the word). She said that she had been noticing that she didn't need my approval as much anymore, because she felt better about herself and her way of thinking.

After she referred to how our discussion of her Mercury in 25° Libra had helped her I mentioned that I also had 25° Libra emphasized in my chart — that it was my rising degree. I told her that I felt a strong connection with her way of thinking. Previously, I had not shared this fact with her because I wanted her to develop the strength to feel good about her way of thinking herself, rather than permitting the likely possibility that a temporary strength might have developed from an identification with me. Now that what might be called "the positive transference" was breaking down, I no longer felt this danger.

We then thought together about the similarities and differences between our personality qualities with regards to 25° Libra. We discussed how we both loved to explore the transcendent cosmic meaning in life experiences. She asked to see my chart, and noticed that I had Mercury in my ninth house and said that my thinking was more about different philosophies (9th house) whereas hers was more about concrete things. A expressed amazement at how the astrological system was "so right on" adding that it was exciting to think about the kind of energies that bring people together.

Feeling close to each other, we ended this session with a warm hug.

## SESSIONS 20, 21, 22, 23

These sessions were characterized by some talking about how A was applying what she had learned in therapy to her everyday life. Looking back, this began the closing phase of therapy. There was an air, on her part, of looking for closure.

There was what might be called a slight relapse before the 21st session where an argument about property rights with her ex-husband "unnerved" her. She felt depressed about this for a few days afterwards, and gave an excellent opportunity to address the question of "cure." By her admission that she had hoped that she would "be able to be strong," which she further defined as "never being unnerved," we were able to come to a process-oriented definition of cure — which encompassed allowing her to feel her experience, accept her weaknesses as part of herself, and to see life as "practice" (in the Zen sense of the word).

In the 23rd session we spoke further about her life plans, pursuing the study of languages, her career as a dental technician, etc. She said that she had decided to take up the study of Sanskrit seriously.

## SESSION 24

Before our next appointment A called me and excitedly asked for an earlier appointment because she had an "incredible dream" that she wanted to share with me. I was able to give her an appointment later that day.

The dream, which I always had her relate in first person present tense, was as follows:

> There is a golden tooth growing from the center of my astrological chart. I particularly notice the root system, which at one point changes from enamel to roots like of a tree. Then further down I find that it is being nourished by a pool of water that's bounded by words in a circle.

(I interrupted at this point to ask if she remembered what the words were and she replied:)

> No, they were symbolic letters that I'd never seen before. But there was a symbol of Mercury in the center of the pool. It feels like a very sacred place, and as I drink the water I feel ecstasy. I then go up to the crown of the tooth. It's gold and it's actually a crown . . . you know, like it's studded with jewels and glowing and everything. I never experienced anything like this in all my life.

After sharing my feeling of incredulity with her, I asked her if she had explored the dream as we had others. She replied that she had and said,

> It feels sort of like a metaphor of my life. It's like I'm a tooth breaking up the food of life into little pieces to find out what it's all about. If I didn't do this my body wouldn't get the nourishment it needs . . . (raising her eyebrows in recognition of what I interpreted as its importance to her life meaning) . . . I'd probably choke. My source of nourishment is my ability to think about words and expand their boundaries (alluding to the Mercury symbol in the pool bounded by words). It feels like the dream is telling me that it's really okay for me to do what I do. That that's one of the things that gets me high.

I asked her, "What about the golden tooth, and the crown?" She said that it gave her a feeling of being like a king, royal and important. I added that the symbol of gold was used by the ancient alchemists to speak of the purification of the psyche and the transmutation of its elements. Alluding to the expression "turning lead into gold" I also said that this is what seemed to me had taken place in her therapeutic process.

She smiled, and then asked me why I had asked her what the words were that were around the pool. I said that I was interested in this because I had read about how words in a circle were often used in spiritual disciplines to aid the person in concentration. It was said that by putting words into a circle, as opposed to a line, the person would be drawn into a center where they could more easily be united with the meaning of the words.[12]

A was very interested in this concept, and I referred her to some books where she could do further reading. I also told her about the temples of Asclepius in ancient Greece where someone would come to be healed. They knew they were healed after having a significant dream (Meier, 1967). The "healing dream," I told her, was the direct means of cure which the process of incubation was aiming towards. We agreed to terminate therapy on this note, leaving open the possibility of her coming back from time to time if she felt the need.

## AFTER SESSION 24

An interesting additional note is the A called me some months later to tell me that she had been accepted at a local college where she was going to pursue her studies of languages. At first I did not recognize her voice, asking "Who is this?" She responded in a joking manner by saying, "It's Golden Tooth!"

## DISCUSSION OF CASE

In questioning those areas that would be most important to discuss in relation to this case, I have chosen four main areas of concentration. We shall examine the reasoning behind my choice to use the astrological "holoscope" with this client, and specifically how I felt it aided her in the therapeutic process. We shall then make it clear how the astrological mode was part of a wider therapeutic whole, and outline briefly how it was integrated with these other therapeutic modalities. Reference shall also be made to certain problems that emerged in relation to the use of astrology and how they were dealt with.

# Why the Astrological Modality Was Indicated

My choice to use the astrological "holoscope" after the fifth session was based on a variety of factors. First, the client's disidentification with her thought processes (i.e., "I tried to shut it off; but I couldn't stop the ideas from coming into my head.") led me to choosing a therapeutic modality which would aid the client in identifying with her thought process so that she could reclaim this alienated part of herself. Although in the first few sessions we worked with Gendlin's (1969) direct referent technique of "focusing" which leads to identification with one's felt experience, it seemed that the astrological

12. See *Mandala* by J. and M. Arguelles, Shamballa Press, 1972

modality could further aid by supplying a structure through which she might see how her unique way of being was worthwhile.

Obviously other therapeutic techniques can also aid the client in the process of identification. The client's lack of ego strength led me to be cautious of pursuing an in-depth psychodynamic mode, for I felt that the client might not be able to handle entering directly into the stuff of the complex at an early stage in the therapeutic process. In cases where there is a greater ego strength, the therapist might use those aspects of the astrological modality which were later used to enter into the stuff of the complex or choose another mode of direct entry.

Due to lack of client ego strength it seemed to be important to use a modality which would establish an **atmosphere of ease** early in the therapeutic process. In this sense I have found the astrological mode particularly helpful due to its seeming superficiality which can aid in lowering the client's threshold of resistance. This client had an affinity with the astrological system and a general distrust toward psychologists developed from an earlier experience with a marriage counselor. Astrology seemed to increase her openness in the early sessions. Also at certain later points in the therapeutic process the client asked to work with her birthchart again due, at least in part, to her feeling of comfortableness in working with this medium.

This fact, that the client herself initially asked to explore her chart, is perhaps the most important factor in suggesting its adoption. Although I have an interest in working with the astrological modality, in most cases in my practice it has not seemed fitting (more on this in the following chapter).

From a psychological point of view one might at first assume that a symbolic mode might be contraindicated in this case due to the apparent looseness of the client's associations in the initial sessions. The astrological perspective, however, gave me a frame of reference which allowed me to see beyond the negative appearance of her behavior. This perspective helped me assist the client in seeing positive aspects of her unique way of associating.

My primary concern was to choose a modality which would enhance the client's feelings of positive regard for herself. It seemed that a symbolic mode would be useful, since I learned from our work in the initial sessions that she felt comfortable with symbolism. Compared with other symbolic modalities, astrology offers in addition a structure for exploring, reframing and validating one's personality qualities, which was important in this case. The symbol of Sun conjunct Neptune, for instance, allowed a reframing of meaning from "looseness of associations" to "expanding the boundaries of aspects of the immediate environment."

## Summary: How Astrology Contributed to the Therapeutic Process

As we reflect on this case, one can see the client's movement from her initial disidentification with her thought processes. In this recapitulation of her process we can see many of those points emphasized in the body of this work. Here it will be shown how astrology seemed to aid this client in these particular areas: in giving the client **permission** to be herself, in **crystallizing** what her unique way of being was, in aiding in the process of **transformation** by which we mean both changing the way **A** viewed herself as well as helping new behavioral patterns to emerge, and in leading the client to a **new experience of her life's meaning.**

When the astrological system was first introduced in the 6th session, it seemed to play an important part in giving the client **permission** to explore whether there was anything worthwhile in her way of thinking. In this session the symbol of Neptune was useful in reframing a negative feeling about her thought processes; this can be seen from her initial nervous statement "maybe it's a symbol of how I space out on specifics" to a smiling "there might be something to my way of thinking." Throughout the therapeutic process, the astrological language seemed to be helpful in allowing the client to look at her way of being in a positive manner thereby changing a sickness orientation to a meaning orientation. Through being given a frame of reference whereby she could see value in her way of thinking, her initial disidentification was changed to an identification with — and owning of — her thought process.

As the therapeutic process deepened, the client increasingly became able to **crystallize** the precise coloring of many of her personality qualities through the use of the holistic astrological language.

It should be clear that a blanket permission or a solely positive way of crystallizing the identity of the client is not our aim.[13] For in the process of crystallization, the symbols took on both positive

---

13. For a thought provoking discussion of the issue of whether to support a client the way he or she is versus trying to change the person, see Enright, J., "Change versus Enlightenment," in *Enlightening Gestalt — Waking Up from the Nightmare*, Mill Valley, California: Pro Telos, 1980.

and negative attributes depending upon the client's unique perceptions. It seems that the symbolic nature of the astrological language was particularly useful: not only in crystallizing both negative and positive aspects of her personality qualities, but in serving as a vehicle for the **transformation** from one to the other. This allowed **new meaning** to be seen and lived.

Let us examine in greater detail how certain astrological symbols aided the client in the above process. We have already mentioned how the symbol of Neptune in Virgo in the third house changed in the client's mind from ''a symbol of how I space out on specifics'' to a symbol for her ''ability to explore and to expand the boundaries of specific things around me and to communicate these observations to others.'' Beyond this the symbol grew to crystallize in a new way other aspects of her personality from her intuitive feeling for teeth as she did the detailed work of a dental technician, to her enjoyment in expanding upon the meaning of words. The important **transformation** that correlated with this positive way of seeing her Neptunian way of being was that instead of wanting to stop these ''spaced out'' thoughts from coming into her mind, she grew to allow herself to question whether there ''might be'' meaning in her Neptunian way of thinking in the 6th session.

The result of this transformation was that the therapeutic goal shifted: from her focus on getting rid of her thought process, to a desire to make her thought process understandable to others by working on the way she communicated (third house). We can see an incorporation of the symbol of Neptune into the client's language in session 9 as we were developing a shared language. In session 16 we can see a positive attitude towards her Neptunian way of being as the client proudly tells me about how good she felt about the way she expanded upon the word ''smart.'' There was a **new feeling of meaningfulness** at this point in relationship to how she felt about this aspect of herself. It should be mentioned that her way of communicating now was different from its characteristics at the beginning of therapy, so that it would be more correct to say that she felt good about her **new** way of communicating.

The symbol of **Mars** was an important vehicle for allowing the client to focus upon the assertive aspect of her communication process. In the 8th session, the symbol of Mars provided a means through which **A** questioned whether she might ''come on too strong,'' and admitted that she did not really feel strength behind her way of communicating. Through the ''focusing'' process which took place in this same session, the client was able to **crystallize** into the form of an image the pattern of her way of communicating. This image was of a girl holding a candle being overpowered by darkness, and led the girl to blow on it like a dragon to increase the flame. From working with this image the client realized that when she was communicating she often overasserted herself like the dragon due to her fear that "no one will ever understand me." This allowed her to **further crystallize** the nature of her behavior, seeing that when someone looked away from her in discomfort that she "would become even more like an Aries" (more assertive) and that this was one of the ways that she had tested to see if people really cared.

By the time of the 14th session the client was able to see a positive aspect in her assertive quality as can be seen by her discussion of how she was glad that she wasn't like her girlfriend who "never speaks her mind." A **transformation** also occurred in the way the client asserted herself. At the beginning of therapy **A** expressed fear of asserting herself in public; and near the end of our meeting together I asked her if she now felt more free in expressing her associations in public. She replied that this was no longer the question for her; she felt less of a need to express herself in that way to many people. From our discussion it seemed that **A** was saying that she was now more discriminating in when and how she expressed herself.

This **centering** in her mode of self-assertion was noticeable in her interactions with me. In the beginning stages of therapy **A** had often gone off on long streams of associations which I could not follow. At the end of the therapeutic process I noticed that she was more in touch with when I was not following her and instead of being afraid to ask me if I was following she would make sure I was with her. There seemed to be more contact with me and less talking to herself. In her relationships, **A** likewise reported that she felt that she was communicating with others instead of associating to herself. This was exemplified in Session 16 when the client remained centered in her associating to her friend about the word "smart."

The transformation which occurred in relation to the client's mode of asserting herself (Mars) was coupled with a change in her receptivity to others (Venus). The process here similarly began with **crystallizing** the nature of her unique way of being receptive. Venus conjunct Moon in the fourth house thereby became a symbol for the client's deep penetration into the meaning of what others were saying and feeling, with particular emphasis upon the textures and sounds of others' words. We further outlined two ways this manifested: a sensitivity to the meaning of words in themselves, and a sensitivity to the meaning others were trying to convey.

In the process of crystallizing the nature of her receptive function, the client became sensitive to the fact that others had trouble following her. By the 16th session we can see that this was no longer the all-pervasive fear of not being understood, but rather became a simple recognition that others had tensions and feelings of inadequacy in not being able to follow her. It was an important realization for **A** that others sometimes handle their feelings of inadequacy by calling her crazy.

In Session 16 we can see exemplified the client's increased sensitivity to these reactions of others and how it resulted in a deeper communication. In her interaction with her friend about the word "smart" the client's sensitivity to his feelings even extended into a more advanced metacommunication process about their interaction which showed an ability to stand outside and "see" the interaction.

A further **transformation** took place in regards to the client's taking responsibility for making sure she was understood. Much growth occurred from the times she went on her associative meanders, hoping that someone would ask her what she was talking about, testing to see if they cared. Instead of sulking in her feelings of noncontact, the client increasingly was reaching out to make sure that she was contacting others for whom she cared.

The symbol of Mercury in 25° Libra seemed to be extremely potent in leading her to further **crystallize** what her way of being was and to discover **new** meaning thereby. In addition to the client's strong reaction in the therapeutic session to its meaning ("the ability to discover in every experience a transcendent or cosmic meaning") it was incorporated into her "healing dream." Although this idea was also to some extent encompassed by our work with the symbol Neptune (expanding the boundaries of things) it seemed that the symbol of Mercury aided her in further **crystallizing** her ability to examine specific qualities of words in searching for their deeper meanings. It indeed seemed that the "cosmic permission" given to enter more fully into discovering more about her ability for questioning the meaning of words was a most important factor in leading the client to pursue her linguistic studies at a major university. I have had only one contact with the client since then, approximately two months after therapy. She told me of her excitement upon being accepted at this university.

# Astrology in Conjunction with Other Therapeutic Modalities

It should be emphasized here that we do not wish to imply that "astrology" was "the cause of" the client's growth in the sense of separating it from the rest of the therapeutic process as a whole. Various other therapeutic modalities played a significant part in the client's process. Here we shall examine how these other therapeutic modalities in conjunction with the astrological mode together formed the therapeutic process. Although our primary focus will be this case, at certain points generalizations shall be made to be of service to others who may wish to attempt a similar integration in their practices or in their lives.

## FOCUSING
Using **Gendlin's** (1969) "focusing" method in conjunction with my work with astrological symbols has proved to be most valuable for it serves to aid the client in establishing a connection between their felt experience and the symbol. From my reading of Gendlin, "focusing" refers to the initial reference of the bodily felt sense and then remaining open to the image(s) that emerges. In my work with this process, I sometimes begin working with an astrological symbol, asking the client to stay in touch with the felt sense that is associated with the image, and then to remain open to allowing an alternate image to come from that sense. Other times in a line with a more strict interpretation of Gendlin's idea, I start with the client's felt sense. It seems to me that the value in Gendlin's mode lies in establishing the felt connection between the symbol and the feeling, not which comes first. By remaining grounded in the felt bodily experience, the client is aided in guarding against the detrimental possibility that sometimes arises with symbolic modalities — that the image will remain intellectual and not deeply felt.

A good example in **A**'s case was in the 8th session where in discussing her view of the symbol Mars she says that it is "supposed to have to do with a strong way of asserting yourself." My feeling here was that **A** was not directly experiencing the symbol's unique meaning to her. I therefore asked her to take the symbol of Mars (the active assertive principle) in Aries (symbol of the light principle just beginning to overtake the dark principle) and to stay in touch with what feeling arose while watching to see if any image arose out of the feeling. From this exercise an image arose that had deep meaning for her. This image (the candle being engulfed by the darkness) led her to realize various aspects of her way of asserting herself that proved important in the therapeutic process.

The "focusing" technique also helped the client later in the 8th session to work through a block she was feeling. In this case I asked her to focus on the block which she reported was "a sort of queasy feeling in my stomach." The images of various life situations that came from this feeling of her boyfriend and her father not listening to her proved to be valuable in leading her to see how great her fear that "no one will ever understand me" was in hindering her relationships with others.

Although numerous examples could be cited to show how the focusing process aided the client in therapy both in conjunction with astrological symbols and without them, the most important point is that the client incorporated this way of working outside of my office. In the very important 16th session where the client was able to confront a boyfriend of hers about the word "smart," the focusing process seemed to be a primary agent in the breakthrough. By focusing on the "queasy feeling" in conjunction with the symbol of "my Venus in Scorpio" (her receptivity) she was able to let go of her tight feeling which came from his looking away, and was able to be both receptive, appropriately assertive, and centered.

## ACTIVE IMAGINATION

The process of "active imagination" discussed by **Jung** also can be seen in Case A. Actually, the work done with the symbol of Mars where the client imagined a girl holding a candle could be seen to be an example of the above process based on the numinous nature of the image; however, we there discussed it in the context of Gendlin's "focusing" process since it appeared as an image after focusing on a felt bodily state. From my reading it seems these two processes are very similar. One distinguishing mark is perhaps more of a concentration on the bodily process in "focusing," while the examination of the image itself appears to correspond to Jung's idea. In this sense perhaps a better example from Case A of the active imagination process was in Session 9 where I asked her to imagine a situation where she was not understood. Here she clearly saw an image of how she asserted herself even more strongly when she saw her boyfriend look away in discomfort. After this experience we were able to examine together more fully the nature of her communication process. In session 14 we went back to this earlier image, this time looking from the perspective of concentrating on her receptive function (Venus). From her identification with her boyfriend this time she was able to see how "he might have trouble understanding me." Through this reentry into the active imagination process, the client was able to step outside of her communication process and gain perspective on it. The new meaning that the client realized was an important factor in aiding her to change this pattern.

## SYSTEMATIC DESENSITIZATION

The "systematic desensitization" process can also be useful in conjunction with astrological work in giving the client a chance to develop a confidence in being able to actualize new patterns of behavior. In the 10th through 13th sessions this process was used to aid the client in establishing the connection between her queasy feeling accompanying her fear of not being understood, and her expressing her discomfort to the person she was communicating to in an appropriate way.

It seems appropriate here to reiterate **Weitzman's** (1967) caution against working on the symptom removal level alone without the accompanying in-depth work on the stuff of the complex. This case points out this problem well for, at the end of the systematic desensitization work, the client mentioned that although she could now confront people with her feeling that they were not listening, she was starting to doubt again whether "there is that much worthwhile in my way of thinking." This temporary regression needs to be placed alongside the fact that I do feel that this work proved to be helpful in her eventual ability to deal with her friend in regards to their discussion about the word "smart." This discussion, it should be remembered, did occur after more work on the meaning dimension, making it difficult to determine whether the systematic desensitization process alone would have been sufficient, and making it almost impossible to determine the extent to which each separately aided her growth.

From my point of view I saw these as two ends of a continuum which were used in circumambulating the complex. The orientation to meaning which astrology can provide in this sense seems to work well combined with the systematic desensitization mode to integrate the dimension of practical application with meaning orientation.

## OTHER PSYCHOTHERAPEUTIC MODES

For the sake of completeness, I must mention the important insights that I have gained from those therapists who have cleared a path before me. From incorporating these ideas into my work with astrology the process has become more whole. One can see the importance of the Gestalt conception of taking responsibility and the Transactional Analysis idea of script analysis in the client's work with her communication process. After outlining her communication process from her initial withdrawing and feeling sorry for herself (poor me) and her subsequent associative rambling, the client was able to recognize that this was an unhealthy script and a self-fulfilling prophecy that indeed led to her not being understood. This analysis of her behavior helped her to take responsibility for being understood.

The contributions of Jung and Assagioli to my understanding of symbolic processes have had a major impact upon my way of working with astrological symbology. Particularly of use has been Assagioli's (1965) method of **Initiated Symbol Projection** and **Imaginative Evocation of Interpersonal Relationships** and the Jungian conception of the **Transcendent Function** which are easily adapted with work done with astrological symbols. In a more general sense their monumental works form an important frame of reference for anyone attempting to work in this area.

An understanding of the "system theorists" is particularly important to the actual therapeutic working with astrological symbols. Their notion of working with the resistance around psychological complexes through "**reframing**"[14] was central to Case A experiencing her unique language style in a new light. The more "A" would be called wrong or crazy in her communications, the more unconnected her communication would become. By reframing her style with astrological symbols, the client was able to perceive the value in her way and thereby gain the necessary strength to work on the interpersonal dimension of her communication with others.

## SUMMARY

In this case illustration one can see a change in the client's way of viewing her way of being from seeing it as "crazy" to seeing it imbued with meaning. The astrological chart seemed to contribute to allowing the client to **crystallize** the unique nature of the qualities of her personality. The new way that the client saw these qualities can be seen as a **transformation** which not only changed her perspective of her way of being, but also seemed to contribute to

---

14. For more on "reframing" see Watzlawick, P., *Change*, W.W. Norton & Co., 1974, Gordon, D., *Therapeutic Metaphors*, Meta Publications, 1978, Grinder, J. & Bandler R., *The Structure of Magic*, Science and Behavior Books, 1976.

behavioral change. She seemed to be more centered in the way she communicated to certain people in her life, and seemed to be more sensitive to what they were feeling. The **permission** given to her to be herself seemed to play an important part in allowing her to enter more fully into investigating her way of being and in pursuing her linguistic studies.

Although a certain degree of dependency remained at the end of the therapeutic process, much adult growth seemed to exist in the client's acceptance of and working with her nervousness and still somewhat shaky feelings about her communication process. There also seemed to be a general experience of **new meaning** in her life as a whole. This can be seen from a note which the client left on my desk at the college where I was teaching. This note was written towards the end of the therapeutic process after a session where we had spoken about her singsong manner of talking.

"I'm beginning to see,
My *Dharma* is me."

## Making Astrological Language More Communicable

It has been a challenge in my practice to discover mediums through which astrological language can be made more easily communicable to the counseling community. The first one we shall consider is the use of historical metaphors to bring forth the meaning of astrological symbols. Rudhyar's book *Astrological Timing* is helpful in this regard, for here he presents an analysis of history using astrological symbols. The therapist can discover in this book a mythological storehouse of metaphors which can be used to constellate life themes in a similar way to the way that mythological material in general serves in complementing the therapeutic process. The following example is of interest both in being an example of expanding the ease of comprehension of astrological symbols, as well as being an example of using astrological symbols to speak of the meaning of phases of one's life's development. This latter concept moves the use of the language into a framework beyond personality qualities *per se*.

## Vignettes — Case B

In this case, a client was using the symbol Uranus conjunct Neptune to explore the meaning of a particular event in her life, her separation from her husband. It is not my purpose to outline the therapeutic process in depth here. As background information, this client had in the past been supporting her husband while he stayed home drinking. During their trial separation her husband had forced himself into her apartment on several occasions and had raped her. Some of the therapeutic work focused on expressing her anger to her husband, exploring the meaning of their relationship and what she got out of staying in it. Throughout the year that we worked together, the client became aware of her need to take care of others, and came to see what she got out of being a victim. She realized how her double messages and her confusion about whether she still wanted to be with him were partially responsible for their continued relationship. The client realized what she got out of taking care of others, and that her role as a married woman helped her to avoid the experience of aloneness. The client came to own that she had little feeling of her worth as a person and that this played a great part in supporting her feeling of not having enough inner strength to assert herself to her husband.

In addition to gaining much strength in being able to express indignation to her ex-husband about his behavior, a new process of examining her own life's meaning apart from her ex-husband began. Although the astrological modality was used for this purpose, it encompassed only one part of her search for meaning. It is not our purpose here to discuss how astrology aided in the client's coming to terms with her life's meaning, but rather to illustrate with one particular example how using a historical metaphor from the astrological language aided her in reframing her view of her life circumstance.

The client requested that I draw up her chart early in the therapeutic process desiring to use it as a tool to focus on her relationship with her husband. During this process the chart was seen to show that a significant cycle was coming to a new beginning. Transiting Uranus (Uranus in the zodiac at that time) was coming into conjunction with Neptune in her natal chart. Since the client had no substantial knowledge of astrology, I searched for an image that would convey the meaning of this conjunction in a way which would make it understandable to her.

According to Rudhyar when this 171-year cycle came to conjunction around 1650 the medieval political system was collapsing almost everywhere, from Japan and India where the Mongol dynasty began to crumble, to France where the nobility opposed the absolute power of King Louis XIV. Old Russia began to collapse and Peter the Great started (after 1689) to build modern Russia, and Holland freed itself from Spain. During the next 171-year period European culture reached its apex in its Classical Era and broke down during the Revolutionary and Napoleonic Era. When Uranus and Neptune came again to conjunction in 1821, in the sign of Capricorn representing the state, Napoleon died and the period of the Industrial Revolution, the era of railroads and the era of new labor-saving machines began.

One can see from these historical events how Uranus conjunct Neptune can be a powerful symbol to represent the disruption of old, effete institutions and laws, revisions of codes and dispositions of governments, new social methods through stress and insurrection, or, more generally speaking, the birth of new life from old structures.

Although working with this image was only a small part of a much larger therapeutic process, it did seem to contribute to helping the client in crystallizing how she also needed to make a new start and separate from her ex-husband. One difference between the use of myth in psychotherapy to work with a client's developmental process, and the use of astrological symbols is that in the latter case the particular mythic configuration is presented in the client's chart. In this case transiting Uranus was in conjunction with the client's natal Neptune at the time we were working.

Seeing that this conjunction was actually present in her own chart at this time in her life seemed to contribute to the power of the metaphor. Lest one accuse us of slipping in the hidden reality point of view under a meaning reorganization cloak, we should make clear again a point that Fingarette emphasizes. He says that there is no reason to suppose that the language in which we interpret therapy (meaning reorganization) is necessarily the best language in which to carry on therapy. Fingarette continues to show how the power of the belief that one has discovered what is present but hidden in one's life (hidden reality) can be most powerful in mobilizing the feeling of will and purpose.

# Case C

A second way that one who doesn't want to develop astrological proficiency can still incorporate it in a limited manner is by the simple **use of the Sun sign as a symbolic vehicle.** I recall a case where the symbol Taurus was useful in constellating new meaning in regards to a person's character. One aspect of her relationship with her father was a long-standing battle over who could hold on to their position the longest without giving in. Working with the symbol Taurus, her Sun sign, seemed to give her new perspective on this pattern, particularly when we did a focusing exercise on the bodily felt sense associated with this stubbornness. An image of a mountain came to the client out of her bodily feeling. From the subsequent work that was done with this symbol the client saw in a new way how their mutually fixed positions prevented them from coming together. She was then able to take steps to change this habitual pattern. The particular issue that we were dealing with was that her father would not come and visit her.

In our subsequent work the mountain became a symbol of transformation (Jung, 1956) which allowed the client to see her relationship with her father in a new way. Addressing the issue of why the mountain (her father) wouldn't budge, she began to examine anew her father's reasons for not visiting her. Whereas before she had assumed that he didn't really love her, now she was able to see the situation from her father's perspective. A reorganization of her meaning schema took place. The client saw that her father probably felt guilty about having left her mother and her while she was young, and that these feelings might prevent him from moving towards her.

The client's problem here was not in being able to express her anger to her father; this had not been difficult for her in recent years and, as a matter of fact, her strong expression of her feelings to him at one stage in their relationship had contributed to his wanting to keep distance from her. Therefore, the focus of the therapeutic work at this point was to explore new ways of approaching her father, and to become more conscious of what they needed from each other at this stage of their relationship. She came to realize that he needed forgiveness from her, and she needed acceptance from him.

These insights helped the client to come together with her father again. A new image emerged for her from the work she did with the symbol of the mountain, "If the mountain doesn't come to Mohammed, Mohammed must come to the mountain." Although the client herself made the initial compromise, her father came for a visit some months later. Her visit with her father was rewarding, for in addition to exploring the roots of their conflicts together, the client experienced important growth in relationship to her fixed way of being.

Although the astrological symbol of Taurus played a small part in the therapeutic process as a whole, it did mark an important phase in her movement. From this example one may see how a very simple use of an astrological symbol may be filled by the stuff of a complex, thereby providing a vehicle aiding in a client's movement.

The final example which shall be given in this section to illustrate possible simplification of astrological language is the use of words deriving from astrological language even when no chart is present. For instance, words such as earthy, fiery, watery or airy can be used to describe personality by those who do not want to use an astrological chart at all. I remember one client who was not open to exploring the astrological dimension; but even though no astrology was used *per se*, still a metaphor stemming from astrological language aided him in getting confidence in his way of being.

# Case D

This particular client was struggling with his upper middle class parents about becoming a carpenter. His parents did not approve, implying that this work was beneath his dignity. A comment of mine which stemmed from noticing how the client was highly sensitive to the aesthetics of my office, led to working with a metaphor. My comment that he seemed to have "an aesthetic sensitivity to the earth" seemed to touch him. In conjunction with a personality quality time trace the client began to remember how much this had always been a part of his life. He traced his sensitivity to the earth back into his childhood where he recalled his interest in arts and crafts at sleep-away camp, and his father's lack of enthusiasm and smug remarks about his creations. As an adolescent he recalled his discomfort sitting in different public places such as airport terminals because it seemed that these areas were never structured to be conducive to people talking to each other. When he brought up these observations to his parents, suggesting alternative designs such as having the seats facing each other, his father responded that "Not all people want to be facing each other, you know."

Although most of the therapeutic work did not center on this metaphor of the earth, it did help in allowing the client to see his as a valid way of being and to appreciate the history of this talent in his life. Furthermore, it seemed to allow the client to own various doubts that he had never before shared with me. He told me how his parents had defined his dropping out of the first liberal arts college as just a rebellious act. Perhaps due to the client's increased feeling of support and positive feeling for his sensitivity to the structure of his environment at this point in therapy he was also able to own that he harbored a secret doubt that maybe the only reason he was doing carpentry was to get back at his parents. "Maybe they're right and it's just good as a hobby."

By continued work with this metaphor of the earth, in conjunction with dialogues with the images of his parents, the client came to see his interest in carpentry as an important part in his life's work rather than reducing it to a mere rebellious act. By speaking through this metaphor we had a shared conception of what this quality was to him, how it had manifested throughout his life, and how it was part of his life's meaning.

In this last example, although no astrological chart was cast, one can still see how an astrological metaphor played a part in reorganizing the meaning the client experienced in regards to his aesthetic appreciation. We do not know in this case whether the client had, let us say, Venus in an earth sign which would symbolize a sensitivity to the earth, Saturn in an earth sign which might signify structuring the earth or whether the two came together in his chart in some combination. It may be of interest for one who wishes to do further exploration in this area to question whether the use of the astrological chart makes a particular image more uniquely specific. For example, would the use of an astrological chart as compared to pure poetic imagination aid a person in differentiating that his earthy sensitivity has to do with music (Venus), perhaps, or with structuring turbulence (Saturn and Uranus) which might lead one to develop earthquake proof buildings?

The discussion in this section has been a beginning in an attempt to broaden the ability of others to use the astrological language. The use of metaphors from historical frames of reference, the use of Sun signs, and leaving the casting of the astrological chart aside altogether are all attempts to widen astrology's scope. The last example hovers on the boundary between astrological language and plain use of metaphor. In the previous chapter we spoke about this as the territory from which poets derive their vocabulary — the ground for astro-poetic language.

## Extended Clinical Possibilities

The parameters for use of the astrological language can be extended to many areas of clinical importance. For instance, from certain of the examples cited in this chapter one can see how astrological language might be of use in **occupational counseling.** By using astrological symbols one has a way to speak of the person's unique talents. This was illustrated in the case of Golden Tooth, where the client experienced new meaning in regards to her talent for listening to the sounds of people's words and expanding upon their meaning. In the example of the young man with aspirations to become a carpenter we saw how even without a chart, language derived from the astrological domain could be useful in speaking of his occupational direction. The use of astrological language in the area of occupational counseling could be most significant; for establishing a connection between one's life's work and one's sense of self is an important part of the experience of wholeness.

The astrological language may at times be of use in **lowering the level of resistance** on the part of the client. This is a most important factor in psychotherapy, for trust and openness are necessary for a healing encounter. One way this may occur is through the system's ability to crystallize differences in type between the therapist and client in a nonjudgmental manner. An example was seen earlier in this chapter under the title "The Astrological Perspective and the Counter Transference."

The astrological language in even its simple form may be useful in lowering the level of resistance in group processes. An example comes from a therapist who works at a local community mental health center. Although this therapist's knowledge of astrology was limited to an understanding of Sun signs, one day she decided to try to use it to "get the energy going" in a group of emotionally disturbed adolescents. According to her, in earlier meetings the group had been reluctant to open up about their negative feelings about their parents. After she asked them what Sun signs their parents were, and several people discovered that their fathers were Tauruses, the group opened up sharing negative feelings. They discussed how their fathers were stubborn as bulls, which led one person to tell stories of how he had been beaten. A new camaraderie was developed in the group.

The astrological language is also useful in marriage and family counseling in providing a holistic language to become conscious of different ways of being. Particularly the idea of seeing the different ways of being of family members as being different places of the wheel of life has proved valuable in certain cases in allowing a nonjudgmental awareness about family members to emerge. Providing a couple with a chart that integrates both charts into a single wheel (called chart synastry by astrologers) can be useful in allowing images of their relationship together to be constellated. A transposition into the Plains Indians' idea of moving around the wheel of life can be used to illustrate how each family member is a symbol for that which needs to be met in order to be whole. Further discussion of this point is beyond the scope of this work.

## General Comments on Areas of Usefulness of Astrological Language

From the discussion in this chapter it seems that the cases most suited to the use of astrological language are those where the therapeutic process calls for exploration of the client's identity. Particularly in those instances where a client feels a lack of self-worth, the astrological language may be able to aid one in being given permission to enter into one's own way of being. Due to its symbolic structure the language can provide a vehicle for transformation and a means whereby new meaning can be experienced in relationship to one's way of being.

Its symbolic quality makes the language applicable not only to work with personality qualities, but also to bringing new meaning to life situations, as was shown in our discussion of transposing the language into the realm of history.

The metaphors that can be generated from the astrological language can be of as much use to the therapist as to the client; for they can lead to constellating the person's talents and problem areas in new ways for the therapist. When I draw up a client's chart it often aids me in my process of centering on those archetypal dilemmas peculiar to that person. It has helped me at times in developing my intuition concerning what is needed in a particular case, as well as in coming up with appropriate images that are capable of aiding in the client's movement.

# CHAPTER NINE

# APPLYING ASTROLOGICAL LANGUAGE TO PSYCHOTHERAPY

In attempting to integrate the astrological language with the psychotherapeutic process certain issues relating to its applicability arise. As with all therapeutic modalities there are certain persons with whom it is more or less suited; and in addition there are problems pertaining to the modality in general. In this chapter questions concerning persons with whom the modality may be contraindicated will first be addressed; and then secondly, considerations shall be given to arguments that are directed to its general theoretical base. As problem areas are discussed, methods will be suggested that the therapist can use to deal with the negative attributes associated with its use.

## Areas of Contraindication

The use of the astrological language is contraindicated in cases of organicity; for in such cases the primary emphasis is to be placed upon the physiological dimension. The use of a symbolic language could only be of peripheral value.

The modality may be contraindicated with those persons who are not at an intellectual stage capable of abstract reasoning. Integrating the astrological language into the therapeutic process would probably tend to alienate the client from therapy and increase feelings of inadequacy.

With clients who have a propensity to spontaneous or over-production of symbols and an overidentification with symbols, symbolic modalities in general are often seen to be contraindicated due to their propensity to lead the client further away from external reality. Certain persons labeled psychotic will be in the grouping and here, especially, the astro-poetic language may not be applicable for the above reason, or at least should be exercised with caution. From an ideographic perspective, however, there may be certain individuals falling into the psychotic classification for whom the astrological language may be of use. For instance, at later stages in the acute psychotic's recovery, I have seen cases where the language is of use to help validate the person's identity, particularly in cases where the person's ontological base had been attacked by significant others. If the astrological language is used here, it should be in conjunction with a modality that grounds the person in the present, so that the symbols do not serve to remove the person from contact with what is happening.

With certain clients labeled introverted neurotic who have an overdeveloped inner world of fantasy, the use of the astrological language requires discretion due to the possibility that it may lead the clients further into their own inner worlds. Again though, a *prima facie* preclusion of the modality does not seem warranted; for here more than in cases of psychosis, there is the possibility that symbols can be used as a bridge to external reality (See Gendlin, 1969). At times, further development of one's introverted world can give an introvert the strength to "come out."[1]

There may be individuals in this grouping who have psychological complexes constellated around their ability to symbolize, due to our culture's devaluation of the dimensions of fantasy and symbolism. Where a conjunctive therapeutic approach (supporting the client's way of being) seems to apply, the astro-poetic language may serve to crystallize the ideographic way that the client uses symbols, and may aid in giving one permission to enter into his or her symbolic capacity. This was illustrated in Case A, where one might have assumed that a symbolic modality was contraindicated due to looseness of associations; instead, the modality seemed to aid the client in discovering new meaning in regards to her identity.

On the opposite end of the spectrum from clients who are too

---

1. For an in-depth study of the question of the positive and negative points of view on narcissism, see Schwartz-Salant, N., *Narcissism and Character Transformation*, Toronto, Canada: Inner City Books, 1980.

oriented to symbols are clients with whom symbolism seems to go against the conscious orientation of the personality. Within this grouping are persons who are, in Jungian terms, of an extraverted nature, or who may have a "rational" orientation to life. Specifically, reference is here being made to those persons who have a strong identification with their conscious personality, and who give little attention to their unconscious processes. When the therapist uses a symbolic mode with such people, they often work with the symbol in a mechanical way, not entering into it. These are the clients for whom the astrological symbol remains on the level of a sign.

Incorporating the astrological language into such cases may confuse or alienate some of these clients, while for others it may provide a point of entry into their inner world of symbolism. In order to capture the beneficial aspects of the symbolic nature of the language, the therapist should probably wait until a later stage in the therapeutic process when the excess of "rational" preoccupation may have been balanced by a line of communication between conscious and unconscious processes. If the astro-poetic language is used with such clients, it may be helpful to incorporate techniques such as Gendlin's (1969, 1981) focusing method to make sure a connection is maintained between the symbol and the felt experience of the person.

# Arguments Against Astrology

## THE QUESTION OF FREE WILL

The most often heard objection to the use of astrology is that it is deterministic and therefore denies free will. From a therapeutic standpoint this would be especially detrimental, if true, for one of the most important aspects of all psychotherapy is encouraging the client to take responsibility for his or her life. Any system which does not leave room for the individual to exercise free will denies this most important aspect of therapy. By doing so people would be led into psychological slavery by projecting their power onto a force outside of their control.

In order to examine whether astrology leads to a deterministic world view, one must first understand that there are different theoretical positions on astrology. Each of these positions has a different theoretical orientation to the free will question. To speak of "astrology" as denying free will obfuscates the differences between these positions.

In this section we shall explore how the free will question relates to each theoretical position. We shall also consider whether astrology, in practice, might produce a deterministic orientation; for if astrology allows for free will in any of the theoretical positions considered, it may still not have this effect in practice. As the causal, synchronistic and symbolic viewpoints are discussed, the reader should keep in mind that these viewpoints are often combined with each other. In our discussion, though, we shall separate them so that their different implications can be examined.

The causal point of view states that the position of the stars at the time of one's birth determines the form of one's personality. Although this theoretical point of view most clearly seems to deny free will, it may be able to be applied by the therapist in a way similar to deterministic psychological systems. Thereby it might allow for free will.

For instance, the Freudian system often posits that a certain traumatic event in one's childhood caused the personality to take on a certain form. The client uses this insight into the origins of a personality trait as a starting point and becomes aware of those habit patterns which "determine" behavior. By so doing the client has an opportunity to deprogram these mechanical ways of reacting to life situations.

Astrology, the causal astrologer argues, similarly leads one to focus on the factors which determine behavior. As one becomes conscious of these factors, the person may increase the ability to be the maker of his or her own destiny.

Although one may question with both the astrological and the Freudian system whether, objectively speaking, there is any reason to believe that this is "why" people are who they are, let us view these approaches simply as belief systems concerning the etiology of personality. One similarity between these points of view is that they both can be seen to rest on a "hidden reality" framework. People's acceptance of either belief system might lead to a feeling that they had discovered the hidden origins of their personality which could function as a highly charged starting point for work on a particular personality characteristic.

A criticism often made against the causal perspective is that it may tend to lead one to place the blame for one's maladaptive style of being upon traumatic events of one's past. From a therapeutic standpoint, concern arises that people might be led away from taking responsibility for their way of being, as is exemplified by the statement, "My parents caused me to be the way I am." Just as the Freudian analyst states that working with parental complexes is a first step to freeing oneself from these complexes and taking responsibility for one's way of being, so might the causal astrologer state that the birthchart is a first step to the client's taking responsibility for his or her destiny. A planet which is seen to cause a mechanical reaction pattern may be met and brought under conscious control.

Although from the above discussion it seems that the possibility exists for free will to emerge from a causal astrological point of view, in practice the astrologer may have a difficult time helping the person to make a transition to taking responsibility for a neurotic habit pattern. It may be particularly difficult from this viewpoint for clients to see how given patterns of behavior were chosen by them and can be changed by their choice.

One reason for this may be that the power of the causal astrologer's hidden reality framework leads people to attempt to justify a way of being by saying that a given planetary configuration predestined their personality to be the way it is. (How the therapist can aid the client who attempts to justify neurotic habit patterns is considered separately in Objection #2.) A more general reason that the astrologer may have trouble aiding the client in making the transition from determinism to free will when using a causal framework is that the astrological discipline is not oriented to modalities of personality change. Although this sort of change is difficult when using a causal astrological framework, it is not impossible if integrated with psychotherapeutic modalities and an understanding of symbolic process. (Again, Objection #2 and case study A give some possibilities as to how such a change may be aided by the therapist.)

The synchronistic viewpoint on astrology was posited by Jung who theorized that there is an acausal relationship between material and psychic processes. As applied to astrology (see Rudhyar, 1936) this means that what is happening in one medium (the stars) is also happening within the human psyche — not that either causes the other to occur. Jung attempts to explain this by saying in *The Secret of the Golden Flower*, "whatever is born or done this moment of time, has the qualities of this moment of time." The connecting link in Jung's view is not cause, but meaning.

In therapeutic practice, this viewpoint may have some of the same problems as the causal view. A person could here say that the qualities of that moment in time, like my personality, had this or that particular limitation. This could lead to an acquiescent acceptance of that limitation. One difference is that the synchronistic point of view is usually coupled with an archetypal understanding and a predispositional rather than a causal world view. This means that although a particular planetary configuration was present at the time of birth, it is not seen as causing anything *per se*; rather its potential is seen as being filled out by the particular environment in which the person is situated. From this viewpoint the person may have more room to explore the unique way he or she manifests a collective pattern than from the causal viewpoint. Although clients may in practice use the synchronistic viewpoint to justify being predisposed to some dis-ease again by incorporating an appropriate therapeutic modality and a symbolic understanding, the therapist may be able to aid in changing this justification into an opportunity for growth (See Objection #2 and the Case Study of "Golden Tooth").

Both the causal and synchronistic viewpoints rest upon a hidden reality framework. Although we have here concentrated on some of the therapeutically detrimental aspects of this viewpoint, such as the possibility of it leading to not taking responsibility for who one was "caused" or "predisposed" to be, or an acquiescent acceptance of the same, there may be positive aspects to the hidden reality belief. As mentioned earlier, at times it may be useful to see the identity quest as an attempt to discover what is present but hidden within; for the power of the archetypal theme of Discovery can augment the process of going into one's depths, mobilizing will and a sense of revealed purpose. To have these viewpoints accomplish this function it helps to integrate them with the therapeutic modalities of personality change mentioned in this book, in particular an understanding of symbolic processes.

The symbolic point of view shifts its emphasis from assuming an objective relationship between the stars and personality and instead emphasizes the use of celestial symbols to explore one's personality. Unlike the causal or synchronistic points of view, one here does not have a fixed assumption that the stars either cause or predispose one's personality; rather the symbol is used to lead the person to discover meaning in his or her way of being.[2]

If the symbolic viewpoint deals with meaning, one might ask, what is the difference between it and the synchronistic viewpoint where a connection through meaning was also mentioned? A confusion arises from Jung's (1960) bringing together of two concepts within his theory of synchronicity. He speaks of meaning as connecting psychical and physical dimensions, but in addition says that "whatever is born or done this moment of time, has the qualities

---

2. This psychotherapeutic function of symbols has been spoken to by Jung (1954), Assagioli (1965), Gendlin (1964), Rudhyar (1966), and is illustrated in regards to astrological symbols in the Case Illustrations Section of this work.

of this moment of time." This seems to posit more than a coincidence through meaning, by its orientation to the objective correspondence between the two realms.

As the symbolic point of view is used in this work we are narrowing Jung's (and later Rudhyar's) theoretical preconception in two ways. First, when this point of view is spoken of, although we do not preclude the possibility of an objective micro/macrocosmic correspondence, our focus is only on that which is of primary relevance to the therapist. This centers on how astrological symbols can aid one in dealing with life's meaning. In a way similar to the way Jung used myths and symbols to aid the client in the process of self-discovery, we shall use astrological symbols, but we shall subtract out his (and Rudhyar's) predispositional stance.

Secondly, the phenomenological "meaning reorganization point of view" forms the theoretical foundation of our symbolic framework, unlike the causal and synchronistic viewpoints which are usually rooted in a "hidden reality" framework. In both of these latter views, people believe that they have discovered the "true" etiological basis from which their personalities grew, whereas the symbolic framework assumes no ontological stance *per se*. Rather, symbols are merely used to reorganize the person's experience of identity; the actual relationship between cosmos and personality is a mystery.

It seems that this combined symbolic/meaning reorganization viewpoint allows for a greater degree of free will than the other two stances, for no *a priori* blocks are seen as influencing the person's character on a theoretical level. In practice this may allow individuals to more readily own how they chose certain habit patterns in response to environmental conditions rather than emphasizing how factors outside of their locus of power may have caused these patterns. By using symbols of these personality patterns as vehicles to explore one's identity, the possibility of transformation may be enhanced.

From a clinical perspective one may question whether a client might not see the patterns of the heavens at his or her birthtime as determining or predisposing the personality to be fixed in a certain way despite the theoretical possibility of the system's use in a symbolic manner. From my work with the system, it does seem that despite theoretical discussions oriented to elucidating the symbolic view, some clients continue to use it in a deterministic manner. Serious questions can be asked as to whether this system may be more pronounced than others in its propensity to lead to certain of the detrimental psychotherapeutic effects associated with a deterministic world view. For this reason, the therapist might well choose not to introduce this language in cases where this potentiality seems to already pervade the client's approach to life in a negative way.

If the therapist does choose to incorporate the language, it should be done in conjunction with a modality which is oriented to personality change. Some suggestions are given in the case illustration section and in the following section on "making an excuse for one's neurosis." If one wished to make a case for using the astrological language in these instances he might say that people inevitably see a given phenomenon in accordance with their level of awareness, and it is precisely the aim of the therapeutic relationship to start from where the client is at. In this sense the *weltanschauung* of the client would come out through working with the astrological system, and could prove useful in working with the client's myth of personality formation.

In closing, though, it should be restated that the practical effects of the determinism associated with the system can loom as an obstacle to the client's growth, while at the same time emphasizing that these obstacles are not insurmountable if used in conjunction with an appropriate psychotherapeutic modality.

## ASTROLOGY IS USED TO MAKE AN EXCUSE FOR ONE'S NEUROSIS

A question arises as to whether astrology serves as a framework through which people can make excuses for their neuroses, rather than allowing them to discover meaning in their life. This is an important question, for astrology is often used this way. In this section we shall consider how the therapist can cope with this problem.

First, it should be mentioned that other systems as well are prone to being used to make an excuse for one's neuroses. For instance, with the Freudian system a person might at first come to the conclusion that "I had to turn out this way because my parents treated me in that manner." As the Freudian analyst knows, this realization is the beginning of a process of taking responsibility for the way one is.

As a matter of fact a general manifestation of neurosis is that such a person often seeks to justify his or her way of being. This has been called "justification collecting" (Perls, 1969). How the therapist aids the person in going beyond the obsession to justify himself is no mere abstract point, and is a general psychotherapeutic problem.

In relationship to its occurrence with the astrological modality, a person might make a statement something like this: "Now I see why I can't express myself in groups. It's because I have Saturn in my fourth house; I wish I had Jupiter there." (Saturn is the symbol of self-containment, whereas Jupiter symbolizes social expression.)

The therapist can aid the person in going beyond the level of justification by using the symbolic nature of astrology. By using it as a symbolic process one can shift the orientation from an interpretive orientation as the **why** one is the way one is, to the process orientation involved when using a symbol to explore **how** one is the way one is.

As applied to the above example, upon entering into the symbol of Saturn in the fourth house, one might see that one talent was feeling intensely the boundaries of one's own inner world. Perhaps it is expressed in the person's forming images in an artistic career, but when it comes to opening up in groups the individual feels bounded in the sense of feeling blocked in any ability to participate in certain topics of conversation. The symbolic mode might allow an image of the person's way of being to emerge. If one man, like White Turtle mentioned in Chapter 2, saw himself like a turtle this might lead him to an experience of new meaning in relationship to a long-resisted personality pattern. By entering into the image of a turtle's head in its shell, the person might come up with new insight as to how to relate in groups. He might decide to share his discomfort with the group, or disclose some of the images that come as his head goes into its shell.

If the person saw socially oriented people and himself at opposite ends of a continuum, the symbol of the astrological mandala might aid him by providing a visual representation of the fact that they each contain a social way of being, but each expresses it in his or her own way. The exact symbol which emerges for the person could give him permission to be social in his own unique way. The transformative power of the symbol is capable of doing more than saying it's okay not to talk in groups because that is how one is meant to be; rather it can lead to new ways of behaving.

Speaking of the symbolic meaning of one's way of being in itself is not necessarily always therapeutically effective. Especially in cases where the client is making an excuse for a neurosis another factor needs to be kept in consciousness by the therapist. This factor is the importance of working with the complex by entering into it. As Reich (1949) points out, and as we have stated in the case illustrations section, it is often crucial to therapeutic progress to deal with the complex itself before one moves to the dimension of meaning interpretation.

Each therapist may have his or her own way of aiding the client in entering the stuff of the complex. As applied to the above example, one therapist might start by asking, "How do you feel in groups?" This leads away from the interpretive question as to why one has blocks dealing in group situations. The therapeutic process might continue with the person imagining himself in an uncomfortable group situation, or the therapist might advise the person to participate in a group. Feeling could then be explored with the person through dialogue, psychodrama, etc. to aid the person in making a transition.

Although all of the above possibilities can be integrated with the astrological modality, Gendlin's (1969) "focusing" technique seems particularly useful in conjunction with the astrological mode. By exploring one's bodily felt sense while a given astrological image is focused upon, a connection can be maintained between image and feeling. This technique had been particularly helpful in working in situations when a client moves into the realm of intellectualization to justify a way of being.

Another way that the therapist using astrological symbols may deal with the problem of justification collecting is by simply confronting the person with one's perception that it seems that he is trying to justify himself. In exploring this with the person, some of the following questions may be helpful. "How does your body feel when you are justifying yourself? Who are you justifying yourself to? What situations do you notice this arising in?" The material emerging from these kinds of questions can involve the person in the experience of his tension, and can lead to ways for the person to work through it.

The general issue here is one of helping individuals to take responsibility for their way of being rather than justifying it. Although astrology is often used to justify one's habit patterns, and it cannot be denied that it may even have a propensity to lead people in this direction (especially when used in line with the causal theoretical position), the therapist may be able to counter this tendency. By using the symbolic nature of astrology along with some of the previous suggestions, the therapist may be able to direct clients to focus on the patterns of their life myths. This in turn may allow them to become increasingly conscious of their role in molding the patterns of their own life.

## PREDICTING FUTURE EVENTS TAKES
## A PERSON AWAY FROM PRESENT REALITY

Rudhyar (1936) says on this point:

> The function of Astrology is not to tell us what will or rather what may, happen in the future but what significance there is in every moment lived or about to be lived. It reveals the quality of particular moments and of the larger cycles rooted in those moments. [3]

One might question whether even though this may be what astrology does ideally, if it has the effect in practice of producing a future orientation on the part of certain clients. This often does occur, but can be compensated for by integrating astrology with psychotherapeutic modalities which are oriented to deal with escapes from the present (such as Gestalt Therapy or Gendlin's techniques). In certain cases it may prove helpful to ask clients to explore what their fantasy is of the future, while the person "focuses" on the chart. To keep the person in the present the therapist might ask how this fantasy feels, and what the person could do to make it more to their liking.

## CATEGORIZING LIMITS A PERSON'S UNIQUENESS

Whether this occurs is a function of how astrology is used. It can be a descriptive system putting people into Sun sign categories, or it can be a symbolic system which can lead one to an experience of the uniqueness of his or her personality.

The transition to the symbolic point of view is not as easy as it may seem from the above statement, although the therapist can aid this orientation by using the astrological symbols in conjunction with the client's own imagination and rootedness in a felt experience of the symbols. The Jungian process of active imagination and Gendlin's focusing method are helpful in this regard, and are demonstrated in this context in Case A.

As this criticism applies to the therapist, one may question whether the astrological language might lead to seeing the client in fixed categories. This is a problem inherent in any descriptive framework of identity for any label tends to limit one's focus. By using the symbolic nature of astrology, the therapist may discover that astrological language has less of a propensity to lead to reductive categorizations than certain other descriptive frameworks.

Still, even symbols may limit one's perception to a certain

---

3. Rudhyar, D. *The Astrology of Personality* Garden City, NY, 1936, 1970, p.88.

structured framework of viewing. From a general theoretical point of view one may then question whether using terms to describe personality serves a positive function or whether it limits the therapist from being in the present. The detrimental effects of psychological terminologies in preventing the therapist from seeing the person as a whole have been spoken of in Chapter One under the title of "systematic myopia." Here we wish to balance this perspective by stating that terms can be used to form as well as to limit, and seem to inevitably arise as individuals create systems that give meaning to their experience.

This is not to deny that the detrimental aspects of systematic myopia may arise with the use of astrology, and the astro-poetic language in general. Our attempt to prevent the possibility of the person's being put into a Procrustian bed is presenting a metasystem which puts the astro-poetic modality into proper perspective. In Chapter Seven, we spoke of how this metasystematic perspective may be useful to enable the therapist to transcend the limitations of the system so as to be present to the living moment.

## ASTROLOGY'S COMPLEXITY IS A DETRIMENT TO ITS CLINICAL USEFULNESS

Some psychologists object to astrology's use as a language saying that it is so complex that the average psychologist let alone the average client would find it difficult to become proficient in its use.

Further, this line of thought continues, even if the psychologist were to become familiar with its intricacies, the resistance that so many people have to what is called a superstitious system would severely limit its use in psychotherapy.

It is true that astrology does take considerable time to master, but this in itself should not preclude its use. New languages often struggle to become understandable; Mendeleyev's periodic table of elements and the Freudian language of the psyche were not easily understandable, yet significantly contributed to human understanding.

Although a complex system may be necessary to speak of the complex differences between human beings, it seemed important to attempt to make the language more comprehensible so that it could be more readily used in the psychotherapeutic process. This aim is accomplished in this work by introducing an astro-poetic language which simplifies astrology by developing certain attributes of its essential nature. This widens the possibilities of use for the therapist in that he may use either the complex language of astrology or the simpler metaphorical language stemming from objects in one's everyday surroundings.

## ASTROLOGY LEADS TO DEPENDENCY
## UPON THE THERAPIST

Although dependency upon the therapist to solve one's problems is an issue of concern in all forms of therapy, and some therapists even argue that it may be important to successful therapy, it may be that this problem pertains to astrology more than to other modalities. I suggest this is due to the fact that it contains a complex foreign language more familiar to the therapist than the client. The therapist can meet this potential problem in some of the following ways.

First, from a holistic perspective, it is important for the therapist to be sensitive to how a client asks for interpretations: whether it is from dependency or from a desire for increased information. As we mentioned in the case illustration, if the therapist acquiesces in the former case the client's dependency may increase; if the therapist refuses in the latter case the most important therapeutic ingredient of genuineness is lost, leaving the client with the impression that a psychological game is being played.

For instance, in the 15th session I answered **A's** question about how I saw the meaning of Venus in Scorpio because in this situation **A** had already told me how she felt about its meaning and was obviously asking for increased information. On the other hand, in Session 8 I did not answer the client's question about why she had a hard time communicating to others if she had so many planets in Libra (the sign of relationship). Here we see exemplified one way that the symbolic nature of the astrological system can be used to deal with the problem of dependency. By asking the client what she felt the answer to this question was, coupled with her "focusing" on the symbol of Mars the client was able to answer this question for herself. She experienced how her excessively strong (Mars) manner of asserting herself created blocks in communicating.

Another way to deal with the problem of dependency is illustrated in Session 17. Here the technique of **dialoguing** seemed to be useful in response to the client's request that I tell her whether the meaning of her Mercury symbol implied that she should be interested in words in themselves or in the meaning that people were trying to convey to her when they used particular words. By suggesting that she attempt to answer this question by giving each of these feelings a voice and have them dialogue, the client came to a synthesis which expressed the ideographic meaning of the symbol for her.

By these suggestions we do not wish to imply that the dependency arising from the use of the astrological system is dealt with easily. Even in Case A, I felt that a dependency existed at the end of the therapeutic process. To counter this predisposition of the astrological mode, the therapist may choose to do additional work on the roots of the dependency, by asking such questions as "How did you learn to look to others for answers to problems arising in your life?"

In summary, I do not see the problem of dependency as insurmountable, and trust that the former suggestions may give others a starting point to deal with this issue.

# CONCLUDING NOTE

For those who are uncomfortable with the manner in which medical model language describes personality, this work has provided a way to expand their linguistic parameters. Astro-poetic language and the perspective outlined herein provides the person with a wider lens through which to view life's meaning and individual identity. By using the universe as one's alphabet, one's "true name" can be spelled.

In our culture the psychological profession holds the power of the name and it is crucial that the utmost sensitivity be exercised in using such; for the vessel that is a human being can become a dungeon or a tabernacle by a shift in name.

# APPENDIX ONE

# SCIENTIFIC STUDIES
# OF ASTROLOGY

That which is looked upon by one generation as the apex of human knowledge
is often considered an absurdity by the next, and that which is regarded as
a superstition in one century, may form the basis of science for the following
one."

Paracelsus

The scientific basis of astrology does not specifically relate to the
theoretical position taken in this work. From the meaning reorganization point of view, astrology has use as a meaning-giving symbolic
system regardless of the objective correspondence between extraterrestrial and earthly factors. In this sense, as with the Rorschach technique, the client may even choose to turn the chart in another direction; the important concern is what that client sees. Still, since usually
one works with the chart the way it is presented, the reader may
therefore question what basis is there to assume that there is any correspondence between the cosmos and life on this planet.

Being of peripheral relationship to this work, and in addition a
question of interest to those exploring our existence, I have included
some of this research in this appendix. Although some studies have cast
doubt on traditional astrological assumptions, our concentration in our
analysis shall be on those points that have been supported by current
research. This line of research seems important to see if causal, acausal
or no relationship exists between these realms of the life process.
Regardless of its results, the language of the cosmos can provide a
holistic way to perceive our existence.

The most often quoted studies used to support astrology are those of Michel Gauquelin, a graduate in psychology and Statistics from the Sorbonne and Director of the Laboratory for the Study of the Relations between Cosmic Rhythms and Psychophysiology in Paris. His wife, Francoise Gauquelin, also a psychologist with training in statistics, was a full partner in Michel Gauquelin's work. Although some of the Gauquelins' research has disproved certain astrological notions, others have confirmed astrological hypotheses at a statistical level of significance. In Michel Gauquelin's works *L'Influence Des Astres* (1955) and *Les Hommes et les Astres* (1960) he published their analysis of over 35,000 charts from five different countries which the Gauquelins had collected of eminent professionals' (listed in *Who's Who*) birthcharts, and then wrote to city halls to obtain the birth times. They found significant relationships between the professions these people were involved in and the planet which was rising over the horizon or at the zenith position at the time of the person's birth. Those planets found to correlate significantly were Mars with scientists, doctors, athletes, soldiers and executives; Jupiter with team athletes, soldiers, ministers, actors, journalists, playwrights; Saturn with scientists and doctors; and the Moon with ministers, politicians and writers. The level of significance of the correlation was 1 * 500,000,000 (West, 1973, p. 169).

After three well-known statisticians studied Michel Gauquelin's second book (Tornier — a specialist in the mathematical theory of probability at the University of Berlin; Faverge — Professor of Statistics at the Sorbonne; and Jean Porte — a critic of his first French experiment), they could find no fault with the statistics, the methods employed in the gathering of the data or in the calculations (West, 1973, p.170). Control groups of horoscopes selected randomly as well as control groups of men in subordinate positions in the same professions yielded results at a level of chance (West, 1973, p.170). Of interest is the fact that it was, for instance, Mars — not Venus — which was correlated with soldiers, which would fit with the ancient symbolic meaning of the planet.

The Gauquelins' second line of research was in the area of planetary heredity (*Die Planetare Herditat*, 1962). Here the data indicated a correlation between the birth sky of parents with that of their children. Using 15,000 matchings which yielded 300,000 positions of planets the Gauquelins found significant results at a level of 1 * 500,000 (Gauquelin, 1970, p.167). They found these results with Mars, Jupiter, Saturn, the Moon and Venus but were unable to disprove the null hypothesis with the other planets. As a control group, the Gauquelins discovered that children who were not born at a natural time (forceps or Caesarean births) yielded nonsignificant results in terms of the correlation between child and parents' birth charts (Gauquelin, 1970, p.168). Michel Gauquelin is always careful to state that he does not want their results to be considered as supporting astrology, but rather they are investigating scientific correspondences.

A recent publication by Francoise Gauquelin (*The Psychology of the Planets*, ACS Publications, Inc, 1982) gives an excellent summary of the character traits the Gauquelins have found associated with the various planets in certain positions of the horoscope. (The Gauquelins discovered character to be the basis of professions in their study of highly successful people. The correlations between certain traits — e.g., courageous — with certain planets — e.g., Mars — in designated positions in the birthchart were even **more** significant than the correlations between planets and professions. Thus, active, courageous, assertive people tended to become highly successful soldiers or surgeons rather than writers.) The trait words which were significant in the research of the Gauquelins are compared to the keywords for the planets used by a selection of both ancient and modern astrologers.

Vernon Clark (1960), a psychologist, attempted to test astrologers' ability to match charts with the correct person without having them present. In his first experiment he sent the birth data of 10 people to 20 experienced astrologers asking them to match the chart with 10 case histories which were sent along with the birth data. The control group of twenty psychologists and social workers were used to control for the possibility that one might, regardless of astrological knowledge, be able to discern which chart corresponded to which case history on the basis of the birth information alone. The level of significance of the experimental group was p = .01; the control group scored at chance. His second experiment testing astrologers' ability to distinguish between the correct horoscope and spurious horoscopes yielded results of p = .001.

Certain weaknesses inherent in Clark's research design limit making definite assumptions. Since the case histories used in the experiments were written by the same person who constructed the horoscopes which were sent out to the astrologers, we cannot rule out the possibility that the case histories were biased in relationship to selecting information, or in presenting it in such a way that would tip off the astrologer as to the corresponding chart.

This lack of double blind does not however affect the results of his third study. Here thirty astrologers were given ten pairs of horoscopes and asked to discern who was handicapped from birth with cerebral palsy. The other horoscope was from a healthy person. The data was obtained from physicians and psychologists who worked with these handicapped people; no data submitted was excluded. The charts were calculated by an independent astrologer. Unlike his earlier studies, no case histories were given to the astrologers, only the ten pairs of birth charts. The t-test yielded p = .01, which indicates a high level of significance for at least 30 astrologers' ability to match the birth chart with the cerebral palsied patients.

The relationship between celestial rhythms and living organisms has been the subject of the research of Frank Brown, Professor of Biology at Northwestern University. In articles published in *Science* magazine (December, 1959) and elsewhere, Brown showed the relationship between celestial cycles and the nocturnal movements of beans, the amount of running performed by rats during the course of a day, variations in the color of fiddler crabs and the sleep patterns of flies. But perhaps his most interesting experiment was with oysters, where it had always been assumed that it was the action of the tides, not the effects of the Moon, which related to the opening and closing of their shells. By taking oysters in light-proof containers from New Haven, Connecticut to Evanston, Illinois, and placing them in pans of specially prepared pans of salt water in a dark room, Brown was able to show that it was the Moon and not the actual motion of the water which provoked the periodicity. Within two weeks the oysters had adjusted their rhythms to the lunar phases of Evanston.

Although Brown had controlled for barometric pressure by his use of special tanks, there are many other possible factors which may be correlated with the rhythms of these oysters, other animals, plants and human beings. This has given rise to hypotheses which point to other correlational factors such as geomagnetic influences, air ionization influences, cymatic influences, radiation influences,etc.

Brown investigated the geomagnetic hypothesis with worms and snails, finding levels of significance above chance. At the Max Planck lab in Munich, Aschoff attempted to show that human beings were also sensitive to geomagnetic fields. By shielding human volunteers in underground bunkers from ordinary electromagnetic fields, he showed that circadian rhythms were changed as compared to volunteer controls who also lived in the underground bunker but in nonshielded rooms (Luce, 1973, p.58). If we question whether human beings are sensitive enough to the small changes in the magnetic fields that result from planetary movements, Dr. Rocard's experiment is of interest. At the University of Paris he found that he was able to condition people to be able to detect with a dowser such small changes in the Earth's magnetic field strength as .3 miligauss (Luce, 1971, p.13). Harvalik also found subjects reacting to magnetic field shifts as weak as 0.007 gamma (Ostrander, 1972, p.38).

The air ionization hypothesis is based upon the fact that the Moon influences atmospheric ionization — electrically charged atoms. Supposedly the full Moon brings more positive and the waning Moon more negative ions. Negative ionization is used in the Soviet Union to speed wound healing and to reduce mental and physical fatigue (Ostrander, 1972, p.34) and one American investigation concluded that negative ions slowed the alpha brain rhythm and brought a feeling of release in people (Pavlick, 1964).

The cymatic hypothesis is based upon the understanding of wave forms, derived from Chaldni's experimentation with the different forms produced on a plate attached to a violin as different sounds were produced. Hans Jenny further refined the technique with his tonoscope. His work illustrates the concept that form comes into being through vibration, and depends upon both the frequency of vibration and the material being vibrated. Since the planets emit waves (Jupiter and the Earth, for instance, emit radio waves), it is conceivable that an equivalent vibration is set up by resonance with some part of the earth which responds to that frequency. Since electromagnetic waves do travel through free space it may be that they influence occurrences on the earth. In this sense the cymatic concept might lead us to question whether the ancient concept of the Harmony of the Spheres should be taken literally. Recent work by Baxter has demonstrated the effect that sound waves have on plants, and it is open to question where this line of research will lead.

At this stage, it is impossible to know whether these hypotheses preclude one another. Without searching for a theoretical conclusion, we can still go on to examine some of the correlational evidence. It seems that many levels of terrestrial activity may be in relationship to the wider cosmos. The famous Piccardi experiments, done by the director of the Institute of Inorganic Chemistry at the University of Florence, show how extraterrestrial fields of force are related to the chemical composition of water. They are important to take into account in working with the calcium deposits in boiler containers (Gauquelin, p. 211).

Since human blood is largely composed of water it is of little surprise that scientists continued their research here. The Takata reaction, a chemical method of testing the albumen in blood serum, was found to be changed when major sunspots interfered with the Earth's magnetic field. During the eclipses of 1941, 1943, and 1948 these reactions were inhibited, and subjects in an aircraft were found to produce the reaction more strongly at heights where the atmosphere was too thin to provide effective protection from solar radiation (Watson, 1974, p. 47). In relationship to blood lymphocytes, Schultz, after making 120,000 measurements, established a relationship between the number of white cells in the blood and number of sunspots (Gauquelin, p. 227). Schultz further found an exact monthly correlation between the leukocyte content in the blood and the Sun's activity (Gauquelin, p. 228). Other diseases correlated with solar activity are heart attacks, myocardial infarctions (heart attacks caused by blood clots) and hemorrhage in the lungs of tubercular patients (Andrews, p. 45; Watson, p. 48). Dr. Becker of New York's Upstate Medical Center in Syracuse found that the frequency of psychiatric admissions correlates highly with geomagnetic force field activity. The probability of the occurrence by chance was 1: 10,000, and the number of admissions in his experiment was 28,642. Becker states:

> Every organism including the human organism demonstrates cycles of biological, mental and emotional activity closely linked to geomagnetic force field patterns and more complex force field interrelationships, both planetary and solar terrestrial in scope. Human behavior is influenced through the direct current central system of the brain by the terrestrial magnetic field, solar and planetary conditions and both high and low energy cosmic radiation. (Becker and Bachman, p.626.)

Other activities correlated with solar activity have been coal mine accidents on the Ruhr; and traffic accidents in Russia and Germany have increased as much as four times the average on days after the eruption of a solar flare.

But these studies could be accepted without one expanding their conclusions to accepting astrological factors, such as planetary aspects and the like, as playing a part in terrestrial activities. Along these lines Dewey's article (1968) "A Key to Sunspot-Planetary Relationship" is of interest, for he there showed that the conjunctions of the planets (with the exception of Neptune) coincide with sunspot activity (West, p. 197). The relationship between the Sun's magnetic fields and planetary positions has been given empirical support by John Nelson, who was employed to research factors interfering with the propagation of radio waves through the ionosphere. He found predictable disturbances occurred when three or more planets were either aligned with the Sun or formed angles of 90°, 30°, and 60° and their multiples. Although this would seem to support the often used aspect relationships of astrologers, one should note that Nelson used heliocentric, not the geocentric, aspects of classical astrology. And he worked with all multiples of 7½°, 11¼° and 18°. Still, in support of astrological symbology was the fact that Mercury (traditionally associated with communications) involved the greatest number of disturbances, and the inferior conjunction of Venus (traditionally associated with a soft receptive quality) was found to significantly reduce magnetic storm activity on the Earth.

In terms of the psychological dimension, Dr. Ravitz, a neurologist at Duke University, has done important research. He has discovered a direct physiological connection between the person and the Moon. Plotting changes in electrical potential emitted by mental patients and normal people, he found that the greatest differences between head and chest readings occurred at a full Moon, particularly in the mental patients. Ravitz hypothesizes that through the modification of the Earth's magnetic field the Moon might be associated with tipping the mental balance in those whose balance is already precarious (Watson, 1974, p.44). Dr. Lehmann has found a correlation between geomagnetic disturbances and excitement on the ward. Other factors such as barometric pressure, temperature, and humidity as well as staff on duty, changes in menu, medication and visiting days were juxtaposed to the hospital calendar of aggressive behavior and these factors were found to not correlate with the cycles of aggression (Luce, 1973, p. 14).

For the world of animals it seems that we are more willing to accept the relationship between them and the cosmos, but the experiment of Franz Sauer ("Celestial Navigation by Birds," *Scientific American*, 199: 42-47, August, 1958) may lead us even further in elaborating on their relationship. Sauer raised European warblers in lightproof, sound-proof rooms. Then in autumn, the season for migration to South Africa, the birds became restless. They were placed in a planetarium so that they could view the night sky. With the autumn sky projected, a bird flew up to the position of usual migration. When the planetarium sky was rotated to show the stars at a different latitude, the warbler corrected its flight direction for that latitude. As a control, when the dome was illumined with diffuse light, the warbler was unable to choose a preferred direction.

Although the skeptic can always pose objections, such as asking for the elimination of the factor of ESP between bird and human etc., this research can give pause to reflect on the possibility that human beings may also be related to the cosmos in ways heretofore unimagined.

Again, the exact mode of interrelationship between these two realms is the subject of continuing research. For instance, the work of McConnell shows that learned information can be passed from the RNA of one "educated" flatworm to another flatworm who has eaten him. Penfield's (1958) studies demonstrate the storage of memory in our brains, and recent work has suggested the hypothesis that the human cell can respond to geomagnetic and extraterrestrial factors. Since the nucleic acids possess magnetic qualities, they may be affected by those geomagnetic qualities spoken of earlier. The Swedish neurobiologist, Heyden (1961) postulated that incoming electromagnetic impulses not only increase the RNA but also change its coding. The changed code produces changed protein and these are the molecular representatives of memory. He conjectured that they have the property of recognizing the same electrical pattern that created the RNA at the time of the original stimulus (Osterman, 1968, p.22).

Although the research generated in this area has been given added weight since Jung wrote this quote, it seems fitting in closing this section.

> Though we know from experience that psychic processes are related to material ones, we are not in a position to say in what this relationship consists or how it is possible. . . . Microphysics is feeling its way into the unknown side of matter just as psychology is pushing forward into the unknown side of the psyche.[1]

---

1. Jung, C.G., *The Collected Works of C.G. Jung*, Vol. 14, Bollinger Series, Princeton: Princeton University Press.

For those interested in going further into the research in these areas:

1. Becker and Bachman, "Geomagnetic parameters and psychiatric hospital admissions," *Nature*, 200, 1963, p.626.
2. Bergier and Pauwels, *The Eternal Man*, New York: Avon Books. 1973.
3. Dean, Geoffrey, *Recent Advances in Natal Astrology*, Browley, Kent, England: The Astrological Association, 1977.
4. Doane, *Astrology, 30 Years Research*, Hollywood: Professional Astrologers Incorporated, 1956.
5. Collin, *The Theory of Celestial Influence*, New York: Samuel Weiser, 1973.
6. Ebertin, *The Combination of Stellar Influences*, Germany, 1972.

7. Gauquelin, F., *The Psychology of the Planets*, San Diego, Ca.: ACS Publications, Inc., 1982.
8. Gauquelin, M. *The Scientific Basis of Astrology*, New York: Stein and Day, 1969.
9. Luce, *Body Time*, New York: Bantam, 1973.
10. Luce, *Biological Rhythms in Human and Animal Physiology*, New York: Dover, 1971.
11. Metzner, *Maps of Consciousness*, New York: Collier Books, 1971.
12. Ostrander and Schroder, *Astrological Birth Control*, Englewood Cliffs: Prentice Hall, 1972.
13. West and Toonder, *The Case for Astrology*, Baltimore: Penguin Books, 1970.
14. Watson, *Super Nature*, New York: Bantam books, 1974.
15. Wheelwright, *The Reality of the Psyche*, New York: C.G. Jung Foundation, 1968. See Osterman, "The Tendency Toward Patterning and Order in Matter and the Psyche."

# APPENDIX TWO

# THE QUESTION OF VALUE IN PSYCHOTHERAPEUTIC SYSTEMS IN GENERAL AND THE ASTROLOGICAL SYSTEM IN PARTICULAR

The attempt to verify that a given system "works" may occur within an experimental/statistical model or within an experimental/phenomenological model. One limitation of the former model is that while it is useful for dealing in generalizations and quantities, it is not as relevant in exploring an individual's experience and the qualities of that unique experience. As Rollo May (1969) points out,

> If you take individuals as units in a group for the purpose of statistical prediction — certainly a legitimate use of psychological science — you are exactly defining out of the picture the characteristics which make this individual an existing person. Or when you take him as a composite of drives and deterministic forces, you have defined for study everything except the one to whom these experiences happen, everything except the existing person himself (p.372).

Psychologists certainly have experimentally demonstrated the importance of the dimension of meaning in mental health (Kotchen, 1960; Davis, 1960) and have constructed tests to measure it ("Purpose in Life Text," "Personal Orientation Inventory," "Life Regard

Index''); but the wish to explore the subtleties of flavor existing within one's experience of meaning seems to lend itself to an experiential mode of inquiry. Since this work deals with the experience of meaning, the focus is directed towards exploring how meaning is experienced as one uses astrological language as a symbolic process.

Attention therefore is not directed to, for example, how many people with the Moon in Cancer would be sensitive by using statistical criteria of measurement. To say that an experimental group with the Moon in Cancer rated significantly higher than a control group on the variable of sensitivity, although providing interesting data on one level of analysis, leaves out the dimension of the person's experience of this quality. It is this later question which is of primary interest to the psychotherapist. Following this line of interest our inquiry shall focus on how, by using a certain symbol (let us say Cancer), the person experiences his or her unique way of being sensitive. Thus our interest is not in describing, diagnosing, or proving that the person is sensitive, but rather to examine the experience that occurs when astrological symbols are used.

The experiential mode of "proof" is recently gaining respectability in our overly rational culture as the experimental/experiential pendulum shifts. In the field of psychology empirical support has been given to this viewpoint by the recent split brain studies (Ornstein, 1973) which have demonstrated that the left side of the brain has a logical analytic function, whereas the right side has a holistic function important to musical ability and other nonverbal modes of experiencing. From such studies there is renewed vigor concerning the importance of both approaches to knowledge in order for the person to be whole.

Choosing an experiential mode of inquiry leads to questions regarding how to measure value in this frame of reference. Experiential approaches, like statistical ones, consist of a given finite province of meaning (Schutz, 1970) and any psychotherapist who sails in experiential waters is asked hard, delineated questions by those on land.

One with keen insight into the methodological problems of psychotheraputic systems might ask, "What is there to guarantee that astrological language does not give an interpretation that is capricious?" This line of questioning might continue, "Any system which claims to be able to identify something must be able to miss the mark and misidentify." How does one determine whether an astrological interpretation is wrong?

These are difficult questions with which all psychotherapeutic systems must wrestle. An interpretation of a dream, an insight into a pattern of behavior, a client's discovery that "ah ha, it stems from my relationship to my father," how does the therapist determine whether there is value in the interpretation?

From a phenomenological perspective, the criteria that each person chooses to measure value stems from the individual's own framework. While the experimentally oriented psychologist chooses statistical means of evaluation, the phenomenologically oriented psychologist looks at the experience of the person and any changes of attitude. This is why hermeneutically oriented thinkers (Beshai, 1975; Ricoeur, 1967, 1970) say that the question of value always rests within a given context, i.e., that it is always inter-subjectively valid. As Gendlin (1969) points out with his **Iofi principle** (instance of itself) any meaning given is an instance of some general methodological category. The kind of meaning that grows from the particular system follows from the framework of which the given meaning is an instance.

Since criteria of value seem to be inextricably connected to one's universe of meaning, an appropriate starting point for our discussion of the "How does one know when an astrological interpretation is wrong?" is to examine certain assumptions behind this question. First, inherent in this line of questioning is the assumption that the clients might be missing the "real thing" they should be focusing upon. Or, in other words, they might not be discovering the "real meaning" of their behavior. Implicit in the question then is "the hidden reality point of view" that there is **a** real meaning behind one's behavior that can be discovered. As we shall discuss later, following this line of reasoning leads to a static rather than a dynamic mode of inquiry.

A second point of clarification is that the question rests differently in different contexts, i.e., when an interpretation is made by looking solely at the chart of a person (chart-centered approach) a different criterion of judgment would be appropriate as compared to using astrological symbols as a way to evoke experiential movement in a client (person-centered approach). The former tack leads to an insight model emphasizing intellectual awareness, whereas the latter is oriented to an experiential model emphasizing felt bodily experience.

In this work the approach to astrological material exists within a person-centered psychotherapeutic relationship where an emphasis is placed upon the experience of the person. Therefore, like others in the field (Gendlin, 1969; Jung, 1931; Fingarette, 1963) the criteria of value is searched for within the felt shift produced and the concomitant behavioral changes. The term "felt shift" as used by (Gendlin, 1978) relates to the new meaning which unfolds from direct reference to a felt bodily state. In speaking of "experience" Gendlin does not preclude intellectual awareness; quite to the contrary he sees the bodily feeling leading to new meaning through the image that is produced by focusing on one's felt experience. The difference between "intellectual awareness" as the term is usually used and the insight growing from direct reference is that this latter meaning is judged in terms of its connection to a bodily feeling.

When one uses symbolic modalities with a meaning reorganization schema in mind, the focus is not upon "correctness" of interpretation. For instance, if a person came to therapy with the expressed complaint of feeling uncomfortable about his behavior pattern of observing, i.e., it made him unable to contact others, the interest would not be in the correctness a particular fixed interpretation except as it affects the client's experience of new meaning. Since multiple meanings can be attributed to any given pattern of behavior, a large number of intellectual interpretations could be given to the above example, such as: "Your nonparticipation and observing people is probably due to being hurt when you have tried to make contact with people in your early life." "Maybe it's due to not being able to watch your secretive parents." "Perhaps it's a symptom of the modern technological age where people are prone to live vicariously."

Even if the therapist does not offer an interpretation, but merely sets the tone by introducing a particular symbol for the client to work with, how does the client evaluate the value of an interpretation? Take an example using the symbol of Uranus for the client mentioned above. Some keywords for this symbol are observing, being outside of a given set of boundaries, and the imagination in general.

First, I should clarify again that the meaning reorganization point of view does not necessarily preclude that the client may hold a hidden reality point of view and believe that now he has discovered the hidden reason why he has always been an observer — "it's because the strength of Uranus in my chart predisposed me to be this way." The emphasis from the meaning reorganization point of view is on how this belief changes the person, not on the "objective" reality of the discovery. If no causal or predispositional stance is taken and the person simply uses the symbol to explore the unique way he "observes" the criterion of measurement still lies in the process of meaning reorganization.

Perhaps by entering into the symbol of Uranus the person would be given permission to be an observer and to let his imagination loose. He may have reported a tightness in his stomach early in the therapeutic process each time he became an observer, while at a later stage in the therapeutic process the client might report that he felt freed to play with being an observer.

The value of this approach would be measured in terms of the change produced, and the thermometer would be the directly felt bodily experience of the client. If the person at the beginning of therapy felt blocked in approaching women because he felt guilty about his observing nature, the value of working with the symbol of Uranus would lie in the change which occurred. Perhaps being given permission to let his imagination loose would enable him to observe a young woman sitting in a coffee house in his local hangout in a new way. The caressing of her lips on the cup and her appreciating the aroma of the coffee that she is sipping might bring an image to him of an impressionistic painter at sunset on a springtime hill in Europe, transposing the ambience of the light into the carefully mixed hues of her palate. Perhaps these images might fill the person with confidence about his poetic imagination, which might generalize to feelings about his personality as a whole. The client might now approach this woman and share his observation with her, and might find less tension arising when he approached people in general.

A further question arises as to how one knows that the symbol chosen was the best one with which to work? This question extends to asking whether another modality entirely might not have produced better results. Jung once responded to this sort of questioning by saying that "no harm will be done if a therapist offers his patients incorrect interpretations. In time, the unconscious will make our errors known" (Rychlak, 1975).

Certainly other ways of working with the above client, or other symbols chosen, could have aided in unfolding other important aspects of the person's world. If one has a world view which rests upon distinctions between good, better and best, the case could be viewed in this light. But the question "Is this particular way the best one?" seems to bring a static criterion of judgment to a process of a different nature. For the point is not so much which way is best, as the process of the therapeutic encounter itself. William James (1908) put it this way, "Truth's being resides in the verification process . . . It's validity is the process of validation."

It thus seems that a process-oriented criterion of evaluation needs to be considered with symbolic modalities. Langer's (1953) discussion of how different criteria of value apply to works of art as compared to logical analytic pursuits may provide some heuristic possibilities here. She suggests using aesthetic criteria for measuring the fruits of the poetic endeavor. As examples, she suggests looking at a word's "semblance," its "import," its ability to "evoke feelings" and its ability "to inspire" might do better as criteria of measurement for this realm than "rightness." The "principle of fecundity," says Langer, may prove useful as a measuring rod for ideas; for this concept emphasizes the generative power of an idea, gives value to expanding the import of a given thing, and emphasizes the dynamic attributes of ideas and their ensuing creations. Langer discusses how the process of Naming with poetic language, unlike discursive language, is selected to express quality and form feelings and intuition rather than to express fact. . .; instead it has the power to make a "virtual reality."

As the process orientation applies to the unfoldment of symbolic processes, if an initial way of looking at one's behavior seems incomplete, the symbolic system must allow the person to move to new horizons. In fact, from the meaning reorganization point of view this is essential to the process of reorganization. The experiential shift emerging from the first interpretation, or way of working, may set the stage allowing a second way of giving meaning which, taken in conjunction with the first, allows the person to experience a new unity. Like the process of poetic interpretation where on one day one particular interpretation seems to click, and on another day another interpretation does, the psychotherapeutic process seems to demand a process-oriented criteria of value. James (1908) said along these lines, "By each of our acts we make new truths possible and old ones impossible."

Thus one would hope that a given meaning schema would allow for moving around the wheel of possible meanings to expand one's interpretative world. When this process orientation is present, the meaning that one rests upon at a given moment is much like a geographic locale; it is a place where one rests for a given period of time. The experience of the person is valued in terms of the horizons of the person's experience as each new meaning unfolds; and as movement occurs from this position new horizons emerge.

In the astrological system the mandala allows for this process-oriented mode of interpretation. For once a given pattern is identified through a certain symbol, its opposite may emerge or any one of many associative links on the mandalic wheel may be brought into consciousness. This parallels Jung's idea of "circumambulation" of the psychological complex. As this applies to our illustrative case, if the person identifies with being an observer, outside of everything, and an imbalance is sensed, a way needs to be found to create movement. If there was an egosyntonic identification with the role of observer, a symbol which leads in another direction might be introduced; in this case perhaps the symbol of Saturn which offers the route to discovering the opposite value of entering into, and being limited by . . . rather than observing from a distance. Movement from a given perspective gained within the astrological system can also come from introducing another framework altogether. This factor shall be discussed in a moment when I extend the discussion to the question of solipsism.

Up to this point one can see that astrology can serve as a symbolic language through which people can explore their life's meaning. The letters exist, their form is partly defined and partly takes form in the therapeutic relationship. The poem that one creates from the letters and the words of the astrological vocabulary, though, would be no better than the poet him or herself. So it can be said that the value of that which is created will stem not only from the center of the system, but also from the center of one's self. In this sense the measuring rod of truth is the divining rod of one's soul.

But just because one experiences movement, just because one reorganizes one's experience of meaning, is this an adequate determination of value? Lest we return to the old days of the doctrine of solipsism, it seems another step must be made. For the experiential approach, one could argue, can be solipsistic. The fanatic of any system, religious or psychological, often says, "It has value to me because I feel it does." What in the astrological system will serve as a check on the problem of solipsism that may exist in our initial statement that the value of a given meaning interpretation must take place within its own framework? This question is often spoken of under the difference between a coherence theory of truth and a correspondence theory of truth, or under the title of internal versus external validity.

The point that we wish to here address is that the biases produced by a given meaning framework as a whole can emerge by allowing interaction with another meaning schema. Although the mandala may allow movement within the system to move to another line of interpretation, a route is also needed to provinces of meaning outside of the astrological system. Otherwise, systematic myopia may result.

As is discussed more extensively in the chapter "Astrology as a Psychotherapeutic Metasystem," the concept of the mandala is also useful in this regard, in that it can keep the system open. By placing the mandala around the astrological system itself, astrology may become desystematized — it is then seen as a language to be used within a larger psychotherapeutic process. In this sense, not only does the astrological system let in other systems, but it is from them that it derives substance. As applied to our example of the observer, the therapist might choose to have the person dialogue with the observer in a Gestalt fashion, focus on the bodily feeling present when observing (a la Gendlin), explore the complex's roots in a psychoanalytic manner, or the therapist might simply confront the person about the imbalance sensed in the person's identification with the role of observer.

This brings us to the second means of checking for solipsism. In addition to the above metasystematic check, the therapist's self, or more accurately put, the therapist/client relationship can serve as a check. This is most clearly illustrated in the section in the text entitled "Making an Excuse for One's Neurosis" discussing how the therapeutic intervention can be used to work with a client who may rationalize neurotic patterns by using astrological language.

Although the therapist's perceptions, the therapist/client dialectic and the particular external system incorporated could all be asked the very same questions concerning bias that is being considered, it does seem that these additional elements introduce a dynamic factor into the system.

The problems with which we are wrestling are part of the realm of the art of psychotherapy. Is the client deluding himself? Is the therapist in the position of influencing the client into accepting his own value system? If we see these questions from Jung's earlier stated point of view, the last check is that which the passage of time brings forth from the person's own unconscious processes.

In summary, the process orientation to the question of value views the question not in terms of "correct interpretation" in the static sense. The therapist uses a given symbol as a fisherman uses a hook. When throwing in the line, the therapist must be sensitive to whether to let line out to give more room, or whether to pull it in. Just as the day's fishing is valued by the process itself, and by that which has taken hold, so when a particular symbol is worked with the therapist must be able to sense how the person nibbles on the symbol and how the felt shift moves one as the interpretation takes hold.

As the therapist and client set sail through the deep waters of the psyche, their journey leaves a wake through the great sea of hermeneutic possibilities.

# BIBLIOGRAPHY

Allport, G. *Personality*. New York: Henry Holt and Company, 1937.
  *Becoming*. New Haven, Conn: Yale University Press, 1955.
Angyal, A. *Neurosis and Treatment: A Holistic Theory*. New York:
  The Viking Press, 1965.
Arguelles, J. & M. *Mandala*. Berkeley, CA: Shambala Publications,
  1972.
Arnheim, R. "A Gestalt Theory of Expression," *Psychological
  Review*. 1949, 56.
Asch, S." "On the Use of Metaphor in the Description of Persons,"
  In H. Werner (Ed.), *On Expressive Language*. Worcester: Clark
  University Press, 1955.
Assagioli, R. *Psychosynthesis* New York: The Viking Press, 1965.
Bachelard, G. *The Poetics of Space*. Boston: Beacon Press, 1969.
Bailey, A. *Esoteric Astrology*. New York: Lucas Publishing Co., 1951.
Barton, A. *Three Worlds of Therapy: Freud, Jung and Rogers*, Palo
  Alto, CA: National Press Books, 1974.
Beck, A.T., et al., "Reliability of Psychiatric Diagnosis and a Study
  of Consistency of Clinical Judgments and Ratings," *American
  Journal of Psychiatry,64119*, 1962.
Berger, P. *The Social Construction of Reality*. Garden City, N.Y.:
  Doubleday and Co., 1966.
Bergier and Pauwels, *The Eternal Man*, New York: Avon Books,
  1973.
Berne, E. *What Do You Say After You Say Hello?* New York: Ban-
  tam Books, 1972.
Boss, M. *Psychoanalysis and Daseinanalysis*. New York: Basic Books,
  1963.
Boulding, K. *The Image*. Ann Arbor: The University of Michigan
  Press, 1961.

Bowman, K. and Rose, M. "A Criticism of the Terms 'Psychosis, Psychoneurosis and Neurosis'," *American Journal of Psychiatry*, 108, 1951.

Bugental, T. *Challenges of Humanistic Psychology*. New York: McGraw Hill Book Co., 1967.

Busteed, M., Tiffany, R., Wergin, D. *Phases of the Moon*. Berkeley, CA: Shambala Publications, 1974.

Campbell, J. *Hero with a Thousand Faces*. Cleveland: The World Publishing Co., 1949.

*Myths To Live By*. New York: Viking Press, 1972.

Cartwright, D. *Introduction to Personality*. Chicago, Ill: Rand McNally, 1974.

Cassirer, E. *The Philosophy of Symbolic Forms, vol. 1, Language*. New Haven, Conn: Yale University Press, 1955.

*Language and Myth*. New York: Dover Publications, 1953.

Casteneda, C. *The Teachings of Don Juan*. New York: Simon & Schuster, 1968.

*A Separate Reality*. New York: Simon & Schuster, 1971.

*Journey to Ixtlan*. New York: Simon & Schuster, 1972.

*Tales of power*. New York: Simon & Schuster, 1974.

Chardin, T. *The Phenomenon of Man*. New York: Harper & Row, 1959.

Clark, V. An Investigation of the Validity and Reliability of the Astrological Technique," *Search Magazine*, 1961.

Collin, R. *The Theory of Celestial Influence*. New York: Samuel Weiser, 1973.

Cox, F. *Psychology*. Dubuque, Iowa: Wm. C. Brown Co., 1970.

Dali, S. *Dali* New York: Harry Abrams & Co., 1968.

Darling, H. *Organum Quaterni*. Lakemont, Georgia: CSA Press, 1968.

Davidson, R. *Astrology*. New York: Arc Books, Inc., 1963.

De Ropp, R. *The Master Game*. New York: Dell Publishing Co., 1968.

Diamond, S. *Primitive views of the world*. New York: Columbia University Press, 1960.

Doane, D. *Astrology, 30 Years of Research*. Hollywood, CA: Professional Astrologers Inc., 1956.

Dobyns, Z. *The Astrologer's Casebook*. Los Angeles: TIA Publications, 1973.

*Expanding Astrology's Universe*. San Diego, CA: ACS Publications, 1983.

Dollard, J. Miller, N. *Personality & Psychotherapy*. New York: McGraw Hill Book Co., 1950...

Ebertin, R. *The Combination of Stellar Influences*. Aalan, Germany:

Ebertin Verlag, 1940.

Edinger, E. *Ego and Archetype*. Baltimore, Md: Penguin Books, 1973.

Eliade, M. *Rites and Symbols of Initiation*. New York: Harper & Row, 1958.

*The Sacred and the Profane*. New York: Harcourt Brace and World, 1959.

*Patterns in Comparative Religions*. New York: The World Publishing Co., 1963.

*Shamanism*. Princeton, N.J.: Princeton University Press, 1964.

*The Two and The One*. New York: Harper and Row, 1958.

Ennis, B. *Prisoners of Psychiatry*. New York: W.W. Norton and Co., 1968.

Erdoes, R. *Lame Deer: Seeker of Visions*. New York: Simon & Schuster, 1972

*The Sun Dance People*. New York: Random House, 1972.

Fagan, C. *Astrological Origins*. St. Paul, Minn: Llewellyn Publications, 1971.

Fingarette, H. *The Self in Transformation*. New York: Harper and Row, 1963.

Foucault, M. *Madness and Civilization*. New York: The New American Library, 1965.

Frank, J. *Persuasion and Healing*. New York: Schocken Books, 1963.

Frankl, V. *Psychotherapy and Existentialis: Selected Papers in Logotherapy*. New York: Simon and Schuster, 1967.

*The Will to Meaning*. New York: The New American Library, 1969.

Freud, S. *The Ego and the Id*. New York: W.W. Norton and Co., 1960.

*Civilization and its Discontents*. New York: W.W. Norton and Co., 1961.

*Character and Culture*. New York: Collier Books, 1963a.

*General Psychological Theory*. New York: Collier Boks, 1963b.

*The Future of an Illusion*. Garden City, N.Y.: Anchor Books, 1964.

*New Introductory Lectures on Psychoanalysis*. New York: W.W. Norton and Co., 1965.

Fromm, E. *The Sane Society*. Greenwich, Conn: Fawcett Premier Books, 1955.

Gauquelin, F. *The Pyschology of the Planets*. San Diego, CA: ACS Publications, 1982.

Gauquelin, M. *The Scientific Basis of Astrology*. New York: Stein and Day, 1969.

Gendlin, E. *Experiencing and the Creation of Meaning*. Toronto, Canada: The Free Press of Glencoe, 1962.

*Focusing.* New York: Bantam Books, 1978 and 1981.

"Focusing," *Psychotherapy Theory, Research and Practice,* Winter, 1969, *16.*

"A Theory of Personality change," *Personality Change.* New York: John Wiley, 1964.

"The Use of Imagery in Experiential Focusing," *Psychotherapy Theory, Research and Practice,* Winter, 1970, 7.

Goldsmith, S., Mandell, A. "The Dynamic Formulation — a Critique of the Psychiatric Ritual. *American Journal of Psychiatry,* 1969, *125.*

Gordon, D. *Therapeutic Metaphors,* Meta Publications, 1978.

Gordon, R. "Symbols: Content and Process," In Wheelwright (Ed.).

Grinder, J. and Bandler, R. *The Structure of Magic.* Palo Alto: Science and Behavior Books, 1976.

Hall, C.A. *Primer of Freudian Psychology.* New York: New American Library, 1954.

Lindsey, G. *Theories of Personality.* New York: John Wiley and Sons, Inc., 1957.

Hall, M. *Masonic, Hermetic, Qabbalistic and Rosicrucian Symbolic Philosophy.* Los Angeles: The Philosophic Research Society, 1971.

Harding, E. *Woman's Mysteries.* New York: Putnam's Sons, 1971.

Henderson, J., Oakes, M. *The Wisdom of the Serpent.* New York: Collier Books, 1963.

Henle, P. "Uses of Metaphor," In P. Henle (Ed.) *Language, Thought and Culture.* University of Mich. Press, 1958.

Hesse, H. *The Glass Bead Game.* New York: Bantam Books, 1946.

Hillman, J. *Revisioning Psychology,* New York: Harper and Row, 1975.

Illich, I. *Medical Nemesis.* New York: Pantheon Books, 1975.

Jacoby, M. *"Psychotherapy in a Non-human Cosmos".* New York: Spring Publications, 1972.

Jaffe, A. *The Myth of Meaning.* New York: G.P. Putnam's Sons, 1971.

James, W. *Pragmatism,.* Logmans, Green & Co., 1908.

Janov, A. *The Primal Scream.* New York: Delta Publishing Co., 1970.

Jenny, H. *Cymatics.* Switzerland: Basilius Press, 1974.

Jocelyn, J. *Meditations on the Signs of the Zodiac.* Blauvelt, N.Y.: Rudolf Steiner Publication, 1970.

Jones, E. The Theory of Symbolism. *Papers on Psychoanalysis.* Baltimore: The Williams and Wilkens Co., 1949.

Jones, M. *Essentials of Astrological Analysis.* Stanwood, Washington: Sabian Publications, 1970.

*How to Learn Astrology.* Garden City, N.Y.: Doubleday and Co., 1971.

Jung, C.G. *Modern Man in Search of a Soul.* New York: Harcourt Brace and World, 1933.

*Two essays on analytical Psychology.* Cleveland: The World Publishing Co., 1953.

"The practice of Psychotherapy," *Collected works.* (Vol. 16). New York: Bollingen Foundation, 1954.

*Psyche and Symbol.* New York: Anchor Books, 1958.

The Structure and Dynamics of the Psyche. *Collected Works.* (Vol. 8). Princeton: Princeton University Press, l960.

*Memories, Dreams, Reflections.* New York: Pantheon Books, 1961.

*Man and His Symbols.* New York: Dell Publishing Co., 1964.

Psychological types. *Collected works.* (Vol 6). Princeton: Princeton University Press, 1971.

*Dreams.* Princeton: Princeton University Press, 1974.

"The Archetypes and the Collective Unconscious," *Collected works.* (Vol. 9). Princeton: Princeton University Press, 1968.

"Psychology and Religion: West and East," *Collected works.* (Vol. 11). Princeton: Princeton University Press, 1969.

Kant, I. *Critique of Pure Reason.* Translated by Norman Kemp Smith. New York: 1929.

Kerenyi, C. *Essays on a Science on Mythology.* Princeton, NJ: Princeton University Press, 1949.

*Gods of the Greeks.* London, England: Thames and Hudson, 1951.

*Goddesses of the Sun and Moon.* New York: Spring Publications, 1979.

Keen, S. *To a Dancing God.* New York: Harper and Row, 1970.

Kelly, G. *The Psychology of Personal Constructs.* (Vol 1). New York: W.W. Norton and Co., 1955 a. (Vol 2, 1955 b.).

*A Theory of Personality: the Psychology of Personal Constructs.* New York: W. W. Norton and Co., 1963.

Klopfer, B., Davidson, H. *The Rorschach Technique: an Introductory Manual.* N.Y.: Harcourt Brace and World, 1962.

Kocklmans, J. *Phenomenology.* Garden City, N.Y.: Doubleday 1967.

Koestler, A. *The Roots of Coincidence.* New York: Vintage Books, 1972.

Kohler, W. *The Task of Gestalt Psychology.* Princeton: Princeton University Press, 1969.

Krag, G. "The Use of Metaphor in Analytic Thinking," *Psychoanalytic Quarterly,.* 1956, *25.*

Laing, R.D. *The Divided Self.* Baltimore, Md: Penguin Books, 1965.

*The Politics of Experience*. New York: Ballantine Books, 1967

Langer, S. *Feeling and Form*. London: Routldge & Kegan Paul Ltd., 1959.

Lecky, P. *Self Consistency*. New York: Island Press Cooperative, 1945.

Leibnitz, G. *Philosophical Writings*. New York: Everyman's Library, 1934.

Levi, S.C., *The Savage Mind*. Chicago: University of Chicago Press, 1966.

Lewin, K. *A Dynamic Theory of Personality*. New York: McGraw Hill, 1935.

Lilly, J. *The Centre of the Cyclone*. Great Britain: Paladin, 1973.

Lindsey, G., Hall, C., Manosevetz, M. *Theories of Personality*. New York: John Wiley and Sons, 1973.

Lindsey, J. *The Origins of Astrology*. London: Frederich Muller, 1971.

Lowen, A. *The Language of the Body*. New York: Collier Books, 1958.

*Depression and the Body*. Baltimore: Penguin Books, 1972.

Luce, G. *Biological Rhythms in Human and Animal Physiology*. New York: John Wiley and Sons, 1973.

*Body Time*. New York: Bantam Books, 1973.

Machover, K. *Personality Projections in the Drawing of the Human Figure*. Springfield, Ill: Charles C. Thomas, 1949.

Mails, T. *The Mystic Warriors of the Plains*. Garden City, N.Y.: Doubleday, 1972.

Maslow, A. *The Farther Reaches of Human Nature*. Baltimore, Md: Penguin Books, 1976.

May, R. "Existential Bases of Psychotherapy," In M. Zax and G. Stricker (Eds.). *The study of abnormal behavior*. New York: Macmillan, 1969.

Mayer, M. *A Holistic Perspective on Meaning and Identity: Astrological Metaphor as a Language of Personality in Psychotherapy*, University Microfilms International, Ann Arbor, Michigan, LD 00166, Vol. 3, Issue 1, March 1978.

*The Mythic Journey Process*. The Focusing Folio, The Focusing Institute Volume 2, Issue 2, Chicago, Illinois 1982.

McCully, R. *Rorshach Theory and Symbolism: a Jungian Approach to Clinical Material*. Baltimore: The Williams and Wilkins Co., 1971.

McDougall, W. *Body and Mind*. Boston: Beacon Press, 1911.

Meier, C. *Ancient Incubation and Modern Psychotherapy*. Evanston, Ill: Northwestern Press, 1967.

Menninger, K. *The Vital Balance*. New York: The Viking Press, 1963.

Metzner, R. "Astrology: Potential Science and Intuitive Art," *The Journal of Astrological Studies*, 1970.

*Maps of Consciousness*. New York: Collier Books, 1971.

Meyer, M. *A Handbook for the Humanistic Astrologer*. Garden City, New York: Doubleday, 1974.

Moon, S. *A Magic Dwells: a Poetic and Psychological Study of the Navaho Emergence Myth*. Middletown, Conn: Wesleyan University Press, 1970.

Moustakas, C. "Heuristic Research," In Bugental, J. (Ed.) *Challenges of Humanistic Psychology*. New York: McGraw Hill, 1967.

Moore, M., Douglas, M. *Astrology the Divine Science*. York Harbor, Maine: Arcane Publications, 1971.

Nash, H. "Metaphor in Personality Theory," *American Psychologist*, 1954, *14*.

Needleman, J. *A Sense of the Cosmos* New York: Doubleday, 1975.

Neihardt, T. *Black Elk Speaks*. Lincoln, Neb: University of Nebraska Press, 1971.

Neumann, E. *The Origins and History of Consciousness*. Princeton: Princeton University Press, 1954.

*Depth Psychology and the New Ethic*. New York: Harper and Row 1969.

Okan, A. *As Above So Below*. New York: Bantam Books, 1973.

Ornstein, R. *The Psychology of Consciousness*. San Francisco: W.H. Freeman and Co., 1973.

Osterman, E. "The tendency Toward Patterning and Order in Matter and in the Psyche," In Wheelwright (Ed.) *The Reality of the Psyche*. New York: G.P. Putnam's Sons, 1968.

Ostrander, S., Schroeder, L. *Astrological Birth Control*. Englewood Cliffs, N.J.: Prentice Hall, 1972.

Otto, R. *The Idea of the Holy*. London: Oxford University Press, 1923.

Pasamanick, B., Denitz, S., Lefton, M. "Psychiatric orientation and its Relation to Diagnosis and Treatment in a Mental Hospital," *American Journal of Psychiatry*, 1959, *116*.

Pauwels, L., Bergier, J. *Impossible Possibilities*. New York: Avon Books, 1968.

*The Eternal Man*. New York: Avon Books, 1973.

Pearce, J. *The Crack in the Cosmic Egg*. New York: Pocket Books, 1973.

Pearson, E. *Space, Time and Self*. Wheaton, Ill: The Theosophical Publishing House, 1957.

Pelligrini, R. "The Astrological Theory of Personality: an Unbiased Test by a Biased Observer," *The Journal of Psychiatry*, 1973.

Perls, F. *Gestalt Therapy*. New York: Dell Publishing Co., 1951.

*Gestalt Therapy Verbatim*. Lafayette, CA: Real People Press, 1969.

Ponce, C. *The Game of Wizards: Psyche, Science and Symbol in the Occult*. Baltimore, Md: Penguin Books, 1975.

Pottenger, M. *Healing With the Horoscope; A Counseling Guide*. San Diego, CA: ACS Publications, 1982.

Progoff, I. *The Death and Rebirth of Psychology*. New York: McGraw Hill, 1956.

Ptolemy, C. *Tetrabiblos*. Cambridge, Mass: Harvard University Press, 1940.

Ram Dass. *The Only Dance There Is*. Garden City, New York: Anchor Books, 1974.

Reich, W. *Selected Writings*. New York: Farar, Straus and Giroux, 1942.

*Character Analysis*. New York: Farrar, Straus and Giroux, 1949.

Ricoeur, P. *The Symbolism of Evil*. N.Y.: Harper and Row, 1967.

Rohovit, D. "Metaphor and Mind," *American Imago*, 1960, 17.

Rosenhan, D. "On Being Sane in Insane Places," *Science*, Jan. 1973, p. 119.

Rudhyar, D. *The Astrology of Personality*. Garden City, N.Y., 1936, 1970.

*The Pulse of Life*. Netherlands: Service/Wassenar, 1963.

*An Astrological Study of Psychological Complexes and Emotional Problems*. Netherlands: Servire/Wassenaar.

*The Practice of Astrology as a Technique of Human Understanding*. Baltimore: Penguin Books: 1968a.

*Triptych*. Netherlands: Service/Wasenaar, 1968b.

*Astrological Timing*. New York: Harper and Row, 1969.

*The Planetarization of Consciousness*. New York: Harper and Row, 1970a.

*Form in Astrological Time and Space*. Lakemont, Georgia: CAS Press, 1970b.

"How can astrology's claims be proven valid?" *Aquarian Agent*, 1970c, 10.

*First Steps in the Study of Birth Charts*. Lakemont, Georgia: CSA Press, 1970d.

*The Lunation Cycle*. Berkeley, CA: Shambala, 1971a.

*New Mansions for New Men*. Netherlands: Servire/Wasenaar, 1971b.

*Interpreting Birth Charts as a Whole*. Lakemont, Georgia: CSA Press, 1971c.

*The Planetary and Lunar Nodes*. Lakemont, Georgia: CSA Press, 1971d.

*The Astrological Houses*. Garden City, New York: Doubleday 1972.

*An Astrological Mandala*. New York: Random House, 1973.

Ruperti, A. "Astrology and the Needs of Modern Man." *Kosmos*, 1971.

Rychlak, J. *Introduction to Personality and Psychotherapy*. Boston: Houghlin-Mifflin, 1973.

Sakoian, F., Acker, L. *The Astrologers Handbook*. New York: Harper and Row, 1973.

Sanford, N. *Issues in Personality Theory*. San Francisco: Jassey Bass Inc., 1970

Sargent, S. "Humanistic Methodology in Personality and Social Psychology," In Bugental (Ed.) *Challenges of Humanistic Psychology*. New York: McGraw Hill, 1967.

Schure, E. *The Ancient Mysteries of Delphi: Pythagoras*. Baluvelt N.Y.: Rudolf Steiner Publications, 1971a.

*The Mysteries of Ancient Egypt: Hermes/Moses*. Blauvelt, New York: Multimedia Publishing Corp., 1971b.

*The Mysteries of Ancient Greece: Orpheus/Plato*. Blauvelt, New York: Rudolf Steiner Publications, 1971c.

*The Ancient Mysteries of the East: Rama/Krishna*. Blauvelt New York: Multimedia Publishing Corp., 1971d.

Schutz, A. *On Phenomenology and Social Relations*. Chicago: University of Chicago Press, 1970.

Schwartz, N., Schwartz, S. "On the Coupling of Psychic Entropy and Negentropy," New York: Spring Publications, 1970.

Shapiro, J., Alexander, I. *The Experience of Introversion: an Integration of Phenomenological, Empirical and Jungian Approaches*. Durham, North Carolina: Duke University Press, 1975.

Shere, J. "Understanding Astrology," *The Telegraph Monthly*. Berkeley, 1972.

Sibbald, L. *The Man with the Water Pitcher*. San Francisco: The Guild for Psychological Studies, 1971.

Singer, J. "The Collective Unconscious: Jung's Most Misunderstood Concept," *Quadrant*. #7. Spring, 1970

*Boundaries of the Soul*. Garden City, N.Y: Doubleday, 1973.

Smuts, J. *Holism and Evolution*. New York: McMillan, 1926.

Stanford, B., Stanford, G. *Myths and Modern Man*. New York: Pocket Books, 1972.

Steiner, C. *Scripts People Live.* New York: Grove Press, 1974.

Stevens, J. *Awareness: Exploring, Experimenting, Experiencing.* Lafayette, CA: Real People Press, 1971.

Storm, H. *Seven Arrows.* New York: Harper and Row, 1972.

Suares, C. *The Cipher of Genesis.* Berkely, CA: Shambala, 1973.

Szasz, T. *The Myth of Mental Illness.* N.Y.: Harper and Row, 1961.

Tart, C. *Altered States of Consciousness.* New York: John Wiley and Sons, 1969.

Terwilliger, R. *Meaning and Mind.* New York: Oxford University Press, 1968.

Torrey, E. *The Mind Game: Witchdoctors and Psychiatrists.* New York: Bantam Books, 1973.

Tripp, E. *The Meridian Handbook of Classical Mythology.* New York: New American Library, 1970.

Tzu, L. *Tao Te Ching.* Baltimore: Penguin Books, 1963.

Velikovsky, I. *Worlds in Collision.* New York: Dell Publishing Co., 1950.

Vernon, W. *Introductory Psychology.* Chicago: Rand McNally, 1974.

Von Franz, M. "Puer aeternus," *Spring Publications.* New York, 1970.

Von Franz M. and Hillman. J. *Jung's typology.* New York: Spring Publications, 1971.

Von Franz, M. *Number and Time.* Evanston, Ill. Northwestern University Press, 1974.

Waters, F. *The Book of the Hopi.* New York: Ballantine Books, 1963.

Watson, L. *Super Nature.* New York: Bantam Book, 1974.

Watts, A. *The Book.* New York: Collier Books, 1966.

   *Psychotherapy East and West.* New York: Ballantine Books, 1961

Watzlawick, P., *Change.* W.W. Morton & Co., 1974.

Weitzman, B. Behavior Therapy and Psychotherapy. *Psychological Review,* 1967, *74.*

West, J. Toonder, J. *The Case For Astrology.* Baltimore: Penguin Books, 1970.

White, R. *The Abnormal Personality.* New York: Ronald Publishing Co., 1948.

Whitmont, E. *The Symbolic Quest.* N.Y.: C.G. Jung Foundation, 1969.

   "Why causality?" *Aquarian Agent,.* 1970.

# INDEX

# NOTES

# We calculate... You delineate!

## CHART CALCULATIONS

**Natal Chart** wheel with planet/sign glyphs. Choice of house system: Placidus (standard), Equal, Koch, Campanus, Meridian, Porphyry, Regiomontanus, Topocentric, or Alcabitius. Choice of tropical (standard) or sidereal zodiac. Aspects, elements, planetary nodes, declinations, midpoints, etc. .... 2.00
**Arabic Parts** All traditional parts and more ......... 1.00
**Asteroids** ⚳ ⚴ ⚵ ⚶ in wheel + aspects/midpoints .... .50
**Asteroids** ⚳ ⚴ ⚵ ⚶ + 15 new ones for 20th century only ............ 1.00
**Astrodynes** Power, harmony and discord with summaries for easy comparison............ 2.00
**Chiron, Transpluto** (only one) in wheel............ N/C
**Concentric Wheels** Any 3 charts available in wheel format may be combined into a '3 wheeler' ...... 3.00
Deduct $1.00 for each chart ordered as a separate wheel.
**Fixed Stars** Robson's 110 fixed stars with aspects to natal chart ............ 1.00
**Fortune Finder** more Arabic Parts — 97 ancient (Al Biruni) and 99 modern (Robert Hurzt Granite) ..... 2.00
**Graphic Midpoint Sort** Proportional spacing highlights midpt. groupings. **Specify integer divisions of 360°** (1=360°, 4=90°, etc.) ........... 1.00
**Harmonic Chart** John Addey type. Wheel format, harmonic asc. eq. houses. **Specify harmonic number** ............ 2.00
**Harmonic Positions** 30 consecutive sets of positions **Specify starting harmonic number** ............ 1.00
**Heliocentric Charts** Sun-centered positions ........ 2.00
**House Systems Comparison** for 9 systems ......... .50
**Local Space** Planet compass directions (azimuth & altitude) plus Campanus Mundoscope ........... .50
**Locality Map** USA, World, Europe, S. Amer., Far East, Austl., Mid East and Africa map — choice of rise, set, and culmination lines or Asc., Desc., MC, IC lines for each map ............ 6.00
**Midpoint Structures** Midpoint aspects + midpoints in 45° and 90° sequence............ 1.00
**Rectification Assist** 10 same-day charts. **Specify starting time, time increment, e.g. 6 am, every 20 minutes** ............ 10.00
**Relocation Chart** for current location. **Specify original birth data and new location** ............ 2.00
**Uranian Planets** + halfsums............ .50
**Uranian Sensitive Points** (includes Uranian Planets). 3.50

## HUMAN RELATIONSHIPS

**Chart Comparison (Synastry)** All aspects between the two sets of planets plus house positions of one in the other ............ 1.50
**Composite Chart** Rob Hand-type. Created from midpoints between 2 charts. **Specify location** ........ 2.00
**Relationship Chart** Chart erected for space-time midpoint between two births ............ 2.00
**Interpretive Comparison Report** Specify natal data for 2 births............ 8.00

## COLOR CHARTS

**4-Color Wheel** any chart we offer in new, aesthetic format with color coded aspect lines ............ 2.00
**Local Space Map** 4-color on 360° circle ............ 2.00
**Custom 6" Disk** for any harmonic (laminated, you cut out) overlays on our color wheel charts ...... 4.00
**Plotted Natal Dial** for use with custom 6" Disk ..... 2.00
**Specify harmonic #**
**Custom Graphic Ephemeris** in 4 colors. **Specify harmonic, zodiac, starting date.**
1 or 5 YR TRANSITS with or without natal positions ............ 5.00
1 or 5 YR TRANSITS, NATAL & PROGRESSED .... 7.00
85 YR PROGRESSIONS with natal positions...... 10.00
NATAL LINES ONLY (plus transparency).......... 4.00
additional natal (same graph)............ 1.00
additional person's progressions (same graph) .... 2.00

## FUTURE TRENDS

**Progressed Chart** in wheel format. **Specify progressed day, month and year** ............ 2.00
**Secondary Progressions** Day-by-day progressed aspects to natal and progressed planets, ingresses and parallels by month, day and year. **Specify starting year, MC by solar arc (standard) or RA of mean Sun** ............5 years 3.00
10 years 5.00
85 years 15.00
**Minor or Tertiary Progressions** Minor based on lunar-month-for-a-year, tertiary on day-for-a-lunar-month. **Specify year, MC by solar arc (standard) or RA of mean sun** ............1 year 2.00
**Progressed Lifetime Lunar Phases** a la Dane Rudhyar ............ 5.00
**Solar Arc Directions** Day-by-day solar arc directed aspects to the natal planets, house and sign ingresses by month, day and year. **Specify starting year.** Asc. and Vertex arc directions available at same prices ............1st 5 years 1.00
Each add'l 5 years .50
**Primary Arc Directions** (Includes speculum) ..5 years 1.50
**Specify starting year** Each add'l 5 years .50
**Transits** by all planets except Moon. Date and time of transiting aspects/ingresses to natal chart. **Specify starting month.** Moon-only transits available at same prices............ 6 mos. 7.00
OR 12 mos. 12.00
summary only 6 mos. 3.50
summary only 12 mos. 6.00
calendar (9 planets OR Moon only) 6 mos. 7.00
calendar (9 planets OR Moon only) 12 mos. 12.00
calendar (Moon & planets) 6 mos. 12.00
calendar (Moon & planets) 12 mos. 20.00
**Interpretive Transits.** SPECIFY STARTING MONTH
**Outer Planets** ♃♄♅♆♇ ............12 mos. 8.00
Hard Aspects Only ☌☍□∠⚼
**Outer Planets** ♃♄♅♆♇ ............12 mos. 10.00
Soft & Hard Aspects △✶⚻☌☍□∠⚼
**9 Planets** ☉☿♀♂♃♄♅♆♇ ............6 mos. 15.00
Hard Aspects Only ☌☍□∠⚼ 12 mos. 25.00
**9 Planets** ☉☿♀♂♃♄♅♆♇ ............6 mos. 18.00
Soft & Hard Aspects △✶⚻☌☍□∠⚼ 12 mos. 30.00
**Returns** in wheel format. All returns can be precession corrected. **Specify place, Sun-return year, Moon-return month, planet-return month/year.** ............Solar, Lunar or Planet 2.00
13 Lunar 15.00

## POTPOURRI

**Winning!!** Timing for gamblers, exact planet and transiting house cusps based on Joyce Wehrman's system. 1-7 days (per day) 3.00
8 or more days (per day) 2.00
**Biorhythms Chart** the 23-day, 28-day and 33-day cycles in ...........Printed { per mo. .50 / 12 mos. 4.00 } black/white graph format.
**4-Color Graph** on our plotter ........ Color 6 mos. 2.00
**Custom House Cusps Table** for each minute of sidereal time. **Specify latitude ° ′ ″** ............ 10.00
**Custom American Ephemeris Page** Any month, 2500BC-AD2500. **Specify zodiac (Sidereal includes RA & dec.)**
One mo. geocentric or two mos. heliocentric ..... 5.00
One year ephemeris (**specify beginning mo. yr.**) ... 50.00
One year heliocentric ephemeris ............ 25.00
**Fertility Report** The Jonas method with Sun/Moon-squares/oppositions to the planets, for 1 year .... 3.00
**Specify starting month.**
**Lamination of 1 or 2 sheets** ............ 1.00
**Transparency (B/W) of any chart or map.**
Ordered at same time ............ 1.00
**Handling charge per order** ............ 2.00

***SAME DAY SERVICE — Ask for Free Catalog***

**ASTRO COMPUTING SERVICES, Inc.**
**P.O. BOX 16430**
**SAN DIEGO, CA 92116-0430**
**NEIL F. MICHELSEN**

*(Prices Subject to Change)*